Photo © Gasper Tringale

From Bill Buford,

"an all-too-rare description of the real business of cooking, its characters and its subculture. I lingered over every sentence as if it were a heavily truffled risotto."

—ANTHONY BOURDAIN,
author of KITCHEN CONFIDENTIAL

Heat

AN AMATEUR'S ADVENTURES AS KITCHEN SLAVE,
LINE COOK, PASTA-MAKER, AND APPRENTICE
TO A DANTE-QUOTING BUTCHER IN TUSCANY

"A dazzling book...The hellish and—he somehow convinces you —sexy joy of being in a top-of-the-line restaurant kitchen, the insane pressure, physical exhaustion, and unexpressed comradeship, as if in an endless boot camp, is brilliantly described...**Above all there is the passion of Buford himself who, as a complete amateur, leapt wildly into the life, drenching himself in it for months on end, slaving, working, slowly learning, and this book is his glory."** **—JAMES SALTER**

GRANTA

GRANTA 94, SUMMER 2006
www.granta.com

EDITOR Ian Jack
DEPUTY EDITOR Matt Weiland
MANAGING EDITOR Fatema Ahmed
ASSOCIATE EDITOR Liz Jobey
EDITORIAL ASSISTANT Helen Gordon

CONTRIBUTING EDITORS Diana Athill, Simon Gray, Isabel Hilton,
Sophie Harrison, Blake Morrison, John Ryle, Sukhdev Sandhu, Lucretia Stewart

FINANCE Geoffrey Gordon
SALES DIRECTOR Frances Hollingdale
TO ADVERTISE CONTACT Lara Frohlich, lfrohlich@aol.com
PRODUCTION ASSOCIATE Sarah Wasley
PUBLICITY Louise Campbell
PROOFS Lesley Levene

PUBLISHER Sigrid Rausing

GRANTA PUBLICATIONS, 2-3 Hanover Yard, Noel Road, London N1 8BE
Tel +44 (0)20 7704 9776 Fax +44 (0)20 7704 0474
e-mail for editorial: editorial@granta.com
Granta is published in the United Kingdom by Granta Publications.
This selection copyright © 2006 Granta Publications.
All editorial queries should be addressed to the London office.

GRANTA in the USA is published in association with Grove/Atlantic Inc,
841 Broadway, 4th Floor, New York, NY10003, and distributed by PGW

TO SUBSCRIBE go to www.granta.com
A one-year subscription (four issues) costs $39.95 (US), $51.95 (Canada, includes GST),
$48.70 (Mexico and South America), and $60.45 (rest of the world).

TRADE SALES QUERIES to sales@granta.com

Granta, USPS 000-508, ISSN 0017-3231, is published quarterly in the US by Granta USA LLC,
a Delaware limited liability company. Periodical Rate postage paid at New York, NY, and additional
mailing offices. POSTMASTER: send address changes to Granta, PO Box 23152, Jackson,
MS 39225-3152. US Canada Post Corp. Sales Agreement #40031906.

Granta is indexed in The American Humanities Index

Front cover photograph:
Communal area of a former sanatorium, now a hotel, Olkhon Island, Eastern Siberia. © Simon Roberts

Design: Slab Media.
Printed and bound in Italy by Legoprint on acid-free paper.

ISBN 1-929001-24-X

ON THE ROAD AGAIN

CONTRIBUTORS

Ann Beattie has published seven novels and seven collections of short stories, most recently *Follies: New stories* (Scribner). In 2000, she received the PEN/Bernard Malamud Award for her stories. She lives in Key West, Florida, and Charlottesville, Virginia, where she is the Edgar Allan Poe Professor of Literature and Creative Writing at the University of Virginia.

George Bowater is writing a book about Turkey.

John Burnside used to work as a computer software engineer and now teaches at the University of St Andrews, where he specializes in creative writing and ecology. He is the author of four novels, a collection of short stories, nine collections of poetry and a memoir, *A Lie About My Father* (Jonathan Cape). His new novel, *The Devil's Footprints*, will be published by Jonathan Cape in Spring 2007.

Michel Faber is Dutch by birth, grew up in Australia and now lives in the Scottish Highlands. He has published four novels, including *The Crimson Petal and the White* (Canongate/Harcourt), and three short-story collections. *The Apple*, his forthcoming collection, will be published by Canongate in September 2006. His work also appeared recently in *Not One More Death*, a collection of essays published by Verso in collaboration with the Stop the War coalition.

Tessa Hadley's second novel is *Everything Will Be All Right* (Jonathan Cape/Henry Holt). She teaches literature and creative writing at Bath Spa University and is currently working on a new novel called *The Master Bedroom*. Her first collection of short stories, *Sunstroke*, will be published by Jonathan Cape in 2007. Her short story, *Buckets of Blood*, appeared in *Granta* 89.

James Hamilton-Paterson left the United Kingdom twenty-seven years ago and, since then, has lived mainly in Italy and the Philippines. His books include *America's Boy* (Granta Books/Henry Holt), a non-fiction account of the Marcos family, and the novel *Loving Monsters* (Granta Books). *Amazing Disgrace*, his new novel, will be published in November 2006 by Faber in the UK and by Europa Editions in the US.

Mark Haworth-Booth has holidayed on Mount Desert Island, Maine, for the past six summers. The island also features in his first book of poems, *Wild Track* (Trace Editions). He is an Honorary Research Fellow at the V&A, where he was senior curator of photography from 1977 to 2004.

Todd McEwen was born in Orange, California, and now lives in Edinburgh. His novels include *McX* (Minerva/Grove Press), *Arithmetic* (Jonathan Cape/Vintage) and, most recently, *Who Sleeps with Katz* (Granta Books). He has contributed to *Granta* since 1987.

Tim Parks was born in Manchester and moved to Italy in 1981. He is the author of three non-fiction accounts of life in northern Italy, most recently *A Season with Verona* (Vintage/Arcade), and eleven novels. He has translated the work of, among others, Alberto Moravia and Italo Calvino and lectures on literary translation at the University of Milan. *Cleaver*, his latest novel, is published by Harvill/Secker.

Simon Roberts is a British photographer. He won the London *Sunday Times* Ian Parry Scholarship in 1998 and in 2004 was identified by *Photo District News* in New York as one of their 'Emerging Artists'. His work has been published and exhibited internationally. *Motherland*, a book of his photographs of Russia (see pages 127–59), will be published by Chris Boot in 2007.

Jeremy Treglown's *V. S. Pritchett: A Working Life* (Pimlico/Random House) was shortlisted for the Whitbread Award for Biography. His other books include *Roald Dahl: A Biography* (Faber/Harvest) and *Romancing: The Life and Work of Henry Green* (Faber/Random House). A Fellow of the Royal Society of Literature and former editor of the *Times Literary Supplement*, he now teaches at the University of Warwick. He is working on a study of the impact of the Franco regime on Spanish culture.

Tia Wallman was born in Columbus, Georgia, and has lived much of her life in Montreal. She sang, once, at the Vieux Colombier and made an LP of English and Irish folksongs in Paris in the Seventies. This is her first published piece.

ISSUE **2**

A
PUBLIC
SPACE

FICTION
POETRY   ARGUMENT
OPINION

APUBLICSPACE · ORG

INTRODUCTION

One of the most beautifully sited cities in the world must be Luzern in Switzerland, and one of the most pleasant things to do in it is to stroll along the Lidostrasse and look across the lake, the Vierwaldstättersee, towards the mountains that rise up straight from the shore on the other side. I went there with my family in April. The atmospheric clarity, the still blue-green waters of the lake, the jagged black mountains, snow-dappled and with small cream clouds moored below their summits—it's like a picture, we said, in the words of millions before us.

Switzerland absolutely fulfils our idea of the picturesque, bred from generations of paintings and photographs, postcards and calendars. Switzerland has the most spectacular scenery in Europe and, ever since 'untamed nature' inspired romantic feeling and became a landscape for recreation, it has set a world benchmark for our notions of natural beauty. Places masquerading as 'little Switzerland' exist in every other continent. Never mind what Harry Lime said about the cuckoo clock (wrongly, in any case, because the cuckoo clock was invented in Germany): what Switzerland gave the Western world was the idea that the drama of natural phenomena alone could make a place worth the journey, without the scholarly excuses of the classical historian, the religious reasons of the pilgrim, the commercial motives of the trader, or the scientific curiosity of the explorer.

Tourists have been coming here for more than two centuries. One of the delightful things about Switzerland is that wilderness is so close to comfort: cold glaciers and peaks can be almost touched from the doors of warm restaurants and railway coaches. Look back towards town from the Lidostrasse and you can see magnificently solid nineteenth-century hotels with names such as the Palace, the Derby, the Château Gütsch; across the bay lies a white fleet of half a dozen elegant old steamers being readied for their summer season on the lake; ahead is the peak of Mount Pilatus, 7,000 feet high, and climbed in 1868 by Queen Victoria on a mule. Invisible to the naked eye are the many small railways and cableways that climb up the hills and mountains, including Pilatus, and that long ago made mules, guides and ice-picks redundant. As well as being a beautiful country, Switzerland is also a beautifully engineered one. By the time the Queen died, even the plumpest Victorian traveller, breathless from cigars and six-course dinners, could reach several of the lower summits without fearing the gradient, and from there see the ice fields and rock faces of mountains which only a few decades earlier, and often by Englishmen, had been scaled for the first time (the Eiger in 1858, the Matterhorn in 1865).

The mechanical conquest of the Alps is a marvellous story, and the best place to see the techniques that made it possible is Luzern's Verkehrshaus, which was our destination that day on the Lidostrasse. The Verkehrshaus is Switzerland's transport museum and its halls are filled with locomotives, automobiles, cable cars and pieces of funicular railway, as well as a steamer's hull and, suspended from the ceiling, many aircraft with the Swiss cross painted on their tails. Models show how things work. Many displays are interactive. We could pretend to be Zurich air-traffic control and give directions for landing and take-off, or imagine ourselves as engine drivers negotiating our way up the pass to the St Gotthard Tunnel. We enjoyed all these, and then I noticed in a neglected corner of the aircraft hall a separate display which would make any visitor wonder where all these forms of travel (but particularly flying and driving) were finally helping to take us: the display made no bones about the terrifying destination—an increase in average global temperatures of somewhere between 2 and 5 degrees Celsius in the next hundred years, bringing rising sea levels, melting polar icecaps, the vanishing glaciers which in Switzerland have already lost half their volume since the latter half of the nineteenth century.

Travel isn't the only cause, but its contribution to the total of the greenhouse gases that warm the world is steadily increasing. Carbon emissions from aircraft occur in the higher atmosphere and have three times the potency of the gases that rise from the ground. The display's captions told their chastening story. Since 1970, the distance travelled in aircraft by Swiss citizens had multiplied by four; more than fifty per cent of passengers leaving Switzerland by air (excluding transit passengers) were flying only 600 kilometres or fewer; eighty per cent of cut flowers arrived by air; civil aviation caused about ten per cent of all Switzerland's greenhouse gas output. What to do? By pressing buttons and watching columns of lights, we worked out that travelling by train from London had saved half as much of the energy as the same journey by air, and cut our carbon emissions by four fifths. Any feelings of smugness quickly disappeared at the next set of captions. To mitigate the effects of global warming—because all we can now do is to modify the severity of the inevitable—we would need to ration the carbon dioxide produced by travelling to an allowance of no more than half a tonne a year for every human being now alive. That translated into 2,200 kilometres by car a year, with no air travel, or 1,000 kilometres by car a year with a return flight from Europe to Bali once every fifteen years.

Fortunately for the climate, a lot of the world's population is too poor to do much travelling at all. But if that were to change, as it almost certainly will in India and China, then a more equitable world hoping to stabilize a changing climate—and prevent, say, the complete inundation of Bangladesh—would outlaw or punitively tax all forms of travel which it judged particularly draining of the earth's resources and harmful to the atmosphere. No government or electorate is yet willing to debate such a possibility, far less act on it; even climate-change lobbyists continue to fly to their conventions, trailing CO_2 on their way. And yet something has changed. Travel no longer seems so innocent or beneficent ('travel broadens the mind'), unless one journeys in some pre-industrial carbon-neutral way, like Thomas Coryat walking all the way from Somerset to India in the early seventeenth century, or R. L. Stevenson on his donkey in the Cévennes, or Queen Victoria getting up Pilatus on her mule.

We left the museum. The snow at the top of Pilatus was still glistening in the afternoon sun. But in the feelings that the sight prompts, something has also changed. The snow no longer seems ordained, falling winter after winter; it may still lie through spring in the lives of our yet-to-be-born grandchildren, or it may not. The lake may be fuller or emptier. Nobody really knows. All we know is that a changing climate is slowly eating away our belief in permanence, of nature continuing as it was before we began to glimpse the consequences of our massive, unknowing interference with it.

This general concern is very new. As recently as 2003, in *Granta*'s issue on climate change, *This Overheating World*, Bill McKibben could write that most Americans still thought about 'global warming' as a problem on a par with 'violence on television' or 'growing trade deficits'—'as a marginal concern to them, if a concern at all'. As to its presence in travel writing—or any other literary form—it is only now beginning to make an impression. *Granta*'s three previous issues devoted to travel, published in 1983, 1986 and 1989, take climate as a given when they mention it at all, and this is entirely understandable since man-made climate change was still a debate confined to scientists through most of the 1980s, until McKibben published the first popular account of it, *The End of Nature*, in 1989.

Travel writing was then in its boom decade. Bill Buford, then the editor of *Granta*, wrote in his introduction to the travel issue of 1983 that the pieces inside succeeded 'not by the virtue of the details they report—exotic as they are—but by the contrivance of their reporting'. All were 'informed by the sheer glee of story-telling, a narrative eloquence that situates them, with wonderful ambiguity, somewhere between fiction and fact'. As a keen reader of travel writers—Naipaul, Chatwin, Theroux—the thought of their 'wonderful ambiguity' had never occurred to me: I imagined that what had been described was what had happened, in more or less the order it had happened in. Now, perhaps, we have a more sophisticated understanding of the omission and distortion that narrative always imposes, and of the sometimes blurry divisions between fiction and exact fact. Still, it seems to me that if travel writing is to be more than a persuasive literary entertainment— if it's to have some genuinely illuminating and perhaps even, these times being what they are, some moral purpose—then the information it contains needs to be trustworthy. How else do you justify the carbon emissions spent in its research?

John McGahern died at his farm in County Leitrim, Ireland, in March, a few days after a small piece on his thoughts about God was published in our previous issue. It may have been the last piece he ever wrote; certainly it was the last piece to be published in his lifetime. He was a great writer, whose best work evoked the people and the landscape of the county he was born in, died in, and lived in for so many years of his life. Perhaps in that way he was among the last of a certain kind of writer—the opposite of a travel writer and increasing numbers of novelists—whose imagination depended on the intimate knowledge of a small and settled community, when its world was steady. He was a delight to know, to edit, and (most of all) to read. *Granta* is honoured to have published him.   □

GRANTA

WE WENT TO SAIGON
Tia Wallman

Tia Wallman in the Imperial Hotel, Tokyo, 1967

When my mother called the Peninsula Hotel in Hong Kong that August of 1967, the receptionist at the front desk simply told her, 'They not here. They go Saigon with father.' It's odd that the fact my sister and I had actually entered a war zone did not register at first with my mother, but I always assumed it was because the young woman in Hong Kong had said, 'They go Saigon with father,' instead of, 'Their father's taken them off with him to Saigon. They left yesterday evening, Mrs Blake. I'm terribly sorry, but they haven't left a forwarding address. Or number. Would you like to speak to the manager?' There's something in the grammar and structure of the English language that lets people down gently. As Paul Scott wrote, it's an ambiguous language: there's plenty of room for deception and dissembling, even comfort, if that's what's called for; if that's what the speaker has in mind. It's the natural language of any peace treaty because it so encourages a sense of *vae victis*, woe to the defeated, without ever seeming to.

But this *They go Saigon with father* was all my mother could get out of the conversation with the young woman at the desk of the Peninsula, which was strange because it was all so stuffy and British back then. In retrospect it seems remarkable to have met a woman who spoke like that, who said *go Saigon father* all in rapid succession like machine-gun fire until my mother finally heard the word *Saigon*. 'My God,' she said, 'they're just children,' and let the receiver fall back into its cradle. By the time my mother had placed her call to Hong Kong from New York City, my sister Joan and I had been in Saigon two days already.

It was unbearably hot and sticky when we arrived in Tan Son Nhut, which was where all Americans crossed into or out of the war zone. I was fifteen. My sister was sixteen. We stood puzzled and glum in the dust. We had disembarked only moments before from a commercial flight, a blue-and-white prop jet which seated sixty people at most, a benign uncomfortable tub that looked as if it'd made the shuttle too many times. My sister and I stood on the tarmac, dumb as beasts in crossfire, wishing we had made a last call, stamped a last card, made a last effort to explain to our mother where we had been and where we were going. *A last even of last times*: I chanted the line from the Samuel Beckett poem I'd read in my ninth-grade English class. The rickety Vietnam Air flight from Hong Kong and its jerky descent into the brown dust rising from Saigon seemed to signal that we were never going to make it back out.

In June my father had sent my sister and me two Japan Air Lines round-the-world tickets. The mail run was generally dull at my New England boarding school, punctuated by a letter either from a Canadian friend or from my mother, and I was not prepared for the hefty brown envelope with its Vietnamese customs' script, stuffed with a thick, ink-laden airline ticket and my father's letter, typed, his jagged, familiar signature at the bottom and its scent of pipe tobacco:

Dear Tia,

You will observe a round-the-world ticket enclosed. I want you and your sister to go from New York to Tokyo. You and Joan will stay two or three days there on your own. Book hotel and flights with Japan Air Lines. They are the best and don't worry about anything. Japan is not like New York and the people are very kind and will help you out to any extent. I'm not worried about a stay in Tokyo at all. Just be back at the hotel by 2300 hours. But you must see a Japanese Opera one evening. I will be in Hong Kong at the Peninsula Hotel, waiting for a wire or a telephone call from Tokyo, giving time and date of arrival (by the 5th of July?) so I can meet the plane. As soon as you receive this letter, make reservations with Japan Air Lines and write me your departure date from New York.

Much love, and see you soon, your Dad, John C. Wallman

P.S. Please dress like young ladies. No mini skirts! And don't say 'groovy'!
P.P.S. The traveller's cheques are not for nonsense but for food and hotel until I see you in Hong Kong.

I almost fainted: the blood drained from my head and pooled in the region of my knees, and without the crowd of onlookers pressing close, I might have dropped. I had not heard from my father in two years and thought he was dead. Six years before, in 1960, my parents had separated. During the custody fight, one midnight in June when my mother was out of town, my father kidnapped his six children. We drove from North Carolina for more than twenty-four hours in a Second World War vintage Rolls-Royce he'd stolen from my aunt and arrived at three a.m. the following day at the door of our new home—an abandoned, vermin-ridden six-storey building on Second Avenue near Forty-seventh Street, condemned but on loan from the Durst Company, where Dad had temporary work. We hid there for seven months, in the alternately stifling or freezing apartment that my father had tried to warm with a fake Rembrandt, with Verdi and Puccini and Mozart, and with a single volume of Dostoevsky—it was *Crime and Punishment*, I think—perched out of reach on the mantelpiece but cracked open for bedtime stories when he wasn't too depressed.

He was completely inept and earnest as a single parent to six children. Even well-behaved children, sensitive to his plight. He drank. He cried out in his sleep. He roared with laughter at Richard Nixon, and Khrushchev's banging his shoe in the UN building one block east. He railed. He wept. He was affectionate and livid, staring from his armchair, entranced by a *Traviata* aria: 'Isn't that the most beautiful thing you've ever heard, duckies? Come sit by your old dad and listen to the greatest thing you'll ever hear.' Intent on making the wreck habitable, he scrubbed the thick layers of dirt in the kitchen, tore off the plaster to the brick beneath, refinished the old pine floors, knocked out the ceiling over the dining room so we children had two communicating bedroom lofts all to ourselves, albeit joined by a crazy, dangling catwalk made of rubbery planks. He punched a hole into condemned building next door to make a modest hovel for himself, inferior to anything he'd mustered for us. He made us welsh rarebit, but he was broke, so he ate dog food from cans. And if he had any cash at all, we ate spaghetti bolognese at the Italian restaurant next door, where it was dark and candlelit and dreamy with the scent of tarragon and mozzarella. We played 'Paper Roses' and 'There's a Summer Place' on the jukebox twenty times running; he was more joyful than normal in these times; he desperately wanted to make it all up to us.

In November, a runner from the court came to take us to our mother who was living with her new husband at a hotel uptown. The police had to be called. My father cried and would not release our hands and then our coats and then he was arrested and then, I think, he ran away. To the Virgin Islands. With the 5,000 dollars my stepfather paid to get rid of him. I heard a friend tell my mother the following year that he'd seen Jack, my father, and that he had opened a raucous bar called the Pied Piper on the island of St Thomas. Her photograph and ours, her friend said, were pinned over the bar.

My sister booked the tickets for August 24 from New York to Tokyo.

'But Dad wrote that we had to be in Hong Kong by the 5th of July,' I said.

'Yeah. Well, it's not that simple.'

This meant that she needed time to arrange everything—passports, photographs, shot cards. We got our passport photos in one of those curtained booths at Grand Central Station that slid out four squashed, oily snapshots in seconds. We got our passports in one day. We took all three injections at once, and our yellow shot cards were stamped and signed by a wary doctor Joan had chosen at random from the NYC phone book. I didn't even ask about dates, times, reservations and accommodation, so I was almost as surprised as my mother when my sister asked me, 'Are you packed?' and showed my mother the tickets the afternoon of the 24th and promised her in her confusion and distress that we'd call from Tokyo, then Hong Kong and be back in two weeks.

'You're joking of course,' my mother said.

'No, Mom. We're really going.'

'Your father bought you a ticket to Tokyo and you didn't think to tell me about it?'

'I thought about it. Maybe you could come with us.'

'Don't be ridiculous.'

My sister flashed the sizeable stash of purple traveller's cheques my father had sent, her ticket, our shot cards, our passports, and the whole business was concluded.

'You're under age,' my mother cried as we bolted, guiltily, from the Drake Hotel suite that smelled of my stepfather's booze and cigarettes. 'I can have you arrested at the airport.'

But we knew she wouldn't have us arrested. She would never have denied us the chance to see our father, particularly as it had been two years since we had last seen him; it was customary for my mother to let us make our own decisions, even the serious ones. She didn't know about Saigon yet, but then neither did we.

My stepfather was a very wealthy New York businessman who was unfaithful with a fat blonde nurse—a dead ringer for Eva Perón. She'd shadowed the marriage all along but we'd met her only once— on Christmas Eve the year before, when she turned up at the door. We were living in the Westbury Hotel then. She waddled through the halls of the hotel dressed in a tight, cheap tweed suit—red and green with gold braid—and a red Santa's cap studded with a white ball, claiming to be Santa's Helper. She banged on the door of our suite, screaming my stepfather's name until he relented and invited her in and we were all introduced. Everyone behaved so well. My mother spoke loudly about the weather and the lights in New York, how they glimmered from shop windows in the snow. Later, when she had retreated to the bedroom to cry so that we wouldn't see, my sisters and brothers and I poured cough syrup into the mistress's Scotch. She said she felt ill and my stepfather put on his stained camel's-hair coat and left with her. My mother finally found him six months later at the Drake, wandering the halls in his underwear.

I don't remember arriving at Tokyo airport in August 1967, only the reckless trundle into the city inside a basket-weave box of a cab. The countryside was not lovely. The grass was spare and pale on a paler red soil and all about us was an earth that couldn't sustain anything. Little grew and what did was unhealthy and orphaned. The air stank of rust and something dead. I wondered if we were driving through a place where a bomb had hit during the last war. Even if this wasn't Nagasaki or Hiroshima, and not *that* bomb but one of the countless others that must have hit Tokyo and its shrubbed outer districts. There was an old raised railway track by the side of the road with iron and broken concrete, and in my innocence I put these broken ties and the odd smell together and assumed it all had to do with the war. The improbability of a smell lingering for more than twenty years didn't occur to me.

'Beautiful,' the cab driver said, swinging his arm stiff to the air.

My sister nodded yes and clamped a hand on my shoulder. 'Very beautiful. It is very, very beautiful,' she said.

'First time? First time Japan?'

'First time. We're coming to see our father.'

'Father? In Japan?' The man frowned momentarily in the mirror, a dot of reflection hardly big enough for his face.

'No,' I said.

'Yes,' my sister interrupted. 'He's at the Imperial Hotel.'

'I thought he was in...' But I stopped because my sister squinted meaningfully, as a lizard at a fly, and I knew she meant not to mention *Saigon*. I surrendered and settled all my attention on the driver, whose black hair and eyes reminded me of my aunt's Chinese lacquer box. If the soil of Japan offered up little of aesthetic interest, the Japanese were fascinating.

The cracked road from the airport eventually broadened and filled with low, exquisite official buildings. The taxi veered and jerked past heavy willow trees lining the streets. The sun was setting. A pagoda loomed ahead, its peaks tweaking the air. The city glowed the most delicate pinky-blue and buzzed, gently, with cars and pedestrians. In 1967, New York was no match for Tokyo: it was a country bumpkin in overalls next to this brocade silk beauty it had bested in war. The United States had no city that came even close. I saw the beauty and only sensed a temperamental, festering quality beneath the order. I loved it. And the sight of my first Japanese men filled me with a sexual longing that I hadn't the experience to identify.

'Do you want to go there?' the driver signalled. *Which door* he meant as we neared the old Imperial Hotel, and we just pointed to the nearest and he pushed us out with our four bags. He was politely agitated when we didn't want to tour the city with him, so he arranged for the man at the hotel door to take our bags inside and insisted we accompany him to the moat around the Imperial Palace to feed the goldfish. He led us to the edge of the moat and purchased the pink-and-white Styrofoam-like rods of fish food and showed us how to feed the sparkling hordes rushing towards us in the shallow water. Gold-and-coral, black-spotted, the huge specimens clustered beneath the lily pads, like quarrelsome siblings, snatching at the hunks the man tossed them. 'Now, for you,' he said, and bought a new handful of fish food. It was my first experience of being treated kindly by a man who was old enough to have been my father's equal and opposite enemy. This man, I'm sure, was in his mid-forties. My father had won his silver star and his field commission at Okinawa.

All the officers had been killed and as the highest-ranking 'non-com' he found, alone, the Japanese base and radioed back its location so it could be 'taken out'. Dad was now in Saigon, in the new war.

'Yes, *hai!* Wallman? Yes, we have your reservation.' The young Japanese man at the desk of the Imperial, unfazed by two tall American teens with a wad of yen, waved a porter to show us our room. After walking down several long corridors, he opened the door to a small, charming room with two beds, a low ceiling and windows ranged across one wall with a door opening on to a courtyard, a garden. Willows, plum trees (bonsai and full-grown), a stream and stone sculptures crowded the open-air central garden, an enchanted forest steaming under the milky-pink tinge of the city at dusk. Now that we'd entered wonderland, only one problem remained: how to reach our father.

For two days we could not raise him on the phone. We called his office at Tan Son Nhut. Nothing. The phone rang intermittently and then clicked dead. My sister finally got through to someone on the base and left a message, but this meant we couldn't leave the room. 'He might call,' my sister insisted every time I begged to go visit something. We made a few forays on to the wide streets and even to a temple, where I stepped accidentally on the monk's mat with my shoes and he, and my sister, were both so disgusted that she dumped me and fled and he ranted for a few seconds and then sat down to weep. My sister, I knew, could hardly bear my ineptitude. 'You are so American,' she said after the temple incident, when I wandered, lost for an hour, over the grounds of the Imperial Palace and the guards ushered me back to the hotel with smirks hardly less hostile than my sister's. 'Do you have any idea what you did, dummy? That mat is his life. To put your dirty shoe on it is like stepping on someone's bed. Or his plate. God, you just don't know anything.' I had hidden the smooth black rock I stole from the grounds. I remember her insisting, later, I stand beneath a willow tree in the small courtyard just outside our room. She wanted to take a photograph with her new Nikon, purchased with the dwindling sheaf of traveller's cheques Dad had enclosed with our tickets.

'Stand there,' my sister said. 'And try to look Japanese.' My head almost reached the highest blossoms of the willow tree. I was clearly out of scale. In the journal I kept I wrote that I was forced to it, forced to be clumsy as I could not fit under such a small, delicate tree. My sister was disappointed with me.

That night my sister tried a half-dozen more phone calls to Saigon. The line was still dead, so she booked our passage to Hong Kong for the following morning. 'We'll find him there,' she said when I pleaded to stay in Japan and wait for him. She had bought us two rayon dresses, 'suitable for travel', and asked me to pose for a photograph wearing mine. I was appalled by the prospect of posing for another picture but my sister said, 'You'll be glad one day, Ti. I promise you. You'll be glad to have this photograph. I'll make you look really pretty in it. Okay? I promise. You just wait until you're old and you have this photograph to remind you.'

I do not remember anything of the flight from Tokyo to Hong Kong except its end, when my sister flagged a cab at the airport and said coolly, 'To the Peninsula Hotel, please.'

'We haven't got any money,' I said to her that first night, staring at the intimidating floor-to-ceiling windows and great Sputnik chandeliers in the restaurant on the Peninsula's second floor.

'We'll charge everything until he gets here.'

I told her in that case I'd have the cheapest thing on the menu.

'And what if he doesn't get here? What will we do then? How are you going to reach him in Saigon? We've tried and we can't reach him. You can't just telephone Saigon in a war. Maybe that's it.'

'It's all right, Ti. We're here now, aren't we? He'll come. He'll just be late,' she said. But her face, which was always so delicate and unmoved, had two small dark smudges under both eyes that signalled years of missed assignations and doubt.

My sister finally reached him, two days later, on August 31 in Da Nang.

'Oh, Christ,' he kept saying. 'How in the hell did you reach me on this phone?'

My sister rolled her eyes. 'Now, Dad, just relax. You said be in Hong Kong and here we are. Of course she's here too, what do you think?' She was silent for a moment and then said, 'Well, you better get here soon because the room costs ninety dollars a day and we only have twenty-four dollars left,' and here she clamped her hand over the phone and grinned at me. 'He says we got him on a top-secret line. He's up near Da Nang doing some fieldwork.'

What's fieldwork? I asked.

My sister only shrugged. 'Boy, is he mad.'

'Really?'

'Uh-huh.'

This took some doing, to make him really angry. It meant we'd surprised him. Before he'd disappeared completely two years earlier, he used to pop up anywhere: in the adjoining seat of an aeroplane flight home from school, or at a school dance, peering over the headmistress's shoulder. He always knew of our whereabouts, even if we couldn't be sure, after the divorce, of his. But the divorce had been so many years before: we'd had plenty of time to grow accustomed to his being a secret agent, even if it seemed the only people he ever spied on were us.

'Jesus Christ,' he said on the telephone. 'Stay right where you are. I'll be on the next plane. You kids. My ducks.' He started to cry.

Forty-eight hours later, we'd quit the gleaming Peninsula. There wasn't enough time to take in the images or the stink of Hong Kong, and I cannot even remember the reunion with my father. It is a blur until we are aboard the Air Vietnam flight. The seat covers were torn and smelled faintly of dung and sour milk, and the stewardess had a huge dark stain down the front of her *ao dai*, and although she was very kind, she looked distracted and her eyes flicked from the stain on her dress to the pilot's cabin, so I thought that this must be the sort of plane that crashes. What were a few more dead, travelling to the city of the dead? What was the point of reaching Saigon safely? Enormous vertical clouds coiled above the city. They never moved but hung there like suspended car exhaust and they were a curious dark brown colour, not grey or black. I asked my father what this meant.

'It's all debris,' he said.

'What's that?'

'Dust, fire, flares. I don't even notice it any more, ducks.'

He patted my head and hugged me and said he loved his duckies more than anything in the world and did I think my old dad would let anything happen to me? Of course I said no. Then the plane tilted crazily to avoid a flock of birds and we dived straight down and Dad yelled, 'Pull the goddamn tip up.' The plane jangled unsteadily to earth, landing in the centre of the dust cloud that rose over Tan Son Nhut.

'Tan Son Nhut is an ugly place,' I wrote in my journal. It was just a series of pale blue tin warehouses, temporary and bland, as if true construction were meant to follow. The heat was suffocating and there were men in fatigues everywhere; it was difficult to see where we were meant to go. My father gripped my sister and me in the rather desperate way he had, left over from his early officer days, and steered us roughly into the nearest tin hangar, which was a waiting room for incoming marines. There must have been a thousand of them sitting inside in the dark, like market fowl, on row upon row of benches, all very neat and unbandaged, and very, very quiet. There had been a steady hum just before we'd entered, but when my father pushed us through the doors and dumped the bags in behind, there was a small communal *pop*, like a flash going off, and then every voice fell dead.

'Bloody hell,' my sister said. 'What are they looking at us for?'

My sister was sixteen. She was dark and attractive in the French way, with slant eyes and olive skin. As anyone who's been to Saigon will understand, she might have been one of the former regime, or Eurasian, dressed smartly, a young Anouk Aimée, delicate and alluring. I was fifteen and perhaps ten pounds overweight, in a blue-and-white-striped cotton shift from Saks which I wore all over South-East Asia that August. Here were these thousand and more boys, hardly older than my sister, who had been trained as *shitbirds* and taught to crack heads, knocked about and ready to knock when their collective turn came, staring at us as if they'd never seen anything so disturbingly normal. And you might be tempted to think it can't have been that easy to enter Saigon as American civilians, teenagers, girls, but it only needed some belligerence and rank, and of course an entire occupying army supporting one's territorial imperative.

'Don't stare, for gosh sakes,' my father said, except it sounded more like 'for *garsh* sakes'.

'Well, they're staring at us, aren't they, Dad, so we're staring right back.'

'You kids, for garsh sakes.' He'd been giving us futile commands like this ever since he'd collected us in Hong Kong. My sister had got into the habit in the past three days of telling him to bugger off when

Joan Wallman in Saigon

he asked her to do something, but then he always said *bugger off* himself, didn't he? He said, 'Oh, bugger that,' to the South Vietnamese officer in uniform who meant to stop us and search our bags, and the man retreated, bleak as a cockroach, and I said to my father, 'Why did you treat him like that, Dad?' and he answered, 'Little beggar thinks he's one of us.'

As we stood listening, like cows flicking their ears for the faintest sounds of conversation, wondering which little beggars were like us and which not, my father signalled to a soldier hunched over the wheel of a jeep, reading a magazine.

'Jimbo! Hey, Jimbo, right on time, my boy. Look who's here. My two ducks, Joanie and Tia. Didn't I tell you I'd get them through? What did Old Baldy tell you?'

'Yes, Sir. You told me,' said Jimbo.

'Joanie's my oldest, and this is Ti.'

'Nice kids, Sir. Nice to have your family here, Sir,' said Jimbo from the front seat, looking at my sister's legs.

'Joanie here is my number one ducks.'

'Yes, Sir.'

'What am I, Dad?'

'You're my number two ducks.'

Jimbo took our bags and put them in the compartment behind the back seat. He wasn't handsome. I could see that. His lips were all dried up, like those on a desert corpse, but this desiccation was, my father said, a trait of the enlisted man. I learned quickly to tell the difference between these and the draftees, who were soft and muddled-looking, like us in fact, like me and my sister. My father was popular with men like Jimbo because he bought them drinks and chatted with them outside officers' clubs if they were on guard duty; he'd smack them on their backs and make rude comments about the ambassador's wife and say things like, 'Oh, ignore the old cow. You know she wanted London and George got Saigon, so that's punishment enough even for old Gladys, heh heh.' He understood perfectly the lowly member of the marine corps who stands at attention outside officers' clubs all over the world, who has gone through his *piss pot* training only to end up a sentinel for prigs.

'Okay, Jimbo boy,' my father said, 'we're all set. Bug out!' and the jeep streaked across the field and made a sharp turn at the enormous green military sign that read TAN SON NHUT in letters far too big for the meagre surroundings.

On the small stretch of road where my father lived in Cholon, chickens and dogs roamed, or hung about in open doorways like reserve troops, looking plunderous if vaguely dispirited, measuring up their foes as they clipped alongside us on the mucky streets. We entered an area of rubble heaps on both sides—now a house, now a heap—a teasing array of buildings plucked off at random. For every house that stood, two lay bombed. The marauding army of chickens and dogs squatted on the upturned soil and ruins, not humans. The Vietnamese had taken directly to the streets and ordered small plots in the mud by covering them over with white cloths. They sat there in circles—heads to the centre, backs to the world—eating rice from bowls.

'Almost there, ducks,' my father said cheerily.

Jimbo hammered down the centre of the road, jerking the wheel to miss a pothole, scratching his groin, and every once in a while spitting a wad of something brown that grazed my ear. We passed an open garbage truck loaded to its rim. A thin Vietnamese man rode on the back, rifling its contents. 'Government-issue truck,' said Jimbo, and made a thumbs-up sign.

Jimbo stopped in front of a white stucco building bound in with a grey metal fence topped with barbed wire. 'Welcome to the Cat House Hotel,' said my father. It was three storeys high and, inside, at each landing on the stairwell, there was a basket stuffed with rifles pointed nose-down, flanked on either side by metre-wide rolls of barbed wire for pitching down the stairs against an intruder. From the balcony of my father's third-floor apartment we could see a good portion of the city, its streets and grey, spotty shacks and, further on, the river that wound its way about Saigon like a rusted wire. Dim. That was all one could say about it. There wasn't much green, so your eyes scraped along the dusty features of the city looking for something cool to settle on, and were disappointed at reaching only the oily, metallic river. The air itself was so wet with unfallen rain, one could catch a hand in it and drag off the moisture.

A dirty latticed window took up most of the front wall. A radio, a desk, a double bed and an army cot were the only furnishings, and it was all very drab save for an ancient notice on one wall that read:

LES FEMMES ET LES BOISSONS ALCOOLIQUES SONT INTERDITES APRÈS
22 H. Which seemed prissy for the French, even colonials.

'It's not bad, is it, ducks?'

He left us in his flat that entire first day. He said he had to return
to Tan Son Nhut and he cautioned us not to go anywhere or do
anything. We lay on the double bed, our hair and cotton shifts sticking
to us, the ceiling fan loping on its axis above. A single whistle of air
blew down and, except for the occasional toot of distant horns, it
was quiet, so boringly, wind-dead, ominously quiet.

'Dibs on sitting next to Dad at dinner,' I said.

'No. I already called dibs.'

'Okay,' I said, rising from my torpor. I meant to argue; my sister
always got to sit next to our father. Then I felt badly for having such
a small thought in such a big place and slumped back to the bed. I
read half a page of *Pride and Prejudice*—it was on my ninth-grade
summer reading list. I had to close the book because my stomach was
cramped with dread—I always sweated profusely over the passage
where the ugly and ungifted younger sister, Mary Bennet, bangs on
a piano. Joan loosened and tightened the mechanics of her new
camera, buried it in her bag and then lay down again on the bed.

'Wake me up if Dad comes back,' she said.

'You mean *when* he comes back.'

'That's what I said, stupid.' She pretended to sleep until dusk,
when my father returned with Jimbo to take us for dinner at a French
restaurant.

In a jeep stuffed with rifles and grenades, we drove through a series
of narrow streets; unhealthy and in some decay, this section of the
city spread and then stopped dead at the river and looked shut up
for some reason. Shut up or shut down. Jimbo jammed on the brakes
and said, 'The Frenchie's.'

Dad said, 'Okay, ducks, grub time.'

The restaurant was on the sixth floor. It was a square, dated-
looking room, shabby, with scrubbed and worn red and black floor
tiles. The seven or eight tables covered in red-checked cloths were
empty. Broad windows on three sides must, at one time, have made
for an impressive lookout. But now everything was brown and
anonymous below. The land was indistinguishable from the water

except for the glum speckles of the streetlamps. My father took the best centre table and just as the last pale shoot of sunlight dropped below the flat horizon a flare went up on the far river bank. It shot straight up and lit the scene with a bare white glow. It burned for only a few seconds before flickering and falling back to earth.

'There you go, ducks,' Dad said. 'It's started. I can set my watch by it.'

'What's started, Dad?'

'The fighting. There,' he said, and as if on cue another flare went up and we heard a tremendous roar and saw three planes. 'Just like day,' my father said, as if we were watching a Fourth of July celebration. 'One minute you can't see your own hand, then *boom*, just like day out there. By God, I tell you those damn things saved my life more than once.' We sat at our table up against the huge windows as the jet fighters approached and dived like eager pelicans into the flare-lit spots. Tat-tat-tat-tat. Crackle and spit sounds echoed in the dark, and there was a pervasive smell of rust and burning hair. A Frenchman appeared. He was short and fat with black hair and a beleaguered look: sighing, sweating, put out by having to cook and serve. He rubbed his stumpy fingers in his stiff apron and smiled with fake cheer. He shouted over the din that there was only water buffalo to be had this evening and perhaps a potato, and good wine, plenty of that, and a crème caramel for dessert.

'I don't want any water buffalo, thank you,' I said, because I'd seen one standing in a ditch, bulky and sad, picking at grass near Tan Son Nhut. My sister declined as well, so we had potatoes and stirred our crème caramels, and the Frenchman sat in a chair against the far wall and waited for us to finish and go. No one else came or went. We must have been there an hour at least, watching my father drink, watching the planes drumming away in a repeated pattern, as if they were firing at nothing at all but just following a map.

'So what are they shooting at, Dad?' I asked.

'Eat up, duckies. Don't leave any potatoes or you'll hurt the old French guy's feelings.'

'I don't see what they're doing out there,' Joan said. 'They go over the same bit again and again. Are they practising or something? It looks stupid to me. This is a stupid restaurant, Dad. What'd you bring us here for?'

'Because you're my number one stinker, ducks.'
'That's all you ever say when I want to ask you about something.'
'You're my stinker, though, aren't you, ducks?'
'I guess so.'
'What about me, Dad?' I said. 'Aren't I your stinker too?'
'Yep. You're my number one and number two stinkers.'
Jimbo came to fetch us and we had a quiet ride back to Cholon. Dad went to sleep on his army cot pressed under the windows. My sister slept on her side of the double bed closest to the door. I waited until I heard Dad snore before turning on the radio to a low sizzle. A voice sang something about *crying in the chapel of love* and then I heard the name Peggy Lee and a voice that sounded suspiciously like Jimbo's cracking dirty jokes. I pulled the radio to my pillow and slept with the speaker to my ear until daybreak.

Most of Dad's male friends I'd met from the Funny Business—which meant, I assume, either the OSS or the CIA—were not at all like Jimbo; they had bent noses or a drooping eyelid or some sort of scar and they were not the type expected to show up on time.

'Fuck,' Jimbo said. Fire rods, gas lines, Government-issue socks, the USMC, the VC and Lyndon Johnson were all f-ing f-ers.
'Who's the fucker now, Jimbo?' I asked.
'Don't call me Jimbo, kids.'
'Sorry, Mr Kowalchuck. Who's the fucker now?'
'Doodle A-hole hand.'
'Oh, I get it.' I exited the jeep and positioned myself as close to Jim Kowalchuck as he would allow. 'Your watch is broken.'
'Fuckin' right.' He spat and rolled a Lucky Strike from one end of his cracked mouth to another.
'Mr Kowalchuck?'
'Yep.'
'What's the difference in f-ers between your watch and Lyndon Johnson?'
'One's a fucker and one's just *fucked.*'
We were parked somewhere in the vicinity of the Continental Hotel. Dad had left us to change money, to get some illegal greenbacks: 'Take the kids for a soda, Jimbo. I've got some funny business to take care of.' He yelled, 'See you soon, ducks.' He was

obviously happy but, as always, addressing my sister rather than me. 'We're gonna get you ducks rigged out in *ao dais* when you get back.' The door slammed and he was gone.

I wonder now what it must have been like for him to see us sitting there in the dirty green jeep: Jimbo was as reliable as a spent grenade and we were so fresh, so deliciously incongruent, his two American babies that he hadn't seen for two crucial years; we were now at our full heights and approximately final shapes. He drew back from me, though. I thought then it was my spots, that I was ugly and he disappointed. I know now it was my wide mouth and slightly swollen features; my growth spurt and sexual development were not to be tidy like my sister's. I didn't sprout straight from child to adult, grave and slim. I had got stuck and looked dumb and sensuous, sketchy; cobbled together from too many disparate family elements to be sleek. I was glad for Jimbo's vague alliance.

'Yes, Sir, Baldy,' said Jimbo under his breath. He slammed the hood and we bolted off to a small French bar in an alley near Tu Do Street. 'Come on, kids. We'll get us something to drink.'

Jim Kowalchuck had other dimensions. I was sure of that. Where a mouth and eyes should have been, Jim Kowalchuck had gone all corroded. He would have spent the duration of the war doing nothing, like an upturned tank by the roadside, if he'd had the chance. He was cataclysmically bored. He didn't want to show us anything, no fighting, no restaurants, no dismal officers' club where the lizards ran overhead. He sat us down at a cosy table in the very back of a narrow, poorly lit bar with straw on the floor. Jimbo ordered a beer and lit a cigarette. He swigged the beer and tapped the fingers of his left hand when it wasn't trembling at his mouth, searching for the cigarette. He jiggled one leg so that his head bobbed as if on a hinge.

'Never you mind,' he said, when my sister asked about two Vietnamese women at the bar.

'They're pretty, don't you think?'

'Nope.'

'I like their dresses,' I said. 'Dad said we could get one. Do you think I could get one like theirs, Mr Kowalchuck?'

'Sure thing. If you want to be measured for one and see them laugh their fuckin'-A heads off.'

'Who's going to laugh?'

'Anybody in a ten-mile radius.'

'Okay. Well, never mind. Can I go up and say hi to them at least?'

'Nope. Drink your beer.'

'Dad said we can get an *ao dai*,' my sister said. 'And Tia's not supposed to have beer. Dad said to get us *sodas*.' Jimbo just shook his head and spat tobacco on the floor. My sister said 'Hi,' to the pretty Vietnamese girls sitting at the bar with an American soldier. They said 'Hello,' and giggled.

'Told ya so,' said Jimbo, as if this explained something.

Later that day, Dad took us to what he called the 'Black Market' in the centre of downtown Saigon. It was a strip of pavement with kiosks running along both sides for blocks. Some kiosks were tented, others were bare of any covering, their wares exposed and colourful. Thick Persian and Oriental rugs lay end to end in the centre, as if a carpet had been spread for a dignitary. In one of the nearest kiosks, Dad had us measured for *ao dais* by three petite Vietnamese women. They giggled heartily with each tape reading: the waist, the upper arm, the ribcage, the neck, the chest. The measurements had to be precise as the over-garment is fitted tight to the torso before it splits into back and front panels to the ankles. The women shook their heads at the prospect of making the willowy satin pants fit these Neanderthal giants. The fabric for everyday wear was a paper-thin, tightly woven silk blend, matt. I chose a sapphire blue from the hundreds of bolts. My sister chose a burnt orange with the non-traditional rounded collar. I asked for black pants but the women said this would not be proper. We must both have white pants because the black was for the farming class, for peasants. The outfits were ready that afternoon. Back in Cholon, when I appeared on the balcony dressed in the *ao dai*, my father said, 'You look beautiful, ducks'—for the one and only time in my life. Then he said I must change, that I could not wear the costume until I got back home and then I must wear it frequently.

Saigon had never been part of the plan. We were supposed to see Japan ourselves and then meet my father in Hong Kong. There had been a third jaunty postscript at the bottom of his letter: 'And don't tell your mother. The old sourpuss has lost her sense of humour.' My mother had a great sense of humour. She just didn't think my father was funny any more. During their marriage, she would say later, he'd shown his true colours. He'd stolen a Persian rug from my mom's Aunt Betty—even though he adored Aunt Betty. When my sister asked, 'Why did you do that, Dad?' he replied, 'Your old aunt has too much stuff anyway.' We could see he had a point.

When he didn't work for two years and sat in the living room quoting passages from Chekhov and singing, 'Abraham Lincoln's mother was a Je-ew,' he boasted that he was working for the CIA and waiting for his next assignment. Then he would hush us up in a stage whisper that we say *not one word*, not one word, mind you, or that would be *it*, about his involvement in the agency. In the last year of my parents' marriage, my father would fall in at three in the morning, bleary-eyed and raving about Arnhem. What were the chances, my mother would wonder, of his employers coming in and carting him off? Did one call the main office in Virginia? He would flash his expired Department of Defense ID in anyone's face—a doorman, the floor walker at Gimbel's—and push to the head of any line, saying, 'Get me such-and-such, I'm in the Funny Business.' His identity photograph showed an ordinary head, handsome, gleaming bald, with two blue eyes. My father was a spy—the low-life variety, a failure: a Willy Loman of spies.

But he was also the sort of father you waited up for, like Santa Claus. There was always a faint expectation of something imminent and celebratory when he was around. He was able to make a good meal and general hilarity from nothing, from what other people would have thrown away. After the divorce and the custody trial the relief—for my mother and me and my brothers and sisters—lasted about two months, until we realized he was actually gone from New York; life felt suddenly diminished, as if we lived in cotton batting.

Dad returned stateside eventually and we saw him three or four times a year until 1965, when he disappeared again without a word. He called from the airport one night, out of the blue, and we drove to Kennedy to meet him. He knew my mother was miserable with my stepfather and his Eva Perón mistress. He begged Mom to go back to him, to bring us, and we'd make a run for it to Cuba or Kenya. I saw my mother relent and tear up in the airport bar. They kissed, but he was still on the next flight out, to South Africa I think. I remember him hugging me and apologizing for not being an ordinary father but I must remember that he did love me and missed me all the time. He had a strange, wild glow about him, as if he'd some treasure stashed, a secret; I thought he intended kidnapping us again. He assured me everything would be all right and he'd be back. Soon. He promised to write. But I heard nothing for two years and thought he was dead. I waited quietly for a postcard for two years and then finally gave up hope of ever seeing him again. I willed myself to forget him and took my stepfather's last name.

Going back into Tan Son Nhut the second afternoon was a less formal affair than I would have thought. We met a GI at the chain-link fence and he passed us through lazily and Jimbo dropped us in the centre of the compound. The dust had disappeared. The sun was radiant. It was only a short distance along a dirt road to my father's office inside one of the pale blue, corrugated-tin structures. I heard *hup-hups* and vague commands but it was quieter away from the main airport buildings. Once inside, there was air conditioning and a cosy room with a tropical flavour. We might have been in Puerto Rico or St Thomas. There were a large chrome drafting table and stools against one wall and a small cherry desk and chair against the opposite wall. The space was narrow but bright and lined from mid-height almost to the ceiling with a cork board cluttered with maps of the Mekong Delta and the demilitarized zone and plans and architects' drawings of bridges and housing. Some towns were circled on the maps and there were areas scratched out with cross-hatching and staked out with coloured pins. Two enormous black Xs had been dragged over the map of the DMZ. There would have been no point in my asking about these. I simply had to look and take in as much as I could.

My father had a gift for three-dimensional reckoning which developed in the army in the Corps of Engineers; when he saw a map, he could stake out the best battle zones with Xs and circles and say to his superiors, 'Here. Tanks here at so many metres, push this way, then pull the others down to this side of the river.' Two of my three brothers inherited this gift and turned it into an aptitude for sculpture, for art, for drawing. I had seen these same Xs and circles in their childhood art journals, only here they were over houses and fields and perhaps a temple. In the centre of the cork board was a letter from me:

Dear Daddy, We are coming to see you soon. I'm so happy you wrote. Where were you? Were you in Saigon all that time? I love you and miss you. XXXXXOOOO From your ducks!!! Your ducks, Tia XXXXOOOOO.

Jimbo stuck his head in the door and said, 'Ready, Sir?' Dad said they would have to be gone for about an hour. They left us at a strange bar inside the compound: an old rickety place no bigger than a shed with two crude, wooden tables and benches inside and a white bar that ran the length of the room. It didn't match anything. It must have been there before the US military ever thought about going to Saigon. Perhaps it was someone's house; it just happened to be in the restricted area and its occupants had been told to shove off.

Dad and Jimbo dropped us just inside the open door. Four or five soldiers slouched at the bar. Sitting alone at one of the two tables was another soldier. *Shunned*, was my first impression—as if he were either the class bully or a simpleton. He jerked his head up as we entered: 'Sit down sit down sit down.'

'Excuse me?' my sister said.

'Sit down sit down I'll get you something. I'll get it. Sit down sit down yeah yeah.'

The GIs at the bar laughed and twisted in their stools and stared at us. We sat with the lone soldier. My sister fared better than me; she never felt obliged to make people feel comfortable, so she just listened quietly and respectfully, and fanned herself.

'Can I git you somethin'? What you want? Can I git it for you? Sit down with me now. Will ya? Will ya sit with me if I git you somethin'? I ain't seen a round-eye in thirteen months. Not one. All slope-eye girls. Can I git you somethin'? Can I? I don't mean nothin'. Won't touch ya. Won't lay one finger on ya but can I git you somethin'? Can I? Just a Coke? Okay? One Coke and that's it. Okay. Okay?'

'Okay.' I had to say something. His eyes were too big and they didn't focus on anything. His hands shook, his nails were bitten to shards, and he made a constant motion as if he were patting an invisible dog. There's a name for his condition now, but back then I could just hear the other soldiers giggle the way people will laugh behind a lunatic's back. Who could pass up a chance like that in wartime, to make fun of someone who wouldn't be hurt, who wouldn't even notice? He jumped up to order three Cokes and my sister whispered not to worry, that he 'just needed proximity to something normal', but this turned out to mean two solid hours of his talking, non-stop, six inches from my face. My sister turned away, stirring her Coke in a glass like a mint julep. I wanted to sock her. The man had black hair that thinned to baldness in odd places—a patch by his ear, a patch where his parting was—so it wasn't natural-looking. I thought maybe he'd been wounded in the head, and I meant to ask him, but never got the chance. His hands and his uniform were dirty, like a mechanic's. He said he'd come in from 'further up'. He expected me to know what this meant.

'Just got here. Just got out the chopper and come here. Just got here. Ain't seen a round-eye for thirteen months, ain't seen one. Round-eye woman. Know what I mean? Been in a cage. Been in a cage up past the line. They couldn't keep me, oh no. I got out the claws of them fuckin' bastards. Killed them fuckers and got out. Know what I mean? Don't mean no harm. Just wanna talk. Okay? Okay?'

Then he would ask where I was from but he wouldn't give me time to answer. I gave up saying anything except 'Okay' and drank my Coke. I think it was his talk that held everything up so it wouldn't collapse, on him, and on us, as we sat there in his cage with him. By the time Dad got back I felt flattened out like a tin can on a road. And wouldn't you know. The man stopped on a dime the second my father entered. It wasn't that he knew my dad. It had to do with light and darkness in a funny way. Dad was such a big man that he blocked out all the light as he stood in the door and this soldier sitting across from us just shut down, froze, as if he were some kind of insect or lizard, instinctively used to the bigger, darker shadow of its enemy. Or maybe he just shut up because he was a good soldier.

'Why did he say he was in a cage, Dad?' I asked.

'Poor bastard. Never mind.'

We were not allowed back into Tan Son Nhut as the day of the election approached, the election of Thieu and Ky. My father told us to do our homework while he went to work.

'In Saigon?' my sister said. 'You don't do homework in a war zone.' She took shower after shower in the mouldy brown-tiled bathroom with its overhead spigot dripping greenish water.

'Well, I'm going to go talk to the Vietnamese man downstairs,' I announced.

'Just don't say anything dumb.'

The man who guarded the huge metal gate of the compound had never spoken to either my sister or me. We had an awkward moment at first; we were both repulsed by the obvious flaws of the other, not realizing what we had in common.

I saw something in his stare of *how big this one is, the colour of a rain cloud, more monkey than woman*. And for my part, being American and so young, I thought *boy, is he ugly*. But we *had* to sit and look at one another, just to see what we could see. I had brought down some playing cards, so I taught him a rudimentary form of poker using matchsticks for chips. When we grew bored with this, I read him passages from *Pride and Prejudice*. I don't think he liked Jane Austen but he was so polite that he sat like a monk through the most frivolous scenes, understanding every few words. At the end of each passage he clapped his hands together like two blackboard dusters and bowed so, I bowed too, and he fixed a rendezvous by signalling a 'V' with two fingers, meaning, I thought, until tomorrow then, two o'clock. But he could have meant something quite different.

That evening, when Dad had not returned by dusk, we lit the single bulb on a wire wound in fly paper and my sister went through all his things: his briefcase, his suit pockets, the wooden bowl under the bed jammed with paper clips, spent shells and some nail clippers. She flipped open his passport and found three red X's in the spaces marked 'spouse' and 'dependants' and whole pages stamped *persona non grata*.

'Hey, what does that mean?' I asked.

'It's Latin, dummy. I'll have to look it up when we get home.'

'What are "dependants"?'

'Us.'

'And who do you think *they* are?'

I sat beside her on the bed and she held, in each hand, two halves of a ripped photograph. The picture was of a young Vietnamese couple, a girl sitting on a man's lap, and they were dressed in Western clothing: she was in tight pants and an open-necked shirt, not an *ao dai*, and he wore khaki pants and a white shirt. They were lovers. Even I could see that.

'Why do you think it's torn?' I said. 'I mean, who'd keep a torn picture like that, with her on one side and him on the other. It's torn right down the middle, to separate them.'

'No kidding.'

'Well, I'm going to ask Dad about this, and the *persona non grata*.'

'You better not, Ti. You promise me you won't. We'll wait until we get back home and ask Mom.'

'Okay. But I'm going to ask Jimbo about the picture at least.'

'You just better wait until we get home. You wait until we get home and ask Mom, or else, get it?'

The last night, the night before the elections, was the worst of the four we'd spent in Saigon. Dad would have said *all hell broke loose* about the fighting that came into the city. The planes rumbled overhead from Tan Son Nhut, one after the other without any break until dawn, each take-off threatening, it seemed, to tear off the roof. At around two in the morning, one of the main bridges was fire-bombed and there were flares and gunfire and explosions. My father sat on the balcony, like Nero peering down at Rome and I could see the ball of fire from the burning bridge just over his gleaming head. Sometimes I heard the tap of his pipe on the cement floor and a burning match, and the occasional sound of spittle as he smoked. You'd think it was impossible to hear these delicate sounds above the din, but they were distinct and local against the other noise: I only had to call out faintly through the open door for him to hear me.

'Dad?'

'Yes, ducks. You still awake?'

'I can't sleep.'

'Come here, bunkins.' He pulled up an aluminium chair and he motioned for me to sit and then held me tightly to his chest.

'What's happening?'

'There's some trouble down at one of the bridges.'

'Will they get over?'

'Nope.'

'But they might get over, don't you think?'

'No, ducks.'

'Well, let's just say, if they *do* get over, how many blocks is it from the bridge to here?'

'A lot.'

'Fifteen? More than fifteen, or less than fifteen?'

'Go to sleep, ducks. Nothing's going to hurt you with your old dad here, understand?

'Dad, are you really in the CIA?'

'Yep.'

'Why don't you get out?'

'You can't get out.'

'You could try. You could come home to New York and get an apartment. You could change your name or something and move back home.'

'It doesn't work that way.'

'Why not?'

'You do things and then you can't go back and then you never get out.'

'Are you ever coming home?'

'Aw, ducks.'

Down by the river a final huge explosion lit the jagged outline of the bridge before it fell, a series of frail sticks flaring then crumbling.

'I'm taking you ducks back out tomorrow. You can't stay here. Now go to sleep.'

But I didn't sleep. I counted the seconds between gunfire the way one counts the delay between lightning and thunder. I said *persona non grata* over and over again to keep it safe in my memory and I tuned the radio to the Jimbo-sounding man and pressed it close to my ear and when I heard my father snore faintly at daybreak, when the fighting stopped and everything was quiet, I fished his passport from the case under the bed and wrote a tiny '6' beneath 'dependants' and traced a faint '1' beneath 'spouse'.

In the morning, my father went off to book our tickets for the afternoon flight to Bangkok via Cambodia. Jimbo came to help us with our bags and I asked him about the previous night's battle down by the river but he only said: 'What your dad bring you to this fuckin-A-hole place for? He nuts?'

'Kind of.'

Jimbo liked this answer, so he showed me a picture of his own children back in Newark.

'That's Shelley and there's my Ricky. He looks just like me, don't he?'

'I can see that he looks exactly like you,' I said, though I did not see this at all.

'Dad talks about you kids all the time. Joanie this. Joanie that. Drive me up a wall.'

'What does he say, Mr Kowalchuck, when he talks about me?'

'All kinda crap. Miss them kids. Those ducks. Calls himself Baldy all the time. "Old Baldy only did one good thing, Jimbo, when he had those kids." *Love my Joanie*, he says.'

'But does he say my name, *my* name, Tia. Does he say *love my Tia* like that, Mr Kowalchuck?'

I remember his hesitation and his shoulders jerked.

'Fuckin' right! *Tia Tia Tia*. I can guarantee he says that name a bona fide one hundred per cent of the whole fuckin' day!'

'Dad never says fuck,' my sister said.

'He don't have to. He ain't enlisted. He gets to fuck whoever he wants.'

I thanked Jimbo Kowalchuck. I kissed him on the cheek which was all plotted over with meteor hits, so this took some courage for a fifteen year old. Plus he had a way of training his eye on you if you got too close, like a cigar-store Indian: resentful and dead.

'Well, shit!' he said, as a sort of thank you, and cheered up considerably just in time for my father to return with his pockets stuffed with US dollars. He smacked Jimbo on the back, *thwack*, and said, 'To the airport, Jimbo my boy,' and we headed off to Tan Son Nhut for the last time.

The funny thing about that summer is that, however selective memory may be, particularly in the way a fifteen year old's is, I can't remember seeing a single dead body. Except the couple in the photograph; I knew the lovers were dead without having to ask.

I had one last conversation with Jim Kowalchuck just before we left. We stood in the dust whirled up by the choppers. My sister was digging her fingers into my arm.

'Mr Kowalchuck, can I ask you a question about Dad?'

'No F-hole way.'

'It's important. I just have to know something. If you let me ask this question, I'll tell Dad not to call you Jimbo any more.'

'Like to see that. Okay. Go on. But snap it up before Old Baldy gets back.'

'We saw this picture in Dad's apartment, torn down the middle, with a Vietnamese girl on one side and a boy on the other. How come he wants to keep a torn picture like that?'

Jimbo shrugged, 'VC.'

'What do you mean?'

'They was VC and they must have got interrogated. Not together, though. What you care about them for?'

And then I said *What does that mean?* and Joan said *Shut up, just shut up* in a whisper, but much louder in a way than if she'd shouted. Jimbo did shut up, which surprised me. I really missed his good humour once we had said goodbye, and I thought my sister was a killjoy. Besides, it was my sister who was the source of all this trouble: she was the one with the obsession for going through Dad's things.

My father flew with us back to Thailand and left us at a hotel in the centre of Bangkok. 'Goodbye, ducks,' he said. He hugged us both and then began to cry. This meant that my sister and I couldn't cry ourselves but instead had to bolster him up. We waved cheerfully as we saw his bleak face in the back of the taxi turn towards us, then fade and diminish to a speck in the crowded street.

In the hotel lobby I bought a sapphire ring from a street vendor. Later, when my sister saw the ring, she desperately wanted one like it, as if all her repressed hopes and wishes had welled up and demanded some token that we'd actually been here, in South-East Asia; that our father had wanted to see us enough to risk our lives. My sister cried in the taxi on the way to the airport. I've only seen her cry twice in my life. She said it was because she hadn't got a ring of her own but I knew this wasn't the real reason because she had said, 'No thank you,' when I offered her mine.

This summer I tried—without success—to find a J. Kowalchuck in the Newark phone book. I need to talk to Jimbo because I only saw my father three more times, briefly, before he died, and because I took the photograph. I hid it in my suitcase and brought it back with me and taped the Vietnamese girl and boy back together. They had been *interrogated*. I didn't even know what the word meant when I first heard Jim Kowalchuck say it.

When I saw the recent pictures of the Iraqi prisoners at Abu Ghraib, the ones tortured by the Americans in this new war, I realized I still hadn't settled questions from the old war in Vietnam and my personal war in Saigon. I started to miss my father in a way I hadn't for years. I used to think he was like a Willy Loman who bungled and loved haphazardly—but in earnest. He didn't know himself in the end, even though he had tried his best, and I was comforted by the fact he had been a failure in the war. But he's left me the task, to find out who he was, like an inheritance, and I have to take it up. But I'm afraid, like a *shitbird* entering a *piss pot* war zone, that I might lose him for ever when I find out more about what he did in Saigon. The thing I am most afraid of is that he may not have been a failure at all; he may have been very, very good at his job.

But I tell myself I could be wrong. These might not have been the events at all. My memories of that summer seem so clear to me but I could be wrong now. I could have been wrong then. Who is there to tell me otherwise? My sister assures me she remembers nothing. She only looks at me in wonder and says, gently, 'Is that so?' 'Did it happen?' 'How can you remember such things?' □

GRANTA

BYE-BYE NATALIA
Michel Faber

Trapped in the dingy, airless Internet cafe, Natalia picks at the frayed black lace of her dress while the photograph of her American penpal loads into the computer. He's sent it at an unwieldy file size, and it's taking ages to come through. A horizontal sliver is slowly, slowly, slowly expanding downwards, giving her a glimpse of the top of Bob's head and nothing more. He's bald, it seems. Or almost bald. She's not usually attracted to bald men. Although Alexander Melnik, the lead singer of her favourite Ukrainian group Inward Path (now defunct, like just about everything else in her life) used to wear a woolly hat onstage, suggesting that he probably didn't have much hair on top, either. She should be more tolerant. There is a lot at stake.

The hem of her dress is unravelling. The lace is old: she likes to tell her friends that it was originally part of the shawl of a nineteenth-century countess who was executed by the Russians. In truth she found it in a basket of assorted remnants at a street market in Kiev and has no idea how old it is. Old enough to be coming to bits, anyway. If only she had a needle and thread, she could mend some of it while waiting for more of Bob's face to manifest on the PC screen. His brow is mostly there by now. It is slightly wrinkled but tanned. He lives in Montana.

Natalia looks at the clock on the cafe wall. She has been sitting here too long already: soon her allotted time will run out and she'll have to pay for another session. Squinting in the gloom—the Internet den is kept dark so that the male customers can enjoy their fight games better—she checks how many *hyrvnias* she has in her purse. Not many.

She considers emailing Bob and asking him to resend his picture, this time at a more manageable size of 50Kb or less. She lifts her hands, preparing to type. Then she lowers them again. She doesn't want to get on the wrong side of Bob. Not that he's nasty—he seems uncommonly well-meaning—but he's a little touchy, a little suspicious. They've exchanged half a dozen emails so far; in the third, she made the mistake of signing off as Natasha instead of Natalia, and he seized upon this as evidence of something fishy. Who exactly was she, he demanded, 'Natalia' or 'Natasha'? She explained to him that in Ukraine, each person has many versions of their Christian name. *Natalia, Natasha, Nata, Natashinka*: it's all the same, she told him. Which wasn't quite true, of course. Some versions were more affectionate than others; you would only use them with someone you were fond of. After Bob's 'who-exactly-*are*-you?' message, she reverted to Natalia in more ways that one.

But this is not the way she wants it. She wants to become intimate with him, to win his trust. She wants, in the end, to be his Natashinka. And that won't happen if she finds fault with his email technique, will it? She must ration the number of times she challenges him. She mustn't waste his valuable American time. She must wait patiently for his unwieldy picture to load. His eyes are there now. They are blue as the Montana sky behind his head.

If she'd remembered to bring her Walkman, she could have been playing her Inward Path tapes while she waited. Natalia's Walkman is her most precious possession: all it needs is a couple of cheap batteries and it functions happily. Such a simple mechanism: society can crumble, governments and wars can come and go, but put a couple of AAs into the Walkman and its tiny spindles revolve at the same speed as ever. Miraculous. Grigory, her old schoolfriend who now works in the faux-Soviet nightclub on Primorsky Boulevard, is the proud owner of a portable CD player that looks like a miniature flying saucer; he makes fun of her ugly grey plastic cassette player with its tarnished stickers. But Inward Path's first three albums never made it on to CD; they were cassette-only releases, for the local fanbase. *Golodomar*, *Antiar* and *Labyrinth*—she owns them all, and a cassette version of their one-and-only CD, *Citadel*. She has played them hundreds of times on her trusty little machine.

Bob's face has pretty much finished downloading. His chin isn't there yet. His mouth is stretched in a toothy smile. The teeth are white and regular. What is it with Americans and straight white teeth? God, they must clamp braces on babies in the womb.

Natalia self-consciously licks her teeth with her tongue. They are not perfect. Two of them are crossed over each other. One of them is chipped. She has lots of fillings, even though she's only twenty-five. Even so, Bob picked her out of hundreds of others on the BlackSeaBrides.com website, so she must have impressed him as an acceptable-looking girl. She didn't show her teeth in the photo, but then she isn't much of a smiler. She likes to look serious. One of her old schoolfriends, Anya, frustrated that her job as a radiologist wasn't paying enough to cover rent and groceries, offered herself to the BlackSeaBrides.com website on the same day as Natalia. Anya posed in a low-cut evening dress that was little more than a nightie, displaying lots of cleavage, a naked leg balanced on a footstool, high heels. She simpered at the camera, as if to say to the unknown men sizing her up: Fancy the merchandise? Well, just say the word and it's yours. Natalia posed in the same gear she always wore: her black Goth dress, lace-up boots, the woollen cardigan knitted by her grandmother. She looked slightly downwards, as if deep in thought. She probably was. She was probably thinking, What...the fuck...am I doing?

Bob's chin has appeared. It's not much of a chin, to be honest. Not the square jaw of the American cowboy hero. But Bob is as close to a cowboy hero as they come in the modern world. He owns a cattle ranch, run by employees chosen by his father. He owns a few horses, a big house and a small apartment in the city. His marriage broke up eight years ago and his kids live with his ex-wife in some other part of the United States. He is lonely. Loneliness radiates from his emails like a nuclear aura, like a giant spill of industrial waste. 'I've done all right,' he told her at the very beginning of their correspondence. 'I got no complaints. But if I could have a person to share all this stuff with, that would be the icing on the cake.'

What was it about her that made this Montana cattle rancher think she might be the icing on his cake? Why didn't he pick one of the hundreds of other Natalias and Anyas and Olgas, all displaying themselves on BlackSeaBrides.com, all listing their vital statistics, their university education, their lack of bad habits and their desire to give themselves to the right person? 'There was something sinsere about your face in the photo's,' he told her in one of his early emails. 'Theres a lot of women just out to take a man for a ride. I could tell you werent like that. And the part where you wrote about your brother in hospital. It shows that you are a caring person.'

Natalia does indeed care about her brother. It's Montana Bob she's not sure if she could care about, even if she were elevated to the status of Mrs Bob, riding her own horse in the American summer. Maybe she could. Surely she could. He seems quite a decent sort of guy, considering the circumstances of their romance, which, let's face it, aren't so romantic. But he's not a sex tourist and he's not a creep. At least, not as far as she can tell. Didn't he tell her about the divorced wife and the teenaged children in his second email? By the standards of Internet matchmaking, that's pretty impressive. Also, he says he likes alternative music! She'll have to ask him what groups he means; it might be a good way of minimizing the age difference between them. Which isn't that huge, actually. Anya is swapping emails with an Iowa computer salesman who's fifty-two. Bob is in his late thirties. Plenty young enough to be into alternative music. Bob writes:

> Here is a picture of me taken by one of my employees. It's not a very good picture but at least it's in focus! The picture of you on the website was really something special. I've looked at it a lot. You have such a soulfull expression in it. And I love your dress, the same dress you are wearing in the photos you sent in the letter. Those photos have been looked at a lot too, I can promise you, but not as much as the website one, because I can blow that up FULL SCREEN and I almost feel you are in the house with me. I hope one day you will be. As my guest. Anyway, I was talking about your dress. The photos were taken at different times in different places but you are wearing the same dress in every shot. Is it your only dress or do you just like it a lot? I like it a lot too. It's excotic and really different. I feel I am ready for something different in my life, something out of the ordrinary. I am ready to learn about foreign cultures and things I never thought about before. I don't want to become an old fart before my time. That's a noughty word—fart. I don't usually use noughty words but in the States, fart also means an old boring person. Not that I have anything against old people. Natalia, I am rambling here. It's late and I'm tired. I will write to you again tomorrow when I am fresh. Please try to write back more often as I get such an enormous buzz when I get an email. It puts a smile on my face all day.

Natalia sits staring at the big tanned face on the computer screen. Marek, the guy who works behind the counter of the Internet cafe, looks at it, too, pretending not to. He knows damn well what's going on here. He's seen it before.

After a couple of minutes, Natalia wonders why she even bothered to wait for the picture to download. It's really not relevant what Bob looks like. He is a rope being dangled down to her from a helicopter as she stands on the roof of a burning building. She has to grab that rope as soon as possible.

Dear Bob,
Thank you for sending your picture. It was very good and clear,
and I can see in it that you are a kind man. Big sky of Montana is
behind you, and it makes me very much wish that I could be with
you under that sky together. Forgive me for writing a not so long
email. I am working most of day and have not so much time for
going to Internet cafe. I will try to go more times, but job
conditions here in Ukraine are not so friendly. Also my brother is
still in the hospital and I go to see him as many times as possible. I
am very glad you like alternative music. What groups are your
favored ones? I like very much The Cure and Sisters of Mercy and
Metallica and Ministry. Some of this music is not easy to buy in
Ukraine but some of our record-shop owners travel now to Poland
to get supplies. But my most favored group of all time is Ukrainian
group called Inward Path. Their words are in English, but full of
poetry of Ukraine spirit. They made many cassettes but I fear they
are not nowadays working any more. This music was important
part of my life.

Natalia sits for another minute, trying to think of something to
add, something that will steer the email towards a natural conclusion.
Bye-bye, Natalia, she types at last.

Outside, it's a brilliant sunshiny day. Odessa is living up to its
tourist-brochure image. All the trees are in leaf. The billboards
are glossy and international. The shop fronts are exactly the same
as what would be on offer in the main streets of London or Paris,
except for the alleyways in between the Prada and Armani stores,
where mangy dogs still scratch themselves and ugly old men still play
cards at rickety, rain-damaged tables. There are sleek new cars
weaving through the traffic, in among the rusted junk heaps driven
by the gypsies. Western pop music is on the breeze. The girls wear
fluffy zip-up tops, pastel nail polish, cute boots, low-slung jeans that
expose their belly-buttons and bum-clefts. Their jeans are artfully
ragged. Poverty chic. It's been months since she saw the old guy with
no feet, pedalling his makeshift buggy in the middle of the road. She
kind of misses him. At least the bent-backed old women are still
sweeping the leaves with their ancient brooms.

Nostalgia for the bad old days: there's plenty of it around, if you look beyond the nightclub wonderland inhabited by Grigory and his pals. The twenty-first century has no use for the idealistic, dowdy drones who kept the gears of communism oiled. Anyone who's too crippled, unattractive or elderly for the new millennium is advised to stay in the shadows and wait to be cleaned away.

At least Natalia has a good job—what passes for a good job in Ukraine. She works in a record shop. Her idiosyncratic, soulful, somewhat gothic appearance is considered a plus for customer relations, despite the fact that most of the music the shop sells is vacuous pop and easy-listening rock, the sort of stuff that should be tossed hastily into a plastic bag by a supermarket cashier. But capitalism wraps its products in more mystery than they deserve, and so Natalia has been installed behind the counter of New Sounds, to suggest to passers-by that she is in some way intimately connected with the arcane, mysterious regions where Art is made, that she has passion and knowledge far deeper than the shop's crassly commercial facade might suggest.

And indeed she does. She could tell you about philology, the subject of her university degree. And she would love to evangelize on behalf of her favourite music; she would love to win new converts to Inward Path, if only New Sounds sold Inward Path albums, which it doesn't. The boss hasn't even heard of them. The boss spends his days in a swivel chair talking to Germany on the phone, nodding at the mention of the latest American sensation, and saying, 'I'll have ten. No, fifteen.'

Natalia's lunch break is over. She hurries back to New Sounds on Sadovaya Street and takes up her position behind the shop counter. Her first customer is an Austrian woman who wants the latest album by Robbie Williams. The woman is disappointed with the price. 'This isn't much cheaper than I could get it at home,' she complains, as though she has caught Natalia in the act of some barefaced scam. 'I'm sorry,' Natalia replies.

It's a balmy Tuesday. The shop closes at six and the summer sun is still high in the sky. Natalia walks straight to the Internet cafe. The gawky young men are pretending to kill enemies with their pale, big-knuckled fingers. Natalia finds her place among them and checks her emails. There's a new one from Montana Bob. No photographs this time, thank God. Not that she isn't curious to see more pictures of the man she may, if all goes well, spend the rest of her life with. It's just that she's in a hurry to go and see her brother, and she hasn't time to sit in the Internet cafe waiting for a gigantic image to load in.

I am mega busy right now. I have acessed your email away from home (I'm in town) but I want to reply anyway. When I'm working I do this a lot—check if there is any message from you. I know I should wait until I have quality time but I can't wait, that's how much it means to me to get one of your emails. Keep them coming! The Cure—what can I say. The Cure are excellent, thier song Fridays I'm In Love was a big hit here in the States. They had some wierd videos didn't they—wierd in an interesting way. Some of my friends have a real thing against The Cures' front man because he is a guy wearing make up. I say you've got to be tolerant in this world. And besides, the guy is using it (make up) to make a living. I would definately rate The Cure one of my top 20 bands from England in the 80-ies. Ministry and the sisters of Mercy I don't know unless you are talking about Christian Rock which is pretty big in these parts. Some of it is good but the messages can get quite heavy, if you're not a heavy church goer, which I am not. I think you can be spiritual without all that stuff. (Don't tell my parents though!)

Anyway, back to music. Metalicca are the best. They have been going for years but they are still at the top of the tree. Seriously rocking dudes. Do you like Black Sabbath? It's not a good idea to even mention thier name around here because people think it has something to do with satanic rights. But in my opinion they are just a great rock band. I like Ozzy Osbourne's solo stuff but Black Sabbath was something special, there was a mystery about it, like they were flying through the sky on a dark stormy night. I know that sounds cheesy but that's the only way I can express it. I must have listened to Sabbath Bloody Sabbath a hundred times when I was at school—the one with the naked women on the front cover! Natalia, please tell me about Inward Path. If they are special to you they must be pretty damn special. And don't worry about the cassettes not working anymore. I am a genius when it comes to fixing cassettes that got tangled up in the machine or snapped or whatever. I take them apart, splice them, put them back together, restore the tension. Good as new. If I wasn't running a ranch I could have had a business fixing cassettes! Except it's all cds these days. And downloads. I don't download music myself, do you? I don't feel something is mine unless I can hold it in my hands. Natalia I am rambling again—and I should be getting on with my job. Must shoot!

Natalia disconnects from the net and checks the clock. As she rummages in her purse for change to pay for her session, she imagines herself getting into bed with Bob. Imagines herself naked, lifting the sheets of a king-sized American bed and exposing the hairy torso and erect penis of a bald, well-meaning guy from Montana. The thought doesn't disgust her. Genuinely well-meaning guys are hard to find. And there is more to the picture than just two people and a bed. Outside Bob's bedroom lies a whole country. A country with properly functioning hospitals and reliably available medicines.

On her way to see Sasha she stops off at a convenience store and buys two bars of chocolate and a packet of apple strudel thingies from Holland. Then she walks towards the Odessa Steps, mingling with the Japanese tourists and European holidaymakers ambling along the boulevards. Her Slavic looks and the bohemian tattiness of her clothing render her immune to the advances of the hawkers; they refrain from pushing kitsch statuettes of Lenin in her face, or handing her leaflets about cut-rate plastic surgery. A young man she vaguely remembers from university stands right near the Steps, holding a live iguana and a Polaroid camera. He tenses up for a moment as he considers pressing the iguana on to her so that he can sell her a snap of her embracing it, then he decides against the idea. He doesn't appear to recognize her. But then, their university days are so long ago. A previous century. Nothing they studied is of any use now. Hot dogs, cappuccinos, Hugo Boss, blow jobs: that's what matters now.

A young Asian couple are smooching picturesquely under the statue of Richelieu, photographed by an accomplice. Natalia doesn't want to spoil their picture by walking through it, but their kiss goes on for ever and she has to get moving.

'Excuse me,' she says, in English. It's the universal language, after all.

She starts to descend the Odessa Steps, but instead of continuing down to the quay, she detours through the trees at the side. A few tourists squint after her in the sunlight, clearly wondering if she's savvy to a tourist attraction not mentioned in the guidebooks. But they won't follow. Their guidebooks are unanimous in advising visitors not to venture outside the designated safe areas.

Behind the trees, the landscape gets messy. There is a well-trodden path through the garbage-littered scrub, an alternative nature trail for dogs. Within a couple of minutes Natalia has reached the encampment.

There are two dwellings: a small concrete hut that was once used by caretakers for storing cleaning equipment and a vacant space under an electricity generator that's been walled shut with sheets of cardboard. A pair of jeans hangs on an improvised washing line spanned between a metal pole and a tree. Yana, a sixteen-year-old prostitute, greets Natalia with a broad smile. Her tangled hair is full of dandelion. A small child Natalia can't recall seeing here before is toddling about, wiping her tiny white hands on her knitted tunic. Dmitry is playing with the dog as usual, enjoying the sunshine. His shirt is open, revealing his lean, wiry body. The dotted scars where surgical stitches have been removed show up white against the tanned flesh. He dances off-balance, waving a cigarette in one hand and teasing the dog with the other. The dog is chewing one of the many ruined shoes scattered around the camp.

'Sasha's asleep,' says Dmitry to Natalia as she approaches the hut.

'Good,' she says.

There are three mattresses crammed into the floor space, so that she must step on to them to enter, careful not to fall. A middle-aged woman she doesn't recognize is sleeping under a mound of grubby windcheaters: probably the mother of the kid outside. The middle mattress is empty except for some pages torn from a colouring book and a scatter of cheap colouring pens. These are the only new elements in the shelter. The walls are still decorated with mildewed posters advertising Monolit Turkelt furniture, a decorative tea towel featuring scenes from Ukrainian folklore, and an ad for a Russian boy band who performed in Kiev in 2002. The broken cassette player still has a tape called *Acid Euro Trance 5* gathering dust on top of it, untouched for all the time that her brother has lived here.

Natalia squats down on the edge of the third mattress, which has

Sasha stretched out on it, nestled next to his junkie friend Andrej. The golden evening sunlight beams in on them. They look handsome and innocent together, both lightly dressed in T-shirts and military trousers. The brilliancy of the light makes them appear freshly washed and unmarked.

'Hi, Sasha,' says Natalia. 'I brought you some things.'

Her brother wakes calmly and sits up, rubbing his eyes. Andrej doesn't stir. Veterans of the streets, they've both trained themselves to recognize which noises they need to worry about and which noises they can afford to ignore.

Sasha takes a cursory glance at his sister's semi-transparent bag of food. 'I don't need it,' he says, serene and surly at the same time. He is two years older than her. He has been a removal man, a house painter; he has been to Germany, Poland, Pridnestrovye. He knows how to take care of himself.

'Maybe you can have some later,' says Natalia, putting the bag down on the spare mattress next to the colouring pens.

'I have everything I need here.'

'Even apple strudel?'

'The people from Way Home brought us a bag of buns earlier on.'

Natalia nods. Way Home is a local charity that tries to lure kids off the streets. Their volunteers distribute cheap food and basic medical supplies, and invite homeless youngsters to relocate to their shelter. Her brother is too old to qualify. 'Did they bring you some condoms?'

'Don't say such words,' says Sasha with a sly half-smile. 'Filthy-tongue Nata. Daddy would wash your mouth out with soap.'

Natalia sighs irritably. 'Daddy's not around any more.

'Is that the fairy tale you tell your American sugar daddy?' Sasha retorts. He's fully awake now and sharp as always. 'Will there be room in his mansion for me, do you think? Maybe a small cot in the corner of the bedroom?'

'You've got it all wrong. He's just a guy I correspond with.'

'Correspond my arse. Does he like boys, too? Maybe if they're young and pretty? You could send him a photo of the way I used to look when I was ten. Who knows, he might go for it. You could sneak me in, wrapped in a blanket. What do you say, Nata?'

'Let's not argue. It's a beautiful day.'

Bye-bye Natalia

They sit together on the edge of the mattress, looking out. Dmitry is still playing with the dog. He seizes the animal by the snout, wrenching the whole head violently back and forth. He knows exactly how far he can go before the dog gets dangerous. Whenever he releases his hold, the dog falls back and looks disappointed, then lunges forward for another wrestle. Natalia and Sasha settle in to the entertainment. The small child stands half hidden behind the jeans on the washing line and watches, too. Yana has disappeared, presumably gone off to beg. No one speaks. The air is punctuated from time to time with whistles, toots and tannoy announcements from the Odessa docks below.

'But seriously,' says Natalia, 'have you got condoms? Clean needles?'

'Stop nagging. You're in no position to lecture me.'

'I'm in the best position of all.'

'Yeah, on your back, with your legs spread.'

Natalia blinks, stares unwaveringly at Dmitry and the dog.

'You know I don't do that any more,' she says.

'What about for your American?'

'He just writes me emails about Metallica and The Cure. I'm trying to get him into Inward Path.'

'Oh, God,' groans Sasha, falling back on to the mattress, his head bouncing off Andrej's thigh. 'Don't you ever give up about Inward Path? They're ancient history, Natasha. You might as well be mooning over Ivan Rebroff or Billy Joel. Do you really think this American guy is going to get excited about your crappy old cassettes by a bunch of Ukrainian heavy metal losers?'

'Inward Path weren't heavy metal. They were dark metal.'

'Heavy...dark...what's the difference...' he mumbles scornfully, laying his punctured arms across his face.

'What about your precious dance music?' she points out. 'You divide it up into about fifty different categories.'

'Let's not argue,' he says. 'It's a beautiful day.'

'I have to go,' says Natalia, wiping her cheeks with her sleeve.

It takes Natalia half an hour to get home on the bus. She lives on the outskirts of Odessa, in a *communalka*, one of the old communist-era apartment buildings. She has a room of her own (with a sink, thank God), and shares kitchen, laundry and bathroom facilities with four other people, none of whom she particularly gets along with. The middle-aged couple and the old pervert are all right, but there's a girl quite close to Natalia in age who really gets on her nerves, watching loud TV that penetrates through the thin walls. This girl, Irina, clogs the toilet with sanitary pads and switches on the worst Russian pop music as soon as she wakes up. She filches Natalia's shampoo, topping up the bottle with water. The communal bathtub always has a pink tidemark around it when Irina's finished with it: the scum of thick cosmetics. 'The cool thing about this cardigan,' she once told Natalia, showing off a fake cashmere number bought for her by her latest boyfriend, 'is that it doesn't look like some senile old bag knitted it.' There are mornings when Natalia can't stomach breakfast because of the stench of Irina's perfume in the kitchen. They've been living together for eleven months and it feels like a lifetime.

Natalia warms up some leftover *golubtsy* in a frying pan, or tries to. The fear of being collared by one of her neighbours makes her too hasty at the stove and the meat inside the cabbage leaves is only lukewarm. She wolfs it down, then guiltily wipes her greasy hands on a tea towel that nominally belongs to Mrs Kotova.

Locked inside her room, she lies briefly on the bed, staring up at the Cypress Hill poster on the ceiling. (She doesn't actually like Cypress Hill—hip-hop rubbish about smoking dope—but the poster is a giant enlargement of their *Black Sunday* album cover and its dark sepia vista of a storm-wreathed graveyard speaks to her.) Every available inch of space on her walls (not that many inches altogether, to be frank) is covered with similarly gloomy imagery: hollow-eyed maidens in chains, demons, snakes, medieval castles shrouded in moonlit vapour. They make her happy, these things. Or, to be more precise, they don't make her unhappiness any worse. The mindless cheerfulness of dance music, the sentimentality of singer-songwriters, the childish naivety of pop: they all grate on her like propaganda. Better to face up to the truth.

Does Bob, way over there in Montana, have any hope of understanding the way she feels? It's hard to gauge how much he really has inside him. When he writes, he likes to keep things breezy. Maybe it's the language barrier? Then she remembers there is no language barrier for him. So maybe he just isn't very smart. Is it important that a man should be smart if all you want from him is that he should save your life? She struggles to recall everything he has ever said. Their correspondence, although only a few weeks old, is already substantial; some of his messages must have taken him hours to write. But what can she remember? At this moment, just that he doesn't care for rap.

If only she had her own computer, she could communicate with him more often; they could exchange messages through the night, when all the world was quiet, their responses flying backwards and forwards at intervals of only a few minutes, almost like a conversation.

Trying harder, she mentally retrieves one of his earliest emails to her—the second, or maybe the third. He showed his profounder side in that. Talked about the emptiness of normal life, the search for something untainted by compromise and commerce, the sense of needing to take a bold step into the unknown, to be prepared to be bewildered and reborn. The email had run for pages and had used words she'd never heard a man use before.

Now she stands on her bed and fetches, from the stack of books and papers on top of the wardrobe, her folder of Inward Path lyrics. She'll pick out her favourite ones and type them into an email for him. He asked her, didn't he? Explaining what makes great music great is impossible, especially in a foreign tongue, but she can at least give him a flavour of Inward Path's poetry.

'Bleeding', from *Citadel*—that's a must. Especially the part that always goes straight through her, where Melnik sings:

As on the day gone by
I talk to you, my faithful blade
You run with crackling flame
So careless so easy
Opening blood stream
Through flesh without pain
In spite of the sand in my eyes
And dust in my mouth
I try to talk through the pressure
Of silence
Trying to touch—like screaming
Come, talk to me, cause I'm bleeding
Desperate heart

Michel Faber

Tries to break out
Through the bones and flesh.

Then there's 'Desolation', from *Antiar*—although the words of that one are actually by Valery Bryusov, a Russian Symbolist poet of the late nineteenth century, which might be too much trouble to explain to Bob. The same goes for 'Into the Night' (words by Eduard Bagritsky) and 'Antiar' itself (words by Pushkin). Although Bob would know Pushkin, surely? Everybody in the world knows Pushkin, even Americans.

Next day, she works at New Sounds till lunchtime and then has the rest of the afternoon off. It's her regular arrangement with the boss, to make up for the weekends she gives to the shop. He waves to her from his position at the telephone, a pen clamped between his teeth. She waves back and heads straight for the Internet cafe.

It's busy today. She has to wait for a computer. Three foreign tourists are seated at the machines that are usually free for her—the less popular machines near the window, exposed to distracting sunlight. She waits patiently, in silence, while the foreigners—Germans, it seems—do what they came for. There are two guys and one woman. One guy checks emails and spends ages lost in thought, staring at the screen through thick glasses. The woman browses through real-estate websites, loading in image after image of flats for sale in Minsk, Odessa, Kharkov, Nikolaev, Kherson, Lvov... She compares the decorative order of various bathrooms and sitting rooms, jots down phone numbers and measurements. The other guy is visiting an Internet chat-room, swapping one-liners with his virtual pals. Natalia's German isn't so hot, but she gets the gist from words like *gefickt*, *Hure* and *Arsch*. His chair, when he's finally finished with it, is hot—so hot that it makes her uncomfortable through the thin fabric of her skirt. Her Montana Bob is a teddy bear among such hyenas.

She has to make this quick. She has an appointment in Krivaya Balka at 3 p.m. and it takes for ever to get out there. Copying out screeds of Inward Path lyrics is unfortunately not feasible. She types the crucial verse of 'Bleeding', and the part in 'Life Grows Weak' about standing before mighty nature like a drop in the sea and a leaf on the wind. She considers typing the whole of 'After Beginning' but settles for the final stanza only:

Was it the stars that sped towards me
Or I into abysmal night
A mighty hand seemed to uphold me
Over the abyss my flight.

Her heart is beating loud in her ribcage. No doubt partly because she's under pressure of time and she dislikes being under pressure of time. But also because she finds it stressful to commit the poetry of Inward Path to an uncertain journey through cyberspace. What if Montana Bob isn't having a particularly profound day?

'They made a very strong rendition of the song "Paranoid" by your old love Black Sabbath on their album of 1994, *Golodomor*,' she adds.

She glances up at the clock. She has five more minutes here before she has to run for the bus. Her heart beats louder than ever. She knows there's something more that Bob wants from her, and that it's been too long since she's slipped him any of it. The tone of their correspondence has grown too cordial; it needs an injection of sex. Not pure, unadulterated sex: he would have trouble dealing with that. But a cocktail of romance, reassurance and a dash of the erotic: that's what he's hanging out for, she can tell. And why not? It's what she wants too.

Bob,
I must go now but I have something significant to tell you, I know you are a good man. There are many bad men in the world and I have been hurt by some of them in my life. I have a lot of love and tender actions that I can give to the correct person, a man who will hold me and take care of me, and I will give him in return a wife to make him proud among his friends and family, as well as in our private place, where the utmost happiness can occur. I have intuition that you are that man.

The Outpatients Department is in one of the shabbiest, most desolate parts of Odessa, an area characterized by defunct factories and dusty roads half-pulverized by heavy vehicles. The clinic is behind a Jewish cemetery. It looks like a mammoth toilet block. It has the words INFECTIOUS DISEASES bolted to the concrete facade, in large totalitarian letters.

Natalia walks into the building side by side with a young man in smart-casual clothing. They have nothing to do with each other, except that they both got off the bus at this stop, and evidently they both have an appointment in this clinic. Natalia wonders how this young man got infected; he's no doubt wondering the same about her. At the entrance of the clinic, he steps back deferentially, motioning for her to enter first. A gentleman.

The clinic isn't busy today. The two Ministry of Health doctors aren't in; one is pursuing his private practice, the other is on vacation. The only doctor on duty is René from Médecins Sans Frontières. René has been treating Natalia for a year now, ever since she got anaemia and almost died. Together they've seen Natalia's blood count creep back towards sustainable human levels. Together they've discussed what Natalia's options will be if the Ministry of Health gets bogged in another corruption scandal and there's a break in the supply of anti-retroviral drugs. Natalia's options are, to be honest, not plentiful. They consist of hoping that the government of Ukraine will grow ever more efficient, compassionate and accountable.

'When are you leaving?' Natalia asks Dr René as he fills a small syringe with her blood.

'Not yet, not yet,' he says, in his soft Belgian accent.

'But soon?'

'Head office says six months.'

'That's soon.'

'I'd like to stay,' says René.

'Then why don't you?' She feels as though she's making a pass at him. Sasha would probably accuse her of trying her luck with every foreigner who comes into range.

'We've discussed this before,' says the doctor. 'Médecins Sans Frontières is supposed to be an emergency aid organization. We go in when there's a crisis and the local authorities aren't coping. We're not designed to be an alternative national health service.'

'If I'd trusted our own doctors, I'd be dead now.'

'But you're alive. And a lot of local doctors are much more knowledgeable about HIV than they were a couple of years ago.

There's no reason why the Ministry of Health can't carry on your ARV therapy.'

'Except that Ukraine is fucked.'

'I'm sorry you feel that way, Natasha.' The doctor is embarrassed, uneasy, and he retreats into gentle banter. 'You were so wonderfully patriotic when I first saw you. Just a few blood cells away from the grave, and you were telling me all about Pushkin.'

'Pushkin can't help me now.'

'You're doing fine, Natasha. Just take it one day at a time.'

He turns away from her, ostensibly to write her name on the plastic capsule containing her blood. She's made him feel bad. She wishes she could make up for it. He is an idealistic young man who'd no doubt be much happier sewing up wounded refugees in Africa than sitting here in a dismal office with a dusty plastic model of the Aids virus on his desk. He has been bashing his head against ex-Soviet bureaucracy for months on end, even sometimes buying medicines with his own money in sheer frustration at the slow grinding of the official gears. Although he and Natalia converse in English, she hears him speak on the phone and to the receptionists, and his Russian is better each time. He must be working his butt off.

'Thank you. Bye-bye,' she says.

'Till next week,' he says, closing his Filofax. There's a photograph of his wife and children sellotaped to the front.

On the bus, Natalia feels so exhausted she keeps falling asleep. Her ear and cheek collide with the window, over and over. The bus becomes crowded as it shudders closer to the centre of town, and she clutches her handbag with the ARV drugs in it. Thieves are bolder nowadays. Odessa is full of tourists and refugees from the collapsed communist empire. Junkies are everywhere.

She dozes and visits Montana in her mind. It won't be like New York or Los Angeles, those vast teeming cities Grigory is so desperate to relocate to. It will be like Crimea, perhaps. But with modern hospitals. No doubt there will be some corruption in the American health care system, too, but at least in America, people are used to demanding, and getting, what they want. They don't queue meekly in grey corridors waiting for permission to die.

There are some days when Natalia feels that every decision she makes is wrong. One trivial misjudgement triggers the next, and then another, and another. Today she jumps off a bus that would have taken her all the way home, because she catches a passing glimpse of the Internet cafe and has a sudden urge to check for news. But the Internet cafe is shut. A sign on the door says, in English, BACK IN 5 MINUTES. She waits fifteen. Then she decides to fill time by visiting Sasha. She goes to a delicatessen and buys chocolate and a bag of *vareniki* dumplings that are going cheap but still look perfectly good. Only when she's halfway to the Odessa Steps does she remember that Sasha doesn't like cold *vareniki*, only hot. Maybe he's less choosy nowadays?

At the encampment, she finds that Sasha isn't there. Gone to Ekaterinskaya Street, says Dmitry. Natalia knows that's Sasha's favourite place for begging. It's a hot spot for foreigners, the sort of faux-traditional avenue where British and American tourists sit at open-air bistros squinting bemusedly at misspelled menus, reassuring each other not to worry about making a mistake because everything is dirt cheap. Natalia sets off, still carrying her little plastic bag of groceries.

By now, she actually dreads meeting Sasha: his begging is excruciating for her to witness. He has a rubbish-skip guitar with four or five strings, brutally out of tune, and he busks with it, performing the worst kind of American soft-rock songs, Bryan Adams, The Eagles, Meatloaf, Bon Jovi, 'A Horse with No Name', 'Hungry Heart', 'We Built This City on Rock and Roll', you name it. He sings them in a weird kind of subdued yammer, like a loud radio overheard at a distance. His sheer awfulness seems to charm the clientele. Some days, he earns more than a schoolteacher or a nurse.

Natalia walks up and down Ekaterinskaya Street. Sasha is nowhere to be seen. Growing hungry, but not wanting to eat the food she's bought for her brother, she buys a Greek salad she can't afford in a convivial-looking cafe. It's lousy. She walks up and down Ekaterinskaya some more. At one point she almost breaks her neck, feeling as though someone has lassooed her around the shins. It's the lace hem of her dress; it's come loose altogether. She lifts it in her fist, unsure what to do with it. If she had something as simple as a pin, she could pin it up. She hasn't got a pin, and there's nowhere around here where she could buy one, even though Odessa prides itself on selling everything nowadays, from turquoise chrome cellphone slipcases to anal sex.

Natalia considers tearing the hem off, but she feels she's made so many wrong decisions already today that she would probably regret it. So she walks to the bus stop, carrying the dangling black lace in front of her like a dog's leash, and goes home.

Four hours later, Natalia takes her seat in front of a computer at the Internet cafe. It's an hour before closing. She has never been here so late before. The place is almost empty; only two game-playing lads remain, injecting their lonesome beeps, buzzes and bombs into the glowing stillness. Outside, there's been a sudden change in the weather: a drop in temperature, stiff winds. An improperly secured billboard flaps loudly right outside the building as Natalia taps out the code to gain entry to her email program. Her wrists are bulky with the sleeves of an ugly nylon windcheater, hardly a fashion item, but she just can't get warm enough. The hem of her dress is temporarily attached with masking tape. She looks ridiculous, she knows.

The game-playing boys laugh. Their laughter has nothing to do with her. Nothing in the world has anything to do with her. The boys have simply had enough of killing and being killed. They're getting up to spend the rest of the night with Mum and Dad.

Dear Natalia,
I can't tell you how happy I was to recieve your email. It was the email of my dreams. Without wanting to put down my first wife, my first marriage would have been a lot better if she had your attitude. I sometimes think that here in America, we take everything for granted and don't treat realtionships with the respect and honor they deserve. I am not saying that I deserve that much respect and honor, I am a guy with faults like anybody, what I mean is love. Love is a miracle and a precious thing. There are so many billions of people in the world, passing each other by in the street, bumping into each other in the grocery store, working together at the office and so on. What do they feel for each other —zero. But just sometimes, out of all those billions of strangers, two people connect. They break through somehow. They show trust and they get trust back.

Natalia, I don't want to scare you off, talking about marriage. I know that sounds wierd, seeing as I found you on a marriage website, but now that we have got to know each other I can see that you are a very special person and I want you to have the special husband you deserve. I am sure you must have felt exposed and unconfortable posing on that website, knowing that thousands of guys were looking at you, undressing you with thier eyes. I admit I was undressing you too, but at the same time I was looking for something else, something deeper. In fact I refused to take the other girls seriously, the ones that had bikini shots and thier jugs hanging out. When I saw you in that dress, it was like being transported back to an older time, a time when love and honor really meant something. A time when a man would bow for a lady and kiss her on the hand and stuff like that. God, I hope you are not laughing. I am serious, my dear Natalia. You are not the only one that has been hurt before, and I don't want to count my chickens.

What I propose is that you come to Montana for a holiday. No heavy expectations, no nothing. I will pay for everything, your fare, all expenses. You can stay in my daughters old room, if you prefer. We won't put a time frame on it. You can take as long as you need to get to know me (and Montana!). Montana is not the most exciting place in America and I'm sure I am not the most exciting guy but I have a good hopeful feeling about this. Intuition, like you said! Well now, Natalia, I have been talking about my feelings and my heart is going boom boom boom, and I think it's time I tried to calm down a little! So back to music. I'm sure Inward Path are a seriously rocking outfit as I don't believe you would be so crazy about them if they weren't. And I look forward to hearing some of thier stuff soon. To be straight with you though, some of thier lyrics are too gloomy for me. Don't you think? I mean, you quoted one, Life Grows Weak, and there's all this stuff about no future, no peace of mind, eyes are bleeding, going insane, I'm lost and destroyed, we'll stay all alone. I don't go for that. Natalia, I am a glass half full instead of a glass half empty kind of guy, if you know what I am saying. There's a lot of sadness and aweful stuff happening in this world and the way I figure it is, you got to be positive or it brings you right down. There's plenty things in my own life I could lose sleep over but I just start each new day thinking OK, this is the first day of the rest of my life. And I think we should put careful thought into choosing the music we listen to, to make sure it's putting something good into our lives instead of something negative. My all-time favorite artist is actually Bruce Springsteen. He is the Boss. I'm on fire, Dancing in the dark, Born in the USA, Born to run, She's the one, Promised land, Jungle land, Hungry heart, Cover me—they are all totally classic in my book. He even has a song called 'I wanna marry you!'

Natalia sits in silence. Her arms are trembling with cold. The flesh of her legs is goose-pimpled. She wishes she were at home in bed, curled up in a ball, blankets wrapped tight around her, warm as an opiate. This Bruce Springsteen thing is bad news, very bad news. Worse news than if Bob had confessed to her that he is a pervert and is very much looking forward to masturbating on to her shoes or her eyes. Sexual disgust she can handle. But Bruce Springsteen…

She blinks in amazement at her own ridiculous fastidiousness, her snobbery, when her life is at stake. What does it matter if the man who is offering to be her husband likes the dullest music in the world? What does it matter that her brother sings 'Hungry Heart' as one of his busking scams on Ekaterinskaya Street, filling gaps in the lyrics with sarcastic Ukrainian, and vamping the 'Huh-huh-hungry' chorus for all he's worth? What does it matter that Bob was probably lying about knowing The Cure? What does it matter what music anyone likes? Viruses and medicines fight to the death inside one's body, a claustrophobic dark-red package of blood and meat where music never penetrates, unless you count the rhythm of the heartbeat. No sound, surely, can ever matter more than that rhythm.

Natalia raises her hands to begin typing her response. Bob will be waiting. What with delays and different time zones, she's probably kept him waiting too long already. She must say yes at once, in case he gets spooked and changes his mind. How much easier it would be if she could just shout 'Yes!', right here in the Internet cafe on Zhukovskovo Street, and have him magically hear her in Montana. Then she wouldn't need to think of a preamble, a way of phrasing her agreement so it doesn't come across as over-eager or too casual or stilted. It's not the important words that are treacherous, it's the little ones that lead there.

Michel Faber

Dear Bob,

How to tell him what his proposal means to her? How to make her assent sound natural and gracious? Is it too soon to discuss the practicalities of airfare, visa, departure date? Should she use the word 'love' in the opening line?

She decides to tackle the Bruce Springsteen thing first. To stop it hanging in the air between them. Then she can write the beginning.

Bruce Springsteen is

That's as far as she gets for several minutes. Then:

a very important song writer in American music and it is natural that you admire him extremely. I

Several more minutes pass. Maybe five. Then:

also admire how he writes always from point of view of very ordinary person even though he has now a big fortune. He is poet of the proletariat. Is that a word in American? It comes from Russian but I think it exists also in English for a long period. Maybe in American there exists different word? Anyway, whenever I hear music of Bruce Springsteen, I

Five, ten more minutes pass while she considers what she can share with Montana Bob about how she feels when she hears Bruce Springsteen. All sorts of statements float into her mind, some honest, some not so honest, some equivocal. At one point, she almost types 'Some days, when I am faced with Ukrainian situation, I wish I could sing truly in chorus with Bruce Springsteen that I was Born in the USA!' A sentence like that would strike a chord with Bob, she's sure. Exactly the combination of warmth, humility, good humour and exotic cuteness he would get off on most. But of course, it's out of the question. Everything is out of the question. She racks her brains for an alternative. The word 'I' hangs suspended on the screen so long that a screensaver comes on. Natalia touches the mouse and the galaxy of ricocheting spheres disappears, replaced by her half-written email and its dangling pronoun at the end. She stares at it until her eyes sting. Finally she makes her decision and clicks a single key with one pale finger.

A box pops up containing a stylized think balloon and an automated question. *Are you sure you want to discard Message 1— Dear Bob?*

Natalia makes the box disappear and disconnects from the net. She rises from her chair. The young guy at the counter almost jumps out of his skin.

'Jesus,' he says. 'I didn't notice you were still here. You were so quiet. Invisible.'

Natalia opens her purse, rummages around in coins of almost no value, pulls out a ten-*hyrvnia* banknote.

'No change,' says the young guy. 'The boss has taken all the cash. It's OK, just pay us next time. You'll be back tomorrow, yeah?'

He stands slightly in the way, as if angling to chat to her for a few minutes longer, in exchange for giving her credit. Natalia blushes, weaves elegantly around him and makes her escape.

'Thanks,' she says. 'I'd better get home.'

Natalia walks the streets. She is in no hurry to get home. Earlier this evening, Mrs Kotova caught her using the Kotovas' electric kettle to make herself a cup of coffee and they had a tense discussion about morality. 'Wear and tear,' Mrs Kosova kept repeating. 'Wear and tear. Every time the electricity passes through the coil, the coil gets pushed a bit closer to packing it in. Every time a towel is touched, every time a mat is trodden on, every time a tap is turned… it all adds up.'

Natalia knows it all adds up. She knows it very well.

A car slows down as it passes her; a gypsy hoping she'll ask him to be her taxi driver. She keeps her eyes straight ahead. The buses don't quit till after midnight. She isn't cold any more. Is it the disease or the medication that makes her body temperature rise and fall so steeply? Right now, she feels as though she could discard her windcheater and her cardigan, just toss them into the breeze and walk in her lacy dress, the raggedy bits fluttering like feathers, her flesh pale under the moon. Night obscures some of the city's modern trimmings; the clean, undiscriminating darkness simplifies the view

Michel Faber

to long, lonely avenues lined with sycamores. With eyes half closed, she could be a nineteenth-century countess, taking a stroll. A masked ball is still in full swing, but she has grown bored and wants a breath of fresh air. She may visit the house of a poet she has taken pity on, a poor sweet boy always on the brink of madness, a doomed idealist who raves about revolution while she dabs his fevered brow with the sleeve of her dress.

Another vehicle slows while it passes. It's the Faith-Hope-Love van, on the lookout for prostitutes to assist. A middle-aged woman Natalia doesn't recognize is at the wheel, no doubt with a hamper of free condoms at her side. Natalia doesn't need any free condoms. She keeps walking, eyes fixed straight ahead.

Eventually, she reaches the faux-traditional restaurant that has the revolving billboard outside. It was here that she had her epiphany, a couple of months ago. It was here that she decided to teleport herself right out of Ukraine, to rematerialize in a new world where Irina's face-powder scum around the bathtub would rapidly fade into the forgotten long-ago.

The restaurant is closed now; its peasant-garbed staff have gone home to their own sordid flats to watch subtitled TV. But the sign is still here, still rotating. BLACKSEABRIDES.COM. 'Unique and beautiful women for correspondence and marriage. Translation, accommodation, flower deliveries available. Visit our website for beach pics, glamour pics, testimonials from satisfied customers. All major credit cards accepted. Sincere females 18 and up always wanted.'

Natalia waits for the sign to turn, curious to see what's on the other side. Nothing, at the moment. Advertising is expensive. Maybe the price needs to drop a little. Not every business in Odessa is booming.

She walks on. Ahead, she can see the luminous marble steps of the museum where her grandmother used to work as a guide. What would her grandmother advise her to do now? Probably give her an earful for being rude. You can't just stop writing to a man who has proposed to you. You owe him a reply, even if it's just to say goodbye.

There's too far to go, she can't walk it. But she'll walk a little further, to give everyone plenty of time to get tired and go to bed. She reaches into her handbag and fetches out the earphones for her

Walkman, fits them snugly into her ears. With a well-practised motion, not even looking inside her bag as she does it, she inserts *Antiar* into the player, presses the middle button. The instant the music starts, she visualizes the cassette cover, vivid as an icon in church, as mysterious and disturbing and thrilling now as it was when she was sixteen: a giant insect poised to prey on a tied-up woman.

The mighty Alexander Melnik could be anywhere now—serving French fries in a Kiev roadside diner, frowning over a laptop in a Moscow-bound plane, teaching Gogol to rich Germans in Cologne, injecting homebrew opiates into his festering thigh in a filthy cellar just around the corner from here—but in Natalia's ears he is reunited with his younger self, without the slightest hesitation, majestic-voiced once more, singing directly into the cells of her body.

'We go into the night!
We go into the night!
Like fully ripe stars, at random we fly...'

Natasha finds a rhythm of walking that's compatible with the furious tempo of Velchev's drums, and smiles, defiant in her intention of playing the same fucking song a million times over, until the rest of the world finally sees the glory of it, or her batteries run out, whichever comes first.   □

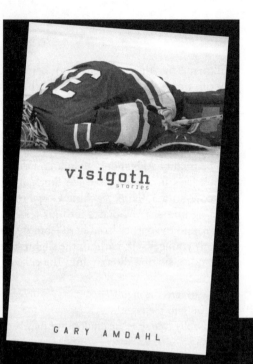

GRANTA

CLOSING TIME
Jeremy Treglown

Cáceres in Extremadura, 1928

W hat claims to be the most important collection of modern Latin American art in Europe is housed in what must also be Europe's ugliest museum. It stands near the centre of Badajoz, in Extremadura, on the border between Spain and Portugal.

To get there, you go south from the cathedral down one of the steep, narrow medieval streets which open on to a modern park, all paved areas and irregularly spurting fountains, beside the bright new Palacio de Congresos. This council building, part funded by the European Union, is a flat white cylinder like a two-thirds-empty gasometer. Beyond it, half-hidden by municipal apartment blocks, is another, taller cylinder, one of unrelieved red brick, approached by a grey ramp with a twenty-foot wall on one side and a series of low concrete parapets on the other. Among the outworks is a net of rectilinear concrete frames like perfunctory triumphal arches. Inside them, the circular tower of the Museum of the Contemporary Art of Extremadura and Latin America is punctured at regular intervals by tiny window openings, one row for each of the four interior floors. The effect is brutal and frightening, and rightly so. The museum was formerly one of Francisco Franco's jails. Its main wings, the spokes of the panopticon, were shorn off as part of the remodelling begun in 1989, but the cruel hub remains.

For all their external aggressiveness, the spacious galleries, early on a Saturday morning in the spring of 2005, were quiet. The Latin American rooms were under reconstruction but those for local art, upstairs, were open and empty of other visitors. Rounding a pillar, looking for a photographic exhibition I had heard about, I surprised two attendants who jumped up from their old armchairs with a haste which seemed needless until it became clear that they had been sitting in an installation: the two chairs, plus a standard lamp in front of a TV set showing a video of someone trying to do an all-white Rubik's cube.

To have turned a *cárcel preventiva y correccional* into an art museum is truly utopian: a high-cultural equivalent of swords into ploughshares. Badajoz, its fortress dominating both the surrounding plains and the long bridge across the now shallow-running Guadiana river, has had to undertake more than its share of such transformations. It was strategically important from Roman times, until Franco's death in 1975 belatedly freed Spain to join the EU. With

Jeremy Treglown

that, the frontier with Portugal lost much of its significance. Previously, the region was often a battleground, not least in the war of Spanish Independence (what the British call the Peninsular War), and was full of military bases. When, in the summer of 1936, Franco's Army of Africa arrived from 'Spanish' Morocco to play its part in subjugating the restless natives of the home country itself, crushing Badajoz was a strategic priority. Show other cities—Madrid not least—what was coming to them if they continued to resist! Badajoz contained plenty of support for the elected Republican government. It was home, for example, to a working men's association founded in 1900, called, after one of Zola's angry socialist novels, the Sociedad Obrera 'Germinal' (the *Germinal* Labour Association). Under Colonel Juan Yagüe—known to his admirers as 'the Hyena of Asturias'—the Moroccan Regulars first submitted the town to heavy artillery attacks and bombing. Then they breached the ancient walls and began to round up any likely Republican sympathizers they could find, driving them through the narrow streets down towards the bullring. There, unseen but not unheard from outside, they were machine-gunned. The number of victims is disputed but Jay Allen, of the *Chicago Tribune*, reckoned at the time that 1,800 were killed in twelve hours. The resulting lake of blood, he wrote, was 'palm deep'.

With a commemorative schizophrenia not uncommon in Spain, the former headquarters of the Sociedad Obrera 'Germinal', which now boasts a memorial plaque, stands in a street named the Calle Regulares Marroquíes (Moroccan Regulars Street). I found no plaque, though, at the site of the massacre. Standing close to where the bullring was shown on my map, I asked an elderly man for directions. He seemed embarrassed. Ah, yes, until recently the Plaza de Toros was here, but it was demolished. Now, we have this new, white building, you see: the Palacio de Congresos.

I was intrigued by how Spain, and particularly Extremadura, depicted itself and its past, and by how the region had been seen by foreigners at different points in time. Plenty has been written about the civil war and the ensuing right-wing dictatorship—the longest in twentieth-century Europe—but what about the years before and since? I was following the route taken by the great English Hispanophile and short-story writer V. S. Pritchett. His first book, *Marching Spain*, is about a journey, mainly on foot, from Badajoz in Extremadura to León in Old Castile during the spring of 1927. 'VSP', as he was always called, was then twenty-six, a little younger than one of his heroes, Robert Louis Stevenson ('RLS'), had been when he made his celebrated trek with a donkey through the Cévennes, half a century earlier. The title *Marching Spain* refers to the 'Spanish Marches'—the border with Portugal—but the book is also about a march. The physical experience of walking through these hot, rocky plains and mountains is as powerfully evoked as what the country and its people were like. Pritchett's zestful narrative was to be described by the southern American author Eudora Welty as 'a stunning announcement of a new writer'.

Marching Spain helped to start a vogue for what, in the 1920s, seemed a new kind of travel writing, one in which the subject was not buildings or art but the ordinary people of any place. Pritchett, disdaining guidebooks, called it 'the architecture of humanity'. In the Depression years, the emphasis by Pritchett and other writers on people in and of themselves had a political edge. Orwell's later *Down and Out in Paris and London* (1933) and *The Road to Wigan Pier* (1937) are the best-known examples. Although the Spain of the 1920s had yet to experience civil war and the Franquista tyranny, it was already ruled by a military dictator, Miguel Primo de Rivera, the latest reinforcer of centuries of feudalism. The *latifundios*—big estates—of Extremadura were among the poorest and the most depopulated regions in the country.

Pritchett wasn't an overtly political writer, but he had recently spent a couple of years in Spain as a newspaper reporter and had prophesied glumly, though as it turned out rightly, that current attempts to change the existing order wouldn't succeed for long. He came from a rackety lower-middle-class background (his father was a serial bankrupt), left school just before he was sixteen and worked as a docklands clerk before, as soon as he was twenty-one, taking off for Paris with the idea of being an artist. At the time, he most wanted to become a novelist, an English Balzac, and what interested him, in his travel writing as well as in the short stories and memoirs for which he is now best known, were individuals: individuals not necessarily at the bottom of the pile, but nowhere near the top of it, either.

Jeremy Treglown

Pritchett arrived at the railway station outside Badajoz one mid-April dawn in 1927. He walked a mile or two through what were then open fields and are now ranks of high-rise social housing, mostly built under Franco, interspersed with advertising hoardings. He crossed the famous twenty-eight-arched bridge, presented his papers to dozing officials at the gate tower and made his way uphill into the town. He doesn't say where he stayed but near the beginning of the barely legible journal he kept on the trip—an intimate, immediate document, with its sweat-stained pages, its maps, lists of expenses and details of how many miles he had travelled each day—there is an address: Arco Agüero 14, Badajoz. It's one of the ill-destined alleys which plunge down from the cathedral ('a hot, stout, and pompous little place, like a country priest who had been doing himself too well') to where the bullring then stood. The name is that of a nineteenth-century general, but what the word *agüero* means is 'an omen'.

Frontier bureaucracy still sustained a variety of long-established clerical jobs in Badajoz and travellers spending a night or two brought in income of their own. There was also, as Pritchett noticed, a strong military presence. As a result, it was a relatively well-off place: more so, he found, than Cáceres, the next sizeable town to the north. The position has been reversed since Badajoz lost its administrative and strategic importance, and since faster transport made stopping there needless anyway. As a result, although you see plenty of modern prosperity—new Citroën C5s and BMW X3s, well-toned women heading for the gym after their school run—there's also a level of poverty more consistent with descriptions of nineteenth- and early-twentieth-century Spain than anything I met elsewhere. Unlike many writers, Pritchett understood trade and work and loved to describe them. To him the old centre was part souk, part a hive of local industry: carpenters, wheelwrights, cart makers, basket makers, potters. Today, while the Arab fortress and its high plaza are being restored, the alleys adjacent to it are derelict. A street market offers a scattering of clay pots and bits of old furniture but vendors outnumber buyers and loping junkies suggest that much of the local business is of a different kind.

Early on the first day I spent in the town, an elegant woman apparently in her sixties—grey hair swept back in a knot, a fur-edged black coat, black jeans, a big, loose leather shoulder bag—hurriedly crossed one of the shopping streets to the west of the cathedral, and bumped into me. As she did so, she wordlessly pushed a half-open hand at me for money. Her face was covered with sores. Startled, and embarrassed to be showing it, I shrugged her off and she disappeared fast around the next corner. During the rest of that day and those that followed I saw her often. I was endlessly walking around looking for something and so was she: our paths were bound to cross. I now wanted to talk to her, but she always swerved away. Once, we were in the same place without my realizing it. I took a couple of photographs of the street market, focused on a young gitano with a rock star's tangle of black hair, hands on hips, filthy shirt and trousers hauled together by a thick leather belt, listening attentively to an older man without ever meeting his eyes. To one side, face averted from the camera as if she's suddenly interested in a terracotta jar, is the woman with grey hair. I didn't see her then and, later, I lost her.

The contrasts you notice on the street aren't between poverty and extreme wealth—I saw none of the latter, at least measured by European standards—but between poverty and a pervasive domesticity, sociability, comfort and ease. One of the differences is laughter.

Early Monday morning. The Gran Café Victoria, close to the Plaza de España. People sit in ones and twos drinking coffee in that preoccupied, start-of-the-week way. Suddenly the room is full of descending confetti. As if in a well-choreographed musical number, everyone freezes. A beat, and everyone looks towards the counter. Another beat, and we all see and understand: an astonished waiter, one hand on an electric food mixer with its top open, the other clutching the remains of a stack of tissues. Then the longest, loudest, most innocent laughter I've been part of since I was a child. Bits of shredded paper still turn up in my notebook.

Travel writing isn't meant to be fiction, but then most traditional fiction pretends not to be, either. One of the many idiosyncratic, affectionately drawn characters in *Marching Spain* is a voluble Protestant convert, a haberdasher whom Pritchett calls Don Benito. They meet in Badajoz and, through him, Pritchett—though himself in flight from his own evangelical inheritance—meets two Protestant missionaries. Travel is foolish, Don Benito believes. He himself has never left Spain. He has even managed to avoid military service in Morocco. Why is Pritchett doing this? What's the good of it?

Pritchett says he may write a book. 'Worse! Madness! Block up the world with bad literature. That you have crossed the province of Badajoz on foot, what does it matter? It is mad.' Pritchett lamely defends himself by saying Don Quixote was mad, too, and Don Benito pounces: Don Quixote is imaginary, a literary creation. 'You are real. What does it matter to the spirit of man if you go across Badajoz? If you must write, imagine something.'

Like others before him as well as after, Pritchett wanted to believe that, in its relative isolation from modernity, Spain had been preserved as a utopia unique in the Western world. He often describes it in terms of fantasy: the inventiveness which, meeting a cheerful small Englishman travelling a few hundred miles for the sake of it, would turn him into a wily smuggler, say, or a husband driven to desperation by having no children, or—a suggestion which, to his bewilderment, Pritchett kept encountering—a German walking around the world. Yet these were not really fantasies. Smuggling did take place across the little-frequented border with Portugal. Pritchett's solitary journey was to some extent prompted by the unhappiness of his childless first marriage. There was even a man with a German name, Franck, who, fifteen years before Pritchett's trip, spent several months walking in Spain and was the author of a book called *A Vagabond Journey Around the World*.

One imaginative aspect of *Marching Spain* is that it's narrated as if the author was a complete newcomer to the country. Yet, as he confessed decades later, 'I knew Spain much better than I pretended.' He had spent eighteen months there as a correspondent from January 1924, travelling throughout the country, not least along its western border. One of the hundreds of articles he wrote for the *Christian Science Monitor* from Spain was called 'On the Road Through Extremadura'. This was in March 1925. The following year, he unsuccessfully offered a book of travel pieces provisionally titled 'Irish Miles and Spanish Leagues' to half a dozen London publishers. Understandably, he drew on some of the earlier material in *Marching Spain*. Chapter thirteen, for example, is set in Plasencia, in northern Extremadura, and includes full, colourful narratives about both a wedding and a funeral there. Until I compared the book with his journal, I hadn't noticed that he only spent one night in the town on this trip, Monday April 25–Tuesday 26: an odd time of the week for a wedding, and a short time in which to have observed two such long rituals so closely. Especially without making any notes on them. He was travelling on foot, after all, and pressed for time. The 340 miles took him only eighteen days, but he thought that 'Not very good going'. There are only so many pages, though, that you can get out of aching legs, a parched throat and unattainable-seeming horizons. He needed colourful episodes, and some of them he imported.

Besides, people had been writing about Extremadura for centuries. A Spanish historian has noted dryly that many pre-twentieth-century English-speaking travellers seem to have thought that it was *un lugar hasta cierto punto virgen*: almost virgin territory—as if they were modern versions of voyagers to the 'New World', so many of whom came from this region. In Pritchett's time, such fantasies were still possible, but only just. He was unaware, for example, that his path was crossed and recrossed by that of a young American ethnographic photographer called Ruth Matilda Anderson, who set off southwards from León in 1926, alone, and spent a couple of years taking pictures of many of the places he passed through. Today, even if you could dream yourself into the situation Pritchett imagined for himself, to do so would seem objectionable. Perhaps that's one of the reasons why travel-writers lately, whether as romantic as Richard Holmes, as naive as Pamela Stephenson on her recent voyage through the South Pacific, or as intellectually sophisticated as Michael Gorra in his 2004 book about being an outsider in modern Germany, have chosen to base their journeys on other people's.

After Badajoz, Pritchett careered north from puncture to puncture over the then unmade, boulder-strewn road to La Roca de la Sierra, in a Ford driven by one of his new missionary acquaintances. Accordingly, I hired a Ford for a day: a Focus Zetec. It took me smoothly and quickly through sprawling suburbs on to the new highway heading past the Parque Tecnológico, the Central Hortifruticola and a military base turned modern housing estate, into a landscape of wheat fields, recently planted orchards and old cork-oak groves full of black pigs, all closely fenced on both sides of the straight road.

Despite signposts to a new industrial estate, and a restaurant-disco complex called Los Sauces further along the road, La Roca is still at first glance the pleasant little market town where Pritchett spent a night. A few old men sat in the newly paved plaza. A few teenagers tore around on scooters. Most people were at work, either in Badajoz, forty kilometres away, or in closer Montijo. Agricultural labour doesn't support many people here any more. In fact, agriculture can be a bit of a joke in newly sophisticated Spain. The day before, the manager of my hotel in Badajoz had told me how the countryside had changed, vigorously miming the activities he used to see in his youth: scores of people ploughing, hoeing, scything. Then he lit an imaginary cigarette, put his feet up on the counter and linked his hands behind his head. 'Now,' he said, 'one man sits in a machine with air conditioning and hi-fi. He might as well still be in bed.'

I was looking for the *posada* where Pritchett had stayed. One or two elderly people came out of their houses to ask what I wanted, though my quest was if anything harder to explain the point of than Pritchett's had been to Don Benito. If all I wanted was a hotel, there wasn't one here any more, but I could easily find somewhere to stay in Badajoz. Meanwhile, others got caught up in the question. A retired farm labourer remembered not only the place where Pritchett must have stayed but its owner, though he was dead and his family long gone. We were talking in the street and he suddenly apologized: he must stop. His wife was ill and he was late doing the laundry. He hesitated. Would I come in? He led me into his house, up the stairs and out through the attic to a tiled rooftop washroom, where he pummelled away in a shallow tub with a built-in scrubbing board of cut stone. Whether absorbed in his task or out of sudden shyness, he grew silent. I asked how things had changed in La Roca over the years. He thought for some time. 'They've paved the plaza.'

I was called back down to meet his next-door neighbour, who wanted to tell me about the local reading group she belonged to and had brought out its curriculum. They had done Andrew Sean Greer's *Las confesiones de Max Tivoli* and Katherine Neville's *El ocho*, and were now on to *Curación emocional*, by David Servan Schreiber, which she said she found helpful. No Spanish books. Another woman asked her nephew to show me the white little municipal library and the more ornate village well. She was French, from Toulouse, her husband Portuguese. The polite, formal boy was there on holiday from Switzerland. In these cosmopolitan, well-educated streets, Pritchett's dirt roads packed with goats weren't unimaginable, but they were beginning to recede.

Not so firmly as they receded from the Ex-100/N-630 heading north to Cáceres and Plasencia. It's called the Ruta de la Plata, from an Arabic word meaning 'paved'. But in Spanish, *plata* can mean 'cash', and it was along this route that bullion from Spain's colonies in South America was moved north from the port of Cádiz to the conquistadors' home towns. Walking here was out of the question. Lorries and SUVs barrelled along, blasting their horns derisively at anyone stupid enough to be on foot and making me stagger in their slipstream. But taking to the fields wasn't easy, either. I began to build up a Ramblers' Association level of resentment against the near-impregnable fences. After ten or fifteen miles, what hurt were not my legs but my hands. Eyes which quickly got used to searching out a loose post at a couple of hundred yards became almost blind to wild garlic and jonquils under foot, larks startled into dipping, switchback flight, storks perched on their untidy nests, patches of gauzy cloud in the miles of sky. And whereas the gregarious Pritchett often met people to talk to along his way—someone on a donkey, a labourer walking home, the ubiquitous herdsmen of the pre-wire-fence era— I spent a whole day in the *vega* without seeing another human being except in a distant jeep: a silhouette with a mobile phone.

If there was less companionship for a traveller in my Extremadura than Pritchett's, there was also less solitude, at least in a sense. Like everywhere else in the 'developed' world, more people are living alone: three million in Spain, twice as many as a decade ago. Yet also like everywhere else, everyone seems to be talking to or listening to or watching someone, though as often electronically as in the flesh. Go into a bar and your order is taken by someone whose eyes are on the plasma screen behind your head. Your fellow drinkers, if not on their mobiles, are also watching basketball, or football, or pop videos, or *La Granja*; or they are communicating intensely with a fruit machine. To try to start a conversation in these circumstances is to intrude on private lives and pleasures. Other kinds of privacy, too, perhaps. In León, earlier in the spring, I got into the habit of having breakfast in a particular bar where, unusually, there was no TV but a range of newspapers. A large proprietor with a malleable face gave orders to his tiny mother, who worked behind a window. He himself cut the ham off the bone in thin dark strips. Circumspect conversations took place between him and elderly men sitting on the bar stools. One morning, the front-page news was the removal of the equestrian statue of Franco from the Plaza de San Juan de la Cruz in Madrid. León, in Old Castile, north of Extremadura, is one of the most conservative parts of Spain and, when the proprietor brought my breakfast, I showed him the picture. What did he think? He lowered his voice: 'They should have left it. It's the past—a bit of history.' Returning to his counter, he muttered something to a couple of men. They turned around, had a good look at me and went back to their papers. Nothing more was said by anyone. If you're over fifty here you were brought up and educated under Franco. If you're a man, you served in his army.

What do you do with the past? Franco had his own ideas about this, ideas beside which the odd statue seems insignificant. During the months leading up to the thirtieth anniversary of his death, the papers were full of stories about local mayors all over Spain who had decided—or decided not—to pull down statues or to redesignate roads which had *nombres no gratos*, unwelcome names: names like that of the savage Civil-War general and propagandist Gonzalo Queipo de Llano. In Salamanca, the Plaza Mayor is decorated with plaques depicting worthies and less-worthies ranging from El Cid through the Duke of Wellington to various monarchs, past and present. The one in the east corner, dedicated to Franco, CAUDILLO DE ESPAÑA, is hard to make out beneath its protesting inundations of red paint. But the main memorial to him would be harder to obliterate. In the centre of Spain, 150 or so kilometres east of Salamanca, fifty north-west of Madrid, it's the biggest crypt in Europe and, along with Franco's remains, contains those of 33,872 victims of the Civil War— from both sides, though it's clear whose side the memorial celebrates. Between 1959 and 1983, well into the post-Franco democratic era, bodies dug up from communal graves were moved to this catafalque inside the Guadarrama mountains. The monument was tunnelled and built by political prisoners over a seventeen-year period between 1941 and 1958, and was clearly intended to compete with the nearby Escorial. It consists of a narrow, cruciform underground cathedral more than 250 metres long: the Basílica de la Santa Cruz del Valle de los Caídos (the Basilica of the Holy Cross of the Valley of the Fallen).

Franco, the only person buried there who died of old age, is in the place of honour beneath the transept. The nave is lined with chapels housing all the others—many of them murdered by Franco's own troops and entombed now, as one angry critic spat out, *junto a su verdugo*, alongside their executioner. The identities of more than half are unknown. Forty-one metres of mountain sit on top of them and on top of the mountain rises an enormous cross, its base surrounded by figures representing Justice, Prudence, Fortitude and Moderation. A satirist couldn't have dreamed it. The whole edifice is higher than the Eiffel Tower. Despite several attempts to set off bombs inside it, hundreds of thousands of visitors come every year. It's claimed that veterans of the German Condor Legion—the Nazi air force which used Guernica as an exercise ground for its new blitzkrieg tactics—have held reunions there.

No one seriously suggests that the basilica should be bulldozed, though there are many ideas about how it could be turned into a different kind of memorial. Some say a good start would be made if Franco's remains were removed by his family. According to a long report in *El País*, time may provide the best solution. The cross has been shaking in the exceptionally strong winds of recent years and cracks are beginning to appear in the granite foundations.

Besides, the bombs that went off in Madrid in March 2004 suggested to many Spaniards that, in our inexhaustible-seeming preoccupation with the horrors of mid-twentieth-century Europe, we've been ignoring developments potentially still more cataslymic as well as more immediate, and with a longer history. No one can travel through Spain without being aware of its Islamic past. Many Moroccans believe that the peninsula was 'originally' theirs, until they were dispossessed by crusaders. By the same token, ever since the *reconquista* many Spaniards have feared that the Moors will one day return. When Franco's Army of Africa landed in Spain in July 1936, it was rumoured that this was what was happening. The superstition resurfaced when the Atocha bombs were found to be the responsibility not of Basque separatists but of Moroccans. There are people with old houses in Extremadura and Castilla-León who will tell you, as they lock their front doors at night, that somewhere in Tangier or Tetouan, a Moroccan family still has a matching set of keys. It's a joke, but also not.

Jeremy Treglown

All post-imperial European countries are ex-colonies, too. Pritchett's route was first paved by the Romans, whose imposing traces can still be seen along it. Most of the towns have fortresses of Islamic construction like the Alcazaba Arabe in Badajoz. With help from the EU, sites like these are being restored. Extremadura and Castilla-León have prospered with the opening up of Spain, not only through the international market for the region's ham, olive oil and cork, but also from tourism. During the weekend *paseo* in towns which in Pritchett's time were impoverished, dilapidated and depopulated, the best way of distinguishing well-off tourists from similarly well-off residents is that the men in the latter category wear ties and hats, that they are carrying their wives' shopping bags and that what they're mainly buying are elaborate cakes. Students, meanwhile, are everywhere. Spain, in common with most developed countries, is worried about its ageing population. Two-thirds of the social services budget for León goes on *los mayores*. What you're most conscious of in the streets, though, are crowds of under-occupied young: well dressed, richly kitted out with iPods and mopeds, noisy, cheerful, sexy and, for now, apparently untroubled about whether and how all this can last.

It would be surprising if Spanish parents of teenaged children—parents whose own adolescence coincided with the early post-Franco transition—weren't even more concerned than others in the West about the downside of contemporary freedoms. Spain is on one of the busier drug routes into the rest of Europe. And then there's the recent, extreme permissiveness about sex. Late-night television here is startlingly pornographic. Like Ireland only more so, Spain can seem to have gone from the nineteenth century to the twenty-first with nothing in between. One of the reasons why the films of Pedro Almodóvar are so powerful, and in Spain so controversial, is that they simultaneously celebrate, mock and mourn the country's shift from Catholic social conservatism to a transgressive hedonism treated in a way no less scandalous for being very funny. Almodóvar was brought up in Cáceres under Franco and educated by monks.

Yet Catholicism, however diminished in national authority, is still a cohesive social and domestic force here. The famous tradition of Holy Week processions is only the most obvious of many examples, though it isn't often described in these terms. My journey north along Pritchett's route was made, like his, soon after Easter. But, like him,

Jeremy Treglown

I cheated a little: in my case by making a kind of reconnaissance trip a couple of weeks earlier, in the opposite direction. This overlapped with Holy Week, which in Spain lasts the whole eight days from Palm Sunday to Easter Day. The atheistic Pritchett hated all the superstitious display. He deliberately arrived after it was over. I, on the other hand, for the first time—and with increasing fascination and enjoyment—watched processions in León, Salamanca, Cáceres and Badajoz. I followed one of the individual *cofradías*—guilds— along its whole route. What did it all mean, not only spiritually and aesthetically, but as part of the lives of those taking part?

These elements can't be entirely separated out, of course. There's no mistaking the devotional seriousness of some of those staggering beneath the massive tableaux—the sinister-seeming hooded men but also, in Cáceres, the bare-headed women and girls who are alone permitted to carry the Virgin Mary and who, like her effigy, wear capes of red velvet. And however one reacts to the baroque gilding, the gory incisions in the statues of Jesus, there's no denying that by midnight the previously tentative squeals of cornets can turn into a rhythmic, penetrating wail that wouldn't have been out of place in the streets of antediluvian New Orleans. And once the bands really get going, the bearers do, too. Part of the art—what the crowds applaud like well-executed manoeuvres in a bullfight—is how smoothly each team of forty or more people gets its float shoulder-high; how neatly it handles a turn in a narrow street or on a steep slope; above all, the moments when the statue is made to take a couple of swaying paces back and then forward, and then to repeat: an elephant doing the paso doble. In western Spain, for all the reconditely theological coverage in the local papers, Holy Week rocks.

Behind the processions lie weeks—for some people months—of preparation. It would be interesting to know what percentage of teenagers in this part of Spain play in a *cofradía* band, with its long training, its weekly rehearsals. Then there are the boys who take posters all over the town, a different one for each guild, and the children who carry candles or collection boxes. Uniforms and robes have to be got ready, and cushions—to protect the bearers' shoulders—repaired. The dressing of every statue, the ornaments, the flowers: as in any carnival, all this is as cheerfully competitive as the music. From a secular, social viewpoint, what matters is not anything intrinsic to these activities but the fact that they involve the young in a range of harmlessly energy-consuming activities which tie them in to the wider adult community of their neighbourhood: people beyond their families and schools who will keep an eye out for them. Don't believe anyone who tells you that the only value of the ceremonies today is that they attract tourists.

No one, in the towns at least, is interested in an Englishman with a notebook. No one, that is, except people watching football in bars. In Extremadura and Old Castile, this happens in an atmosphere of sober, connoisseurial calm, a bit like a sheepdog display in Wales. On a Sunday afternoon when a big game is on TV, the place will fill up with families—an old woman in a wheelchair pushed by her son and his girlfriend, parents with small children, a hunchbacked teenager with his siblings, groups of middle-aged friends. If you leave your seat, you lose it, but no one spills your drink, or theirs. It's common to see glasses left half full when people go home. Meanwhile, conversations have gone on and, while exciting passages of play hold everyone's attention, the reactions to a goal or a foul are phlegmatic. Regional loyalties, so intense in Pritchett's time, have broadened. When I talked with a waiter from Madrid about Real Madrid's victory over Barcelona that day, what he mentioned first, with evident pride, was that the game had been watched by eight million people all over the world. Yet even nationalism has been modified by Spain's having become part of Europe. The British, with their mix of insularity and transatlanticism, can find it hard to grasp that so many continental Europeans, especially the young, are patriotic about being European. Few more at present than the Spanish, for whom accession to the EU so quickly followed their breakthrough into democracy.

All this would be too much to read into a few football matches, but it was unmistakable that being a compatriot of David Beckham and Michael Owen—the latter then still playing for Madrid—made me welcome in some Spanish bars. People were keen to tell me that Owen's goals came from on average fewer minutes of play, and fewer strikes, than those of Ronaldo or Raúl, and that Beckham's fitness allowed him to cover more ground than anyone else in the game. As for 'Leevairpull', with its Spanish manager and prominent Spanish players, it is of course essentially a Spanish team: one whose

Champions' League victory caused almost as much enjoyment here as in England, if of a much quieter kind.

Better to be talked to about football than not at all. Still, I ungratefully, and possibly wrongly, felt that it was of little relevance to what I was supposed to be doing. Pritchett was no sportsman and the hard-pressed people he met in 1927 didn't have time for games. Where could I find the kinds of conversation he had had—with ideologues, fantasists, the lovelorn and the lost?

I decided to find a way of staying in an 'ordinary' household. I wanted the equivalent of a B&B. The assistant in the tourist office in Cáceres translated this immediately as a *casa rural*. My preference was for a hamlet called Segura, today almost a shanty town, a satellite of Cáceres—or rather, of Nuevo Cáceres, its latest suburban development—which I had passed on the bus. Pritchett had arrived there late one night, exhausted after a mountainous walk of thirty-five miles. He had been promised a *venta*, the most basic of inns, but there wasn't one. Groping in the dark through an outcrop of rocks, he was startled to hear the screech of a peacock and assumed that it meant civilization. He found a door into a small stone hut: a forge. The blacksmith and his wife said at first that they had nowhere for him to sleep, but they gave him water. Reviving, the traveller told them where he had walked from, where he was going. They gave him food. Briefly alone with him, the woman asked about his family and lamented her own childlessness. Then the cottage filled up: the smith's father, his two younger brothers. Two sacks of straw were brought in for Pritchett, and a couple of mule blankets. When the family noises subsided, they were replaced by a carillon of sheep, goats and cattle outside the house, each with its own bell. Pritchett slept poorly. In the middle of the night, a pair of dogs which had been shut out burst through the boarded window and landed on top of him. At dawn, labourers began to arrive with ploughshares and pieces of wheel to be mended. Pritchett was given eggs and coffee. It wasn't the night's rest he had hoped for, but he had heard and seen more than he would have in a commercial lodging, and Cáceres was only half a day's walk to the north.

If there was no inn for Pritchett in Segura in 1927, in 2005 there was a *casa rural* and I had its phone number. I spoke to a harsh-voiced woman and we agreed on my time of arrival. The cost seemed high—sixty euros a night—and she told me there could be no meals apart from breakfast. She showed surprise that I asked about this, and even more that I had no car: most people bring their cars, she explained, and travel around. There are good restaurants in the towns. But, yes, there was a bar within walking distance, and I could enjoy the countryside around the castle.

I took this to mean a nearby landmark. Pritchett had been guided to Segura by an ancient tower, the 'Torre de Moro'. But when I belatedly asked for the address of my *casa rural*, it was the Castillo de las Seguras. The term 'country house', it seemed, is as ambiguous in Spanish as in English. It was too late to back off and I arrived in a mood of frustration compounded by social chippiness. What was the point of going in search of 'the architecture of humanity', only to end up somewhere worthy of the Landmark Trust? True, I now had an explanation for the peacock which had guided Pritchett to the blacksmith's door, but I wouldn't learn much about modern Spain from the guest sitting-room, a dark great hall with a tree stump smouldering in its cavernous fireplace, the walls covered with stuffed birds and mounted heads and horns, each with the date when it was shot—several very recently: a kind of wildlife version of Franco's Basilica. In the garden, these doubts were confirmed by an encounter with the owner, a short, handsome, dark-haired man in his forties wearing white trousers, a white linen shirt, black shoes and a double-breasted blazer with shining buttons. He was picking at a rose with secateurs. He introduced himself: José Miguel Carillo de Albornoz. He asked politely but with apparent indifference where I lived and where I had just come from, and why. He said I was the first of his paying guests to have come from England. The enterprise was new. The castle had always been in his family but it no longer had any land. Once, everything you could see from here belonged to it. Gesturing over unbroken plains towards a distant line of mountains, he shrugged. The place had to pay its way, somehow. He described in some detail the improvements he had been making.

My Spanish is not bad but if I lose the thread I become inattentive; or perhaps it's the other way around. My host said something about the television—was that all right? Assuming that he meant that it wasn't working, I said I didn't mind at all. Picking up on what I'd briefly told him about Pritchett, he asked if I, too, were a writer and when I said yes, he replied, '*Perfecto.*' It seemed an odd reaction—the guest quarters conspicuously lacked books—but I assumed it was a way of bringing the conversation to a close. I went in, slept for a while, and then set off in search of the Torre de Moro.

The woman with a harsh telephone voice turned out to be a shy and solicitous maid. She had a daughter at school in Cáceres. Her husband, she said, worked a long way away. Diffidently, she directed me to the nearest place where I could get supper: La Cabaña, a bar-restaurant attached to a petrol station and lorry park, twenty minutes' walk from the castle along the hectic main road. A loud game show on TV, a couple of hyperactive fruit machines, a display case of knives for sale, another of legs of ham, another of doughnuts. At the bar, a local policeman with dusty trousers and a loosely slung revolver, like someone out of the Wild West. At a table, two men with a laptop open between them. With her eyes on the TV, the waitress dangled a plate approximately in front of me: *arroz a la cubana*—warm rice in tomato sauce covered in half-melted cheese and a fried egg. I drank a lot of wine.

The next morning felt better. Pritchett's tower had been easy to find yesterday, a romantic, stork-filled ruin in the middle of a wide field of cattle. The word he had heard as 'Moro' was Mogollón, one of the family names of the people at the castle. It was interesting that he either hadn't cared or hadn't noticed, even in daylight, that where he was walking was a feudal estate. Did it mean he was more or less of a republican than I had thought? Today, I would ask about the forge. Breakfast for one was laid at the end of a long table in the sitting room. The stuffed heads looked down companionably.

Then, in came a blue-jeaned blonde with dark eyes, followed by my host, followed by a small bearded man with a large TV camera. Cheerful introductions and an air of expectation. I asked if they needed me to move out of the way. No, no, José Miguel protested happily, this was the TV crew he had mentioned. How soon could I be ready? A new man brought cables and lights. I improvised with my coffee. José Miguel disappeared and I took the chance to ask the blonde what was going on. Did I really not know? She laughed the laugh of one who is recognized wherever she goes. She was Lujan

Argüelles, a presenter on Cadena 3's Monday late-night show *Siete Días, Siete Noches* ('Seven Days, Seven Nights'). They were making a feature partly about José Miguel and his novels, partly about the history of his castle. The angle was new kinds of tourism in Extremadura. Was it true that I was writing a book about a famous English author who had stayed here?

José Miguel's novels?

Sure, didn't I know that he was a *muy famoso* writer of historical fiction?

On cue, he opened the door and beamed.

In stumbling Spanish, I talked to the camera about Pritchett, displayed the opening page of his chapter titled 'The Venta de la Segura', described his uncomfortable night in the *herrería*. José Miguel promised to show me the forge. I answered questions about the *casa rural* and praised its comforts by contrast with those of the smithy. How good that one may enjoy a holiday in a countryside so beautiful while having directly the experience of a little of its history! (Surely my bill would be reduced.) They filmed me lying on my bed with a book, looking enquiringly into the opulently tiled bathroom, gazing at the stuffed heads.

For the rest of the day José Miguel was busy with the crew all around the castle, but he pointed me towards the smithy. Immediately to the south of the thirteenth-century keep stands a substantial square house which belongs to an uncle. Against the outer side of its garden wall, behind an outcrop of granite rocks, leaned a small, single-storied white shack, its tiled roof falling in. The low main door led directly into the paved forge with its furnace. The building belonged to the estate and was still in use until fifteen years ago. A living room led off to the right, two tiny bedrooms to the left. The window through which the dogs jumped on to the recumbent Pritchett is still there. I poked around for a while in dust and ashes.

A hundred yards up the slope, Lujan Argüelles and her crew were filming the castle's arched, crenellated, crested gateway, the round and square towers restored in 1927, José Miguel said, by his grandfather, and a low battlement which he likes to sit on when he's expecting visitors. Pritchett must have seen all this as he sat outside in the cold dawn, eating his eggs. He had to walk straight past it as he set off for Cáceres. A British historian recently described conditions in places like Extremadura in the 1920s—conditions the Republicans were committed to changing: 'At the mercy of seasonal crops, climatic fluctuations and the personal whim of their employers, thousands of landless labourers...lived in abject poverty, while the handful of families who owned vast areas of land in those regions enjoyed enormous social, economic and political influence.' (Even today, a quarter of Spain's agricultural subsidy from the EU ends up in the hands of one per cent of farm owners.) With a trade like a blacksmith's, one was a little less badly off. Still, the rich man in his castle, the poor man at his gate: there couldn't have been a more perfect example of 'the architecture of humanity' at its most divisive. In the very year that Pritchett had slept on straw in this hovel with the smith, his wife, father and two brothers, the castle behind was having an expensive make-over. Why had he left this out? Was it too obvious? Or was the tired walker in too much of a hurry to reach Cáceres before the sun got seriously hot?

If Pritchett had missed a story, I nearly missed a better one. The filming seemed to have gone well and, once the crew had left, José Miguel relaxed and became very friendly. The following day he showed me the castle's grand main floor, upstairs, where he lives when he's not in Madrid. Family portraits, a chapel with an early fresco, a dining room with modern still lifes and a collection of old china. We stood in his study looking at a picture of the Palacio de Ovando in Cáceres, which once belonged to the family and contained its main library. Then he showed me his own books, talking about them with the undisguised southern European pride that the British easily mistake for boasting. Here was his novel about Sor Juana, which had sold 50,000 copies. This one told the story of Isabel de Monteczuma, the Aztec princess brought back to Extremadura by one of Cortés's followers as a prize. Here was a very important book, his most recent, a biography of Monteczuma himself: José Miguel inscribed it for me. And the previous one, El Comendador de Alcántara, about his ancestor Frey Nicolás de Ovando y Flores, first governor of the Indies at the beginning of the sixteenth century, responsible for the slaughter of native chiefs including Queen Anacaona and well deserving, the blurb says, his fama de sanguinario. A contemporary observed that he was extremely shrewd and a very capable ruler of men, but not of Indians.

Two days earlier, I'd had José Miguel Carrillo de Albornoz down as an idle aristo playing at gardening while he waited for the shooting season to open. If, like Pritchett, I had left early the next morning, and if I had mentioned the episode at all, that—subject to the libel laws— would have been how I would have described him. Now he was turning out to be a thoughtful, sensitive, melancholy but impulsive and often amusing man, a writer torn between the romance of his family background and the brutality and injustices on which much of its recently evaporated fortune was founded. Joining me as I watched the Pope's funeral on TV, he blurted out in English that it was a good thing he was dead. 'This Pope was a sixteenth-century Pope, a fifteenth-century Pope. He undid the work of Vatican II. I am a hundred miles from the church today.' Then he relented a little: 'He was a strong spirit, this Juan Pablo.' He joked that the Pope's death had probably been arranged by Elizabeth II as a way of delaying her son's marriage to Camilla Parker Bowles: 'She is a powerful woman, your Isabel.' I said it was a pleasure to see the Spanish king and queen in the front row at the funeral, and not President Bush, who was placed behind them. 'We are in Europe,' José Miguel said simply—not, I noticed, 'They are Catholics.' Later, he mentioned the 'terrible' campaign to make the Spanish Queen Isabella I a saint and showed me a cutting in which he was quoted as denouncing her for having murdered thousands of people. When I stood up to go and pack, he unexpectedly embraced me and said, 'You're a good guy, Jeremy.' Touched, I went to pay the bill (full price) and waited for my taxi outside the back door. José Miguel returned to clipping shrubs, a lonely-looking figure, but we kept bumping into one another. Behind the castle there is a derelict pigsty on the scale of a palace courtyard—certainly no less commodious than the forge, and much better designed. As I stood admiring it, José Miguel came around the corner. 'My uncle, he said he wanted to have pigs here. I said no. No more pigs. Please.'

Between Cáceres and Plasencia, still in Extremadura, the train crosses the Tagus. In Pritchett's day there was no road bridge: pedestrians took a ferry. For reasons of his own ('I am not ashamed of my fears for they are my adventures') he walked dizzily across the rickety railway bridge instead, half jumping, half crawling from sleeper to sleeper. You couldn't do that now, not least because the old bridge has been submerged by a reservoir which enables Spain to extract the last of the river's energy before it wanders across the border towards Lisbon. In any case, the train costs only 3.75 euros for an eighty-minute journey with a reserved seat in a clean, uncrowded, air-conditioned carriage, taking you through unspoiled landscapes of gorges, moorland and mountains. There's a station named Rio Tájo, where an elaborately uniformed station master saluted with a furled red flag as the train passed without stopping.

The banks of the reservoir below, which spreads west as far as Alcántara, are a beautiful place to camp and fish in the spring, when the water is high. Or if. In April 2005, despite the last of the melting snow pouring from the mountain tops, there were wide, white beaches of sand and fissured, tussocky clay. It could have been late August. 'The Tagus,' Pritchett wrote, 'the Duero, the Ebro, the Guadiana, and Guadalquivir are the rivers that do not dry up in the summer.' No one would risk that statement now.

A main cause of Spain's comparative poverty in the nineteenth and early twentieth centuries was that it had missed out on the industrial revolution. This wasn't, as some foreign historians used to imply, a mere matter of laziness and incompetence reinforced by religious bigotry. Early industry needed water, consistent and plentiful water: for mills, for boilers, for transport by river and canal. Before the petrol-driven engine, nothing else would do and Spain—after Greece, the second driest country in Europe—didn't have it. Today, once again, water is precious: as precious in some parts of southern Europe as in North Africa. How will Spain fare in the growing struggle for resources?

As I continued north, stopping a night in Plasencia before going on by bus to Salamanca, I read about new airbrushings of Franco. Following the example of Madrid, Guadalajara—where in 1937 the Fascists, mainly in the form of Italian troops, suffered their first defeat by the Republicans—hauled a bronze statue of the uniformed *caudillo* off its feet, along with another memorial to him. In Cáceres, there are notices explaining that this or that palace was constructed by knocking together the former homes of Moors, but nothing to indicate that it was on one of these balconies—potent emblems of Christian reconquest—that Franco had himself proclaimed Generalísimo and head of state in 1936. There are still more conspicuous blanks in Salamanca, despite the presence of a museum of the Civil War. Salamanca was at the heart of Spanish Catholic conservatism. It was here that the country's battle against the European Enlightenment was most successfully fought: here that the university refused to teach Hobbes, Gassendi, Locke, Newton, Descartes. Early in the Civil War, Franco made the city his headquarters, as did his brother-in-law and leading adviser, Ramón Serrano Suñer, who had moved his family into the bishop's palace. The liberal intellectual Miguel de Unamuno, meanwhile, supposedly Rector Perpétuo of the university, having spoken bravely and directly against Nationalist glorifiers of war, was shunned by his colleagues, hounded from his post and driven into virtual house arrest.

The historian Paul Preston tells us that in Salamanca the future Franquista state was planned and, as town after town fell to the Fascists, a card index of some two million Republicans and trade unionists was built up to facilitate post-war reprisals: executions, labour camps, the new prisons. The files are now in the museum's research archives but nothing about any of this appears in the public display cases. There's a heavy emphasis, on the other hand, on the history of Freemasonry, presented as if it were the chief resistance movement against Fascism. International involvement in the war, especially on the Republican side, is well illustrated but undermined by the fact that the captions are exclusively in Castilian (not even in Catalan, though it was from Catalonia that much of the strongest opposition to Franco came). I learned, though, that there was a funny side to Fascism: its propaganda. One postcard of the time shows Spain as an island defended by three soldiers against an invasion from the east by pig-faced fat devils with green bodies and webbed feet, whom they are throwing back into the sea.

If Franco is being disappeared, the same isn't true of the conquerors of South America. Many of the leading adventurers came from Extremadura and Castilla-León and most towns on this side of Spain have their Plaza de los Conquistadores, their Avenida Hernán Cortes, their Calle Francisco Pizarro. In Salamanca, there's a whole district in which all the streets are named after old colonies—Argentina, Bolivia, California… Such things are more noticeable to a foreigner. American visitors to Bristol, mindful of the slave trade, can be startled by finding

Jeremy Treglown

Black Boy Hill and Whiteladies Road still on the map. But all that was long ago: sensible not to pretend it never happened. Besides, the days of Spanish exploitation of Latin Americans have gone.

Or have they? One night, I did some emailing in a *locutorio*: walls of computers with webcams, a rank of curtained phone booths. It was a Friday and crowded. A whole family next to me was trying to get into the same shot. My keyboard was covered with other people's cigarette ash, my desk with other people's Coca-Cola. A dour old man took the money between phone calls of his own. I hoped to get answers to some of my messages so, next morning, I went back early. Everything had just been thoroughly washed and there was a no-smoking sign on the reception desk. A neat young South American woman in an overall was polishing the desks. I had a couple of replies, one with an attachment which I couldn't open. She sorted it out. The place was empty, so we talked. She was Bolivian, an illegal immigrant; call her Juana. She worked there every Saturday and Sunday, 10 a.m. to 2 p.m., 4.30 p.m. to 10 p.m. It was a cash business, so the job was a responsible one. The rest of the week, she looked after an elderly woman in the town, but she also had to be at the *locutorio* late on two week-nights, to cash up. Because she had no papers, the owner didn't pay taxes or social security for her and could sack her whenever he wanted. She had a room in a flat rented by other South Americans. Did she like it here? She needed to be here to support her family in Bolivia. But, no: she hated the food, always the same. And the people were *racista*. Why? I don't know what I meant by the question, but her answer was simple: 'Because we're in Extremadura.'

I knew that there was a Mexican cafe in the town I was about to move on to, a bus ride away. The old woman whom Juana cared for was spending Tuesday in hospital, so she would have some of the day free. She agreed to come over. I met her in the middle of the morning. She was fashionably dressed in a white embroidered cotton top and jeans but noticeably nervous of the traffic, or perhaps of me. She was worried about when there would be a bus home so we found that out and booked her a seat. Now she cheered up. It was the first time she had been out of the town she worked in since she arrived a year ago. She wished she had brought her camera. I had one and she asked me to photograph her: in front of a church, under a tree, on a bridge, in a garden. All this happened quite quickly, even efficiently. She found a one-hour printing shop and told them we would be back on time.

After coffee, she wanted to go into the cathedral. She went around very slowly, pausing before gloomy baroque paintings, lighting candles. Then she needed to phone her employer's hospital. I had left my mobile behind, so we went to a *locutorio*. She didn't know the area code and the student working there seemed over-helpful, in a way I didn't identify until I realized how few Latin Americans, or for that matter blacks or Asians, you see in Extremadura, by contrast with Madrid or Barcelona. You don't notice what isn't there. Outside, Juana and I were looked at quite often: a look which could have been about a pretty young woman with an older man, or could have been something else, or both.

Back at the printing shop, while I was paying, Juana extracted not only the pictures of herself but the negatives. No, I couldn't have one. No man had a photograph of her, *ninguno*. It would be unlucky for her. The pictures were for her family, to show them she had been to this beautiful place.

In the Mexican bar we ordered enchiladas and she repeated her dislike of Extremeño food: *frito, frito, frito, cerdo, cerdo, cerdo*—all fried stuff, all pork. Instantly at home with the girls working there, she helped herself to a beer and began to tell me her story: an older man had made her pregnant when she was seventeen; they hadn't married but he wouldn't let her go to university. Later, they had another child. He supported them well and helped the rest of her family—her mother in La Paz, her father living separately in Peru, her brother, three sisters. But he was jealous and violent. She couldn't stand it any more but if she left him she had to make money. The friends with whom she now lived had recently moved to Spain. Juana contacted them and came out, ostensibly for a holiday. The friends helped her to find a job. Her children, a boy of twelve and a girl of five, were with her mother. She became tearful. Because she had no papers she couldn't return to visit them even if she could afford to: she wouldn't be allowed back into Spain. That was one reason for working in the *locutorio*: she could talk to them every week and with the webcam they could even see each other, but it was 'agony that we can't touch, agony'. The enchiladas came and again she brightened up. She covered her mouth with both hands in mocking embarrassment. 'I sleep with two *animalitos*,' she said, 'a toy duck and a toy dog.'

Lunch over, she suggested we go to the market to buy fruit. A young Spanish man, seeing us come out of the bar, nudged his girlfriend and pointed surreptitiously, but the stallholder was friendly and, again it seemed, extra-attentive. Juana picked over the produce disdainfully, agreed with a show of reluctance to be bought apricots and a pineapple, then added some vegetables and, as we left, muttered fiercely about these filthy people who never wash their food: in Bolivia, we are poor but we are clean.

We sat on a park bench in the shade, surrounded by palaces, churches, a convent: carved balconies, crested doorways. Unprompted, Juana made a sudden speech. 'My country had a culture and a government which the Spanish destroyed. They invaded my country because they wanted to rob it. They took our silver and our gold. Those buildings were paid for by these robberies. Bolivia is poor because of this—this is why my family can't live unless I come here.'

Then it was time for her bus and, again, she grew quiet and anxious, but brightened at finding it already waiting. She gathered her fruit and vegetables and her photographs, kissed me on both cheeks and said goodbye, without thanks. A couple of months later, she emailed me to say that she had found a new job in another town, another *locutorio*. She had been given a permit and a contract. She was saving to visit her children.

Marching Spain ends sombrely. Despite Pritchett's resistance to religion, his refusal to use a guidebook and his emphasis on 'the architecture of humanity', once he had crossed the northern mountains of Extremadura into Old Castile and walked as far as León he felt obliged to visit the great cathedral there. He powerfully if sweepingly describes its narrow nave ('The naves of all cathedrals are cruel; they are the undeviating spears of the faith'), its 'agonised' brilliant stained glass, the freezing air. (All art selects, exaggerates, finds patterns. What I noticed as much was the breadth of the cloisters and the cheerful paganism of the dazzling floral designs in many of the windows.) Almost as soon as he has gone in, he is told that the building is about to close, *se van a cerrar*, and he's back in the street outside. The book's last words repeat the phrase as a statement about Spain: it is about to close.

Pritchett gives a vivid, sometimes funny, sometimes troubling picture of an impoverished region on the brink (though he never explicitly says this, and perhaps didn't consciously realize it) of a vicious war and a stifling dictatorship. His last page is a big gesture, yet, thinking back about the book in the light of it, one finds other premonitions: a passing question about the likelihood of revolution by someone on the boat coming over; the number of soldiers Pritchett noticed in Badajoz; a conversation in Cáceres about the colonial war in Morocco; his instinctive distrust of Salamanca, with its high cloistered walls, 'a place that shuts the stranger out...an ascetic place without heart or intimacy'.

His anti-Catholicism was not only very English, both of its time and for centuries before, but in tune with prevailing Spanish Republican sentiment. Yet perhaps Spain can't be fully grasped without a feeling for Catholicism. Even the impact of Almodóvar's films is diluted unless—if only by suspension of disbelief—you experience them as blasphemous. The Spanish Civil War was many things but one of them was a victory of religion over secularism: a fact which, along with the Nationalist self-identification with the *reconquista*, can now appear even more frighteningly prophetic than the war seemed in other ways at the time. While Pritchett half anticipated Fascism, though, he couldn't have guessed what would follow it. Many people wished for, but no one seriously expected, the increasingly outward-looking, tolerant, prosperous, democratic European Spain of the past quarter-century. In León, a lavishly illustrated guidebook was left beside my bed, like a new Gideon's Bible. It began: 'It is in your power a book-guide that will do more pleasant your stay in Castile and León...a booming community that bets resolutely by the tourism of quality, that adds many attractives that are a must... We will keep on going up.' *Seguiremos subiendo*: perhaps this was twenty-first-century Spain's version of *se van a cerrar*. But then there were those parched mudflats on either side of rivers that should have been in full flood. And anniversary pictures of the Atocha bombings: people with their clothes bloody and shredded; a woman sobbing into her mobile—images of kinds we had seen all too recently, have seen again since and will go on seeing. Whatever any Western intellectual guessed in 1927, it wasn't that by the century's end religion would once again be a global force, more dangerous than ever before. Or that we would be turning the very air we breathe into a weapon of mass destruction.

Among the landscapes I had passed through, every bit as thrilling as in Pritchett's descriptions, there was one which wasn't underpopulated: the foothills of the dramatic Sierra de Béjar above Hervás, where he left the main track to climb overland. It was a holiday and the roads were busy. In nearby Baños de Montemayor, all the hotels were full, treatment sessions at the state-of-the-art Roman spa booked up. Embarrassed families crossed the village street in dressing gowns, carrying their towels. Hervás, too, has several hotels, both in the village and in the surrounding countryside, and, like other Spanish places, has turned its monastery into a luxury *parador*. Historic sites are clearly signposted, notably the Jewish quarter, where, as a plaque records, twenty-five families lived productively until the fifteenth-century reign of Isabella and Ferdinand: *Los Reyes Católicos*. Then, those who refused to 'convert' were forced to make the harsh mountainous journey of exile westwards via Ciudad Rodrigo into Portugal. Their names are listed: Cohen, Haben Hayiz, Samuel la Rica... Crowds now strolled through these winding, narrow lanes, video cameras at the ready.

I walked out of Hervás, hoping to identify Pritchett's route, and found a narrow path leading to a reservoir, where I sat for a time. Behind and ahead of me, half a dozen groups straggled along in walking boots. On a wider, rocky track crossing mine, a couple with rucksacks stumbled as they showed each other their text messages and then flattened themselves against a stone wall while two families lurched past in cars, leaning out of the windows to see how much further up they could drive. A sudden roar: a posse of quad bikes, revving to overtake. Below stood a ruined mill with a piece of graffiti: UTOPIA ES PENSAR QUE EL MUNDO PUEDE SEGUIR ASÍ POR MÁS TIEMPO. Utopia is thinking that the world can go on like this for longer. □

GRANTA

HOW TO FLY
John Burnside

I flew for the first time when I was nine years old. Nobody saw it happen, but that didn't bother me: the Wright Brothers' earliest ascent had also been conducted in the strictest secrecy and, until public pressure forced them out of hiding, any number of successful flights had gone unwitnessed. Of course, Orville and Wilbur hadn't attempted to do what I was doing: like Blériot and Santos-Dumont, they were changing the known world, but they weren't committed to flying in its purest sense. They were mechanics, not angels; what I wanted was something that they had never even considered and, though I knew I was destined to fail, I wasn't prepared to settle for anything as mundane as a flying machine. Though I admired those early aviators more than anyone else in history, I knew, even then, that the people we think of as pioneers were pioneers only of machine flight—which, for me, was as different from actual flying as a conjuring trick is from natural magic. I didn't want to soar with the aid of an engine; I wanted a miracle, a triumph of the will. I wanted to fly unassisted, like a bird, or a medieval monk.

Like Elmer of Malmesbury, for example. According to the legend, Elmer, dressed in his usual monk's habit, but with home-made wings fastened to his shoulders and ankles, climbed to the top of the abbey tower and threw himself off, travelling a distance of around 600 feet before he crashed to the ground, breaking both legs. It was a windy morning in the year 1010. Apparently, Elmer had spent long hours observing the jackdaws that congregated around the abbey, and he felt sure that he had discovered their secret; according to the story, told later by William of Malmesbury, he really had flown for some distance before he suddenly lost faith in his abilities and panicked, a little like Peter, who, having clambered bravely out of his boat on the Sea of Galilee to follow Jesus across the water, suddenly became afraid and began to sink. It took some time for Elmer's legs to mend but, as soon as he was well enough, he began preparing for his next flight, convinced that his fall had resulted partly from his own lack of conviction and partly because he had forgotten to provide himself with a tail. Had it not been for his abbot, who forbade any further experiments, Elmer would almost certainly have tried to fly again; instead, he lived a long and studious life, possibly surviving until 1066, when he was able to observe the passage of Halley's Comet, just as he had done when still a young boy in 989. Or so William tells us.

Monks, it seems, had a particular obsession with flying: not much of an advertisement, perhaps, for the religious life. Even more interesting than the case of Elmer of Malmesbury is that of Giuseppe da Copertino, who, several times during the first half of the seventeenth century, was observed to rise into the air unassisted by a number of independent and more or less reliable witnesses. His abbot was similarly upset by the news of his flight—or, possibly, his levitation—and demanded that Giuseppe desist at once. This he could not do, his ascents being altogether involuntary, so he was obliged to become a recluse, where he presumably practised his art unobserved, until his eventual reassimilation into the fold. There he remained until he died at the age of sixty. Those who saw him fly say he rose straight up into the air without warning, and hovered there for a time with a faraway look on his face, a look of ecstasy perhaps, or the expression a sleepwalker assumes on his nocturnal perambulations.

Possibly because I wasn't a monk, my own attempt at flight, that first day, was modest by comparison. On a clear, almost windless afternoon, out on a patch of open ground near Cowdenbeath, Fife, I climbed to the top of a disused pit building and jumped off the roof. The only mechanical aids I employed were a grubby old bedsheet tied to my wrists and ankles with twine and a pair of swimming goggles to protect my eyes. I didn't travel any great distance but I did feel a tension in the sheet at my back, and I landed further from the building than I might have expected, floating a moment, it seemed, my arms and legs splayed wide, my hands making tiny, ineffectual swimming movements, before I hit the ground, hard, and rolled sideways into a patch of broken bricks and nettles. I was lucky not to break anything, but I was also heartened by the notion that I really had flown for two or three seconds. By the end of the week, those two seconds had been transformed in my memory to half a minute; a week after that, I was back, with more sophisticated wings, and high hopes of a genuinely *perceptible* flight. It never happened. The sheer number of my eventual failures should have been more than sufficiently convincing but, no matter what I did, and no matter how graceless and painful my falls were, I continued to believe that willed flight was possible.

Of course, I wasn't interested in air travel; what I wanted was to *fly*. My family weren't the kind of people who could afford to travel by aeroplane—in those days holidays happened in Blackpool or Clacton—but that didn't trouble me at all. I didn't want to go up in the air according to a schedule, piloted by a stranger, shoehorned into my seat alongside a hundred other people. I wanted to go solo. I wanted to fly—and, in spite of my poor record, I remained convinced that it was possible. All I lacked was the knowledge: as with so many things back then, the key to the problem was more science. What I needed, I realized, was *an instruction manual.*

I found Richard Ferris's *How to Fly* at a church jumble sale. It was published in 1910, by Thomas Nelson and Sons, one of those chunky, durable hardbacks aimed at the more serious child, alongside *How It Is Made* and *How It Works* ('Splendid books for boys, telling them just what they want to know'). The front cover showed an aviator in a perilously fragile craft—something like a tea-chest fitted with wings and the wheels from an old pram—soaring among clouds in a sky of faded cerulean. Maybe it was the colours that first drew me to the stall where the book lay, innocently priced at sixpence, between an old-fashioned bicycle pump and a tattered golliwog; more likely, though, it was the fact that the pilot, an intent, hunched figure in a flying cap and what looked like a safari jacket, was not only alone in his craft, but barely *in* it at all. His head and his entire upper torso were completely open to the elements: flying like that, in this makeshift crate, he would have felt the cool air of the upper atmosphere on his face, he would have smelled the ozone, tasted clouds. That picture alone was probably enough: the first page, however, closed the deal, and my sixpence was duly passed over. What I read that day is with me still:

> The air which surrounds us, so intangible and so commonplace
> that it seldom arrests our attention, is in reality a vast, unexplored
> ocean, fraught with future possibilities. Even now, the pioneers of a
> countless fleet are hovering above us in the sky, while steadily,
> surely, these wonderful possibilities are unfolded.

This thrilled me. I had visions of a thousand souls wandering the heavens, each in his own, solo craft, powered by nothing but human will. I didn't connect this vision of flight to the aeroplanes I knew about: those were nothing more than huge buses, chugging along from stop to stop. To buy a ticket and board an aeroplane wasn't flying; it was air travel—and air travel was what businessmen did or families off on holiday to Malaga. When I studied the contents page of this marvellous book, what I saw contradicted every tenet of air travel that I knew about: 'The Air', 'Laws of Flight', 'Balloons: how to operate', 'Balloons: how to build' and, best of all, 'Biographies of Prominent Aeronauts'. The men and women who jetted to and fro above my head in commercial aircraft weren't aeronauts, they were passengers and, from what I had seen at the pictures, they didn't do anything at all, except drink gin and tonic and look out of the window at passing clouds. They weren't exposed, they couldn't taste or smell or feel the sky, like Claude Grahame-White, 'the most famous of British aviators', or Léon Delagrange, who gave up a promising career as an artist to smash the world speed record in 1909, 'travelling at the rate of 49.9 miles per hour', but was killed the following year 'by the fall of his machine'. Those men had flown: compared to them, the ever-increasing company of airline passengers might just as well have been on a Sunday afternoon coach trip to the Trossachs, with flasks and sandwiches and scarves to keep them warm.

So, to my child's mind, air travel had nothing to do with flying; but it only became a lie, as such, in the late Sixties and early Seventies. By then it was hopelessly accessible; by then it had been sold too hard, it was too remote from the ether and it was too safe. The sight of a modern plane passing overhead presented none of the beauty and awe I experienced when I studied plate twenty-two of *How to Fly*, a grainy photograph entitled 'The Wellman Dirigible *America* starting for Europe, October 15, 1910'. Here, a cigar-like airship tilted dangerously above what looked like unlimited ocean, utterly vulnerable and just fifty feet from the cold, dark water. This was flying. It was easy to doubt aeroplanes, because they had been reduced to machine noise and safety features; it was easy to doubt the pilots in old war films, with their immaculate uniforms and ridiculous moustaches. It was easy to doubt the happiness of air hostesses, because they smiled so hard—and it was impossible not to doubt the moon landings, because Neil Armstrong and his colleagues were so very serious. Like everything else we saw on television, Apollo was all Fifties rhetoric and odd haircuts, another outmoded and surprisingly cheapskate pantomime to divert us from the nagging sensation that something true was happening elsewhere. Remembering it all now, I can't tell one event from another: the badly lit, pockmarked dust of the moon surface blurs with the badly lit face of the dead president's brother on the kitchen floor of the Ambassador Hotel, the look in his eyes betraying the ordinary realization that history repeats itself in the most casual ways, and the same people get away with the same crimes, time and time again.

People were flying off in all directions: to Acapulco, to the moon, to spy on the Russians, to bomb the Vietnamese. Aeroplanes were passing overhead all the time, but nobody I knew was on them. Once, flying had been an adventure; now it was merely glamorous. Once, the men and women who took to the air needed courage and skill; now all they required was money. Once upon a time, people had really flown—people like Amelia Earhart and Amy Johnson and Antoine de Saint-Exupéry; now they, and the flights they had taken, were as remote, and just as unreal, as imperial Japan. By the time I first boarded a plane, anybody could do it and so, by definition, it wasn't worth doing. It was a chore. For a long time, looking out of an aeroplane window was like watching television: nothing I saw was entirely real, it was all travelogue, just a step away from cinematography. I half expected a commentary, in a well-practised Oxford English accent, telling me what to look for in the landscape below, or naming the types of cloud that I could see on the tiny screen: *cumulus, stratus, cirrus, nimbus, mammatus, contrail, altostratus, cumulonimbus.*

I fell in love with Amy Johnson when I was fourteen. I had more or less given up on the idea of flying; now, what interested me was the possibility, not of defying gravity and floating away into space, but of disappearing altogether. I still had dreams where I glided downstairs, or along an empty street, my feet just millimetres above the ground, but, more often, I saw myself from outside, walking in new snow, or in brilliant sunshine, and vanishing—gradually, one step at a time—into thin air. It seemed an obvious progression: after flying came the disappearing act and so many of the great aviators had done it. Saint-Exupéry, for example, had simply melted into the upper atmosphere, the author of my favourite book—*Wind, Sand and Stars*—becoming the very elements he most loved. I could never quite believe that any of the great aviators had crashed: I couldn't see them spiralling into the ocean, to drift for a few hours or days waiting vainly to be rescued, while the sharks circled and closed in; I couldn't see them consumed by fire, or cut to pieces; I could only imagine them as lost. Which is to say: I could only imagine them in some blessed, deeply sensual state, one degree from angelhood, the air bright and sharp on their faces and in their lungs, as they slipped through some invisible barrier that only the lost can detect. By the time I was fourteen, this was what I admired and longed for: to disappear, to be lost, to arrive at an unimaginable elsewhere. Why would I want to fly, if I could vanish? To become a Saint-Exupéry, or an Amelia Earhart, had less to do with aeronautics than with invisibility.

The most invisible aviator of all was Amy Johnson. Her story is not unique in the annals of flight, but it is perhaps the most austere, and almost certainly the most beautiful. She is best known for her solo fight, in May 1930, from Croydon to Darwin, Australia, a passage of 11,000 miles, which she completed in nineteen days in a single-engine Gypsy Moth. The following year, with co-pilot Jack Humphreys, she flew from England to Japan; in 1932, flying solo again, she set the England to Capetown record. Throughout the Thirties, she pursued non-stop flights to the United States and India, with her husband, Jim Mollison. When war broke out, she joined the Air Transport Auxiliary, where her duties were fairly routine—and it was on one of these ordinary flights, rather than above some faraway ocean, that she disappeared, crashing into the Thames estuary on January 5, 1941. She was the first ATA pilot to be killed: it seems she parachuted out of her stricken craft, but drowned in the icy water, silent and unseen.

Amy Johnson was the first real infatuation of my life, but I wasn't very much interested in her biography. What I cared about were her solo flights. It was only by flying solo that an aviator could reach the borderline between this world and the invisible, and it was only by being lost that she could *cross* that line, falling out of the sky and into forever, alone, blessèd, untouchable. That was what disqualified Amelia Earhart from flight's highest echelon: she did make solo voyages, and she did disappear, during an attempt, in 1937, to be the first woman to fly around the world—but she was not alone. Her navigator, Fred Noonan, was in the aircraft with her when she went down, and presumably perished with her, somewhere near Howland Island, in the Pacific Ocean. Sometimes I dream of her solo Atlantic flight, between Harbour Grace in Canada and the north Irish coast, (she had been heading for Paris, but severe weather conditions forced her to land near Derry), and I honour her as one of the great flyers, but, like so many others, she can only be numbered among the missing, not ranked with those who truly disappeared. To disappear, you had to be alone. That, for me, was the fundamental rule of flying.

The missing are so many. I think of them as limbo people, stranded in some wide departure lounge of the afterlife, bluish phantoms touched with ozone and jet fuel. Otis Redding and Glenn Miller are sitting together by a window, talking about music; Thomas Selfridge, the first man to die in an aircraft accident (September 1908), is having a drink with Admiral Yamamoto and Leslie Howard; Buddy Holly is flirting with Carole Lombard. In another of the many seating areas, Dag Hammarskjöld and Yuri Gagarin are discussing history; while Patsy Cline is surprised to find that she has so much in common with Rocky Marciano. Ronnie Van Zant and Steve Gaines are forming an *a capella* singing group with Jim Reeves and Ricky Nelson. It's a crowded space, and everybody here is waiting for his or her own particular flight, though whether they are going back to where they came from, to start again in a different guise, or are on the way to some other, quite unknown destination is impossible to tell.

For particularly mundane reasons, I've spent the last twenty-odd years of my life on aeroplanes. This came under the heading of business travel, mostly: another step away from being an aviator, and even lower than passenger status. Yet, oddly enough, such a debased form of air travel was exactly what I needed, in order to investigate the metaphysical possibilities of flying. Who is more invisible than the business traveller? In an airport, who do we notice: the pretty girl with the rucksack, the young Indian family travelling halfway around the world to visit friends in Pittsburgh, or the man in the grey suit? If the journey of a thousand miles begins with the first step, then my first step was to vanish into the crowds at the airport, the man nobody saw, the one who slipped through unnoticed, a non-first-class, unaccompanied, middle-management type, one of those people with nothing to say and no one to say it to. It was wonderful. I would sit by the window and gaze out as the plane prepared to touch down at Schiphol or JFK, and I would register, with infinite care, the usual details: the airport buildings; the lights; the fields around the runway; the rather pretty, oddly provincial sprawl of Long Island. Every now and then, something different would happen, or I would be overwhelmed by the strange beauty of the descent: the endless simmer of Buenos Aires, say, and the great silted mass of La Plata; the sudden apprehension of the Pacific, as the plane headed into San Francisco; the giddy sense of archipelago that came and went in an instant, just above Copenhagen. Finally, no matter where I touched down, there was always the feeling, as I recovered my bags and headed for the exit, that I was in a place where nobody knew me, a place where I could simply disappear. I could walk to the rank, get into the first taxi and go somewhere other than where I was supposed to go. There was a fictitious account running in my head, of a man more or less identical to me, who would be observed getting on to the shuttle bus, in a dark raincoat, carrying a brown leather bag, somewhat tired, perhaps, or a little preoccupied, but not looking or acting in any way out of the ordinary: just a man getting on or off the shuttle bus, never to be seen again. By now, there was more room to disappear. People took less notice; the world was less accountable. Eventually, in principle, it wouldn't matter if I disappeared or not. I could keep my appointments, I could return my rented car on time and catch the flight home, and I still wasn't entirely there—and this is why the real pioneers weren't Orville and Wilbur Wright, or Louis Blériot, or Charles Lindbergh, but Amy Johnson and Amelia Earhart and Antoine de Saint-Exupéry. Because the real accomplishment of the twentieth century wasn't, as Ferris put it, that 'Man has learned how to fly!', it was that, quietly, and with no sense of a breakthrough, people were learning how to *vanish*.

The last time I flew was somewhere between Kautokeino and Lakselv, far inside the Arctic Circle, in the Norwegian province of Finnmark. It was early May, but I was still driving on snow tyres when I left the tiny, unheated *hytte* that I'd borrowed in Kautokeino and headed east towards Karasjoka; by the time I reached the hazy white turn in the road that would take me back north, to Lakselv's tiny civilian airport, the snow had almost stopped and the sun was out, glittering on the rivers and thaw-streams, illuminating the land so that what had seemed like grey, monotonous scrub a few minutes before was now full of subtle colour: the rich browns and soft purples of the birch twigs; the pale yellows and greens of *Salix lapponica*; the soft oranges and blue-greys and reds of the mosses and lichens. Towards Lakselv, the land is owned by the Norwegian military: in places, it is forbidden to stop, except in cases of emergency. Normally, I pay attention to the warning signs that are posted everywhere along this route, but that day, I ignored them. I wanted to go for a last walk in this sudden theatre of light and colour: just a short hike to carry home the silent chill of the tundra in my bones and my nervous system. I pulled in and positioned the car so it couldn't easily be observed from the highway, then I struck out, heading along a reindeer track beside a wide, frozen lake, picking my way through the snow, listening to the thaw-streams as they trickled down the gentle slopes, a sound I'd heard before, in the work of the Sami poet and musician, Nils-Aslak Valkeapää, long before I ever saw Finnmark.

I didn't go far. It was still cold, and I had to be back in Lakselv that night, to return my hire car; besides, I was nervous about the military. I skirted the lake for a while, letting the May sunshine warm my face, then I turned back. The great thing about the sub-Arctic is that a few days, or an hour, or even a couple of minutes can be enough: it is a land full of signs, a land of sudden, local miracles. All you have to do is learn how to find them. That day, I thought I'd had my gift, with the sun and the colours and the sound of the thaw-water; then, a few hundred yards from where I'd left the car, I disturbed a flock of ptarmigan and they flared up out from the snow-covered scrub, white birds in a field of white, their wings whirring, a sound like tiny wheels turning in my flesh—and suddenly, with no sense that anything out of the ordinary was happening, and perhaps for no more than a few seconds, I was rising too, flaring up into the air, just like the birds, wingless, dizzy, my head full of whiteness. I don't want to make of this any more than it was: it lasted less than a minute, and it was in no way mystical or even inexplicable. At the same time, though, I do want to give that moment its due, because I did take to the air, I did fly and, for a few moments, I was one of those birds, attuned to the flock, familiar with the sky. Some miracles are purely personal and may be entirely imaginary, but they are miracles, nonetheless. I'd disturbed ptarmigan like this more than once—it's difficult not to, out on the tundra—but I had never felt this sensation before. For the first time, I had come close enough, and I had been caught up, carried away, offered the gift of a moment's flight.

Later, I dropped off the car and found a place to stay for the night. It was a quiet, rather austere guest house, the only one in town that was open. My room had a picture window, with a view of snowy birch trees and a low, dark wood beyond. The plane back to Tromsø departed around two o'clock the following afternoon; I had plenty of time, and nothing else to do but take it easy—a guarantee, if ever there was one, that I would find it impossible to sleep. When I'm away from home, I only sleep well when things are happening: in transit, say, or in busy cities, with traffic and voices all around me. That night, in a world of indelible stillness, the snow muffling any sound that might have filtered through the birch woods, the guest house itself utterly deserted, I lay awake for a long time, listening to the silence, remembering the feel of the tundra; then I got up, packed my kit-bag, and went down to the kitchen, where some bits and pieces had been left out for breakfast. I had a few slices of Gjetost cheese and some coffee and, feeling warmed and milky inside, I set out to walk the mile or so to the airport. It was six o'clock in the morning.

That far north, the nights are white, even in May. I walked in a cold, chalky light, the only human creature awake on the northern *vidda*, it seemed, and I took my time, stoking up my solitude rations, tuning in to the rhythm that comes off the earth in the sub-Arctic, a rhythm like no other, a pulse that lingers for days, or weeks, in the fabric of bone and flesh: a pulse that is almost a sound, like a drumbeat, or a harmonic. I didn't want to go back to the occupied world; I wanted to stay there, to stay in tune with this land, to gaze up at this sky. The Finnmarksvidda is high and wide, close to the sky, a place for clearing the senses, for becoming far-sighted, and I knew that to go back was to be diminished in so many ways, to close down a little. Yet I had no choice: there were chores to do and promises to keep. By the time I reached the airport, I was resigned to life as the person I seem to be, in the civilized world.

The *vidda* had one gift left for me, however. Because Lakselv is a remote, tiny airport at the very top of Europe, it is never busy and, in winter, it almost falls out of use. Once a day, it seems, a plane comes in, discharges its few passengers, then turns back and returns to Tromsø, rising from this narrow coastal town and crossing the high plateau *en route*, allowing its passengers a privileged glimpse of the steep, snow-covered sides of the *vidda*, one of the most beautiful landscapes I have ever seen. The rest of the time, it is quiet—though not, perhaps, as quiet as it was that morning, when I walked into the foyer and found it silent and deserted. It was darker indoors than out, which gave the place an eerie feel, and I walked through to the departure area, from where I could look out at the runway. Nobody was there. The runway was covered in snow, like the land round about, and had it not been for the airport building I could have been in the middle of nowhere. I sat down, facing out into the whiteness. Time had stopped. Everything was still. I was alone in the world.

People who live in the sub-Arctic, like the inhabitants of prairies and deserts, are more gregarious than city folk: not being surrounded by strangers all day, even the most solitary among them learns to appreciate a little company. I understand that, and I understand the practical reasons for valuing one's neighbours, when they might be needed at any moment, but I prefer to be alone in almost any circumstances, and this empty place, this deserted airport, was a double gift: first, because it allowed me to sit quietly and spend a last few hours with the self I am when I am far from home, and, second, because it was filled with a dream of flight, a room full of sky and the group memories of aviation. All I could see were a runway and a windsock, but that was enough: the spirits of Amy Johnson, of Antoine de Saint-Exupéry, of Léon Delagrange were there all around me, suspended on the air, perfected and eternalized, in the snow and the grass under the snow, in the clouds and the ozone, in the wind that gusted across the runway and in the pulse that rose from the earth and passed like a current through my body, even here, in this modern airport lounge. The spirits of the vanished were there with me, and I was with them, alone in a cold white place, and capable of disappearing in my own right, at any moment. I sat a long time, that day, waiting for my flight—and some of me is sitting there still, enjoying the stillness, becoming the silence, learning how to vanish. Every day, in every way, I am disappearing, just a little— and it feels like flying, it feels like the kind of flight I was trying for, that first time, when I was nine years old—but it has nothing to do with the will, and it has nothing to do with *trying*. If it happens at all, it happens as a gift: and this is the one definition of grace that I can trust. The air which surrounds me, so intangible and so commonplace that it seldom arrests my attention, is in reality a vast, unexplored ocean, fraught with possibilities. Even now, the pioneers of a countless fleet are vanishing into brightness and, steadily, surely, all the wonderful possibilities continue to unfold. □

GRANTA

CARY GRANT'S SUIT
Todd McEwen

Eva Marie Saint and Cary Grant in 'North by Northwest'

1.

North by Northwest isn't a film about what happens to Cary Grant, it's about what happens to his suit. The suit has the adventures, a gorgeous New York suit threading its way through America. The title sequence in which the stark lines of a Madison Avenue office building are 'woven' together could be the construction of Cary in his suit right there—he gets knitted into his suit, into his job, before our very eyes. Indeed some of the popular 'suitings' of that time ('windowpane' or 'glen plaid') perfectly complemented office buildings. Cary's suit reflects New York, identifies him as a thrusting exec, but also arms him, protects him: what else is a suit for? *Reflects and Protects*...a slogan Cary's character, Roger Thornhill, might have come up with himself.

But, as Thoreau wrote, 'A man who has at length found something to do will not need to get a new suit to do it in.' Cary may cut quite a figure but as a person he is meaningless, so far. We find him in the Suit, but certainly he has not found himself, or 'what to do'.

The recent idiom of calling a guy a 'suit' if you don't like him, consider him a flunky or a waste of space, applies to Cary at the beginning of the film: this *suit* comes barrelling out of the elevator, yammering business trivialities a mile a minute, almost with the energy of the entire building. The suit moves with its secretary into the hot evening sun, where we can get a good look at it: it's a real beauty, a perfectly tailored, gracefully falling lightweight dusty blue— it might be a gown, you know. It's fun to think of it as 'dusty' blue because of what befalls it later. It's by far the best suit in the movie, in the *movies*, perhaps the whole world. The villains, James Mason and Martin Landau, wear suits of funereal, sinister (though sleek and pricey) black, while their greasy henchmen run around in off-the-peg browny crap. 'The Professor', head of Intelligence, bumbles about in pipe-smoked tweed and a revolting shirt of old-man blue.

In 1959, the year *North by Northwest* was released, America was a white-shirt-and-black-suit nation: the 'revolution', if you want to dignify it that way, was ten years off. There's a nice photograph of Ernest Lehman, who wrote this picture, sitting in Hitchcock's office, a typically late Fifties black-and-white office, natty in a white shirt and narrow black tie. Some could make this look good but if you were *forced* to dress this way, if you worked for IBM, say, it contributed only to the general gloominess of the age. Sometimes you can find yourself wondering if life itself was conducted in colour then—even the 'summer of love' was largely photographed in black and white. Don't let anyone kid you: the Sixties were dreary.

Outside on Madison, the white shirts blind you, but not one of them is quite so white as Cary's. (As someone with a slight experience of applying theatrical make-up, I have no idea how they kept it off these white, white collars. It drives me nuts.) Non-streaky Cary's daring and dashing in the most amazing suit in New York. His silk tie is exactly one shade darker than the suit, his socks exactly one shade lighter. In the cab he tells his secretary to remind him to 'think thin', which commands us to regard his suit, how it lies on his physique.

A friend of mine in politics said to me once, 'I love wearing suits. They're like pyjamas. You can go around all day doing business in your pyjamas.' It has to be said that his suits were pretty nice, particularly so for *Boston*; whether he meant that he did his business half asleep only his constituents could say.

The suit, Cary inside it, strides with confidence into the Plaza Hotel. Nothing bad happens to it until one of the greasy henchmen grasps Cary by the shoulder. *We're already in love with this suit* and it feels like a real violation. They've mistaken Roger Thornhill for a federal agent called George Kaplan. They bundle him into a cab and shoot out to Long Island, not much manhandling yet. In fact Martin Landau is impressed: 'He's a well-tailored one, isn't he?' He loves the suit. But next moment Cary tries to escape—there's a real struggle, they force all that bourbon down his throat... (He later thinks they'll find liquor stains on the sofa, but if there was that much violence why aren't there any on the suit?) Cut to Cary being stuffed into the Mercedes-Benz—he's managed to get completely pissed without even 'mussing' his hair. On his crazy drink-drive, the collar of his jacket is turned the wrong way round. That's *all*. He gets arrested, jerked around by the cops, conks out on a table and appears before the judge next morning, and the suit and the shirt both look great. But this is the point in the picture where you start to worry about Cary's personal hygiene. Start to ITCH. Cops aren't generally too open-handed with showers.

It's back to the bad guy's house, then back to the Plaza, looking good. I always hope he'll grab a quick shower in the hotel room— he keeps gravitating towards the bathroom. There's a good suit moment when he tries on one belonging to Kaplan, the guy he's looking for, who doesn't exist. Kaplan's suits are stodgy, old-fashioned, unbelievably heavy for a summer in New York—with *turn-ups on the trousers*. So much for the sartorial acumen of the US government. 'I don't think that one does anything for you,' says Cary's mom, and boy is she right. She also jokes that Kaplan maybe 'has his suits mended by invisible weavers', which is what happens to Cary's suit throughout the picture! His suit is like a victim of repeated cartoon violence—in the next shot it's always fine.

Off to the United Nations, where the Secretariat looks even more like Cary than his own office building. He sublimely matches a number of modern wall coverings and stone walls here and throughout the picture. He pulls a knife *out* of a guy, but doesn't get any blood on himself. There's a curious lack of blood in *North by Northwest*; it must be all to save the suit, though there must be ten or even twenty of them in reserve, no? Cary evades the bad guys again and scoots over to Grand Central Station, where they have, or had, showers, but he's too busy...

2.

This is what's ingenious about this picture, at least as far as the SUIT goes—Cary's able to travel all over the country in just this one beautiful suit because the weather has been *planned for the suit by Ernest Lehman*! It's the perfect weather for an adventure in this suit, and that's why it happens. At the same time, there's a CREEPINESS about the whole escapade generated by our own fears that in some situation Cary will be inappropriately dressed (Cary GRANT?) and this will hinder him; or that the thin covering of civilization the suit provides him with will be pierced and here he is, thousands of miles from home, with not so much as a topcoat. Men ought to admit that they can experience suit-fear: the fear of suddenly being too cold in the suit you thought would do (in Glen Cove, Long Island, even on a summer night) or too hot (the prairie, to come). Exposed, *vulnerable*. Cary does have some money though, we know that, so he could buy something to wear if he had to, assuming his wallet isn't destroyed along with the suit. But it would be too traumatic to see this suit getting totalled, that would be way beyond Hitchcock's level of sadism. This feeling of exposure, the idea of having suddenly to make a desperate journey in just the clothes you have on, comes up in *The Thirty-Nine Steps* (book and movie): Richard Hannay is alone in a desolate landscape in inappropriate town clothes when a menacing autogiro spots him from the air...

In the suit are a number of subtle tools for Cary. It's so well cut you can't tell if he's even carrying a wallet (turns out he is). Here's what he's got in that suit! He goes all the way from New York to Chicago to the face of Mount Rushmore with: a monogrammed book of matches, his wallet and some nickels, a pencil stub, a hanky, a newspaper clipping and his sunglasses—but these are shortly to be demolished when Eva Marie Saint folds him into the upper berth in her compartment. (Really this is a good thing, because Cary Grant in dark glasses looks appallingly GUILTY.) All this stuff fits into the pockets of the most wonderful suit in the world. Does the suit get crushed in the upper berth as his Ray-Bans are smashed? No. Cary keeps his jacket on in the make-out scene that follows. The suit defines him, he's not going to take off that jacket. I know this feeling.

3.

When Cary and Eva Marie walk from the train into La Salle Street station the next morning, he's wearing a purloined red-cap's outfit, open at the neck and showing a triangle of snowy-white undershirt. She has the same white triangle peeping from under the jacket of her dark suit, which rather matches the suit James Mason wore the night before. But here are two little white triangles who spent the night together on the train. There might be an opportunity here in Chicago for a shower, you itch, but it looks like he chooses merely to loosen his shirt and have a quick shave, with Eva Marie's minuscule razor. His suit was temporarily stuffed into her luggage while he made his exit from the train in disguise. Has it suffered? Has it hell. It looks like a million bucks; his shirt still blazes out. But now comes the suit's greatest trial, the crop-dusting scene at 'Prairie Stop'. This begins with Cary and the farmer eyeing up each other's attire across the hot highway. The farmer wears a clean though saggy brown suit and a slouchy hat. Going to town? Here Cary gets covered in dust from giant trucks passing by (a deliberate and somewhat comic *attack on the suit*), sweats like a pig (or should— *we* do), has to throw himself into the dirt, gets sprayed with DDT by an evil crop-duster plane, then practically gets run over by a tanker; he grapples with its greasy undercarriage and writhes around on the asphalt.

After all this, and having fled the scene in a stolen pickup truck, Cary has only his hanky with which to make himself presentable at the Chicago hotel where he thinks 'Kaplan' is staying. Still, he's done a pretty good job with it—he looks like he's been teaching school all afternoon—just a bit chalky. His tie is still pressed and the shirt is white, even the collar and cuffs. You cannot violate the white shirt of the Sixties. You might kill me but you will never kill this shirt.

Eva Marie enters this scene in a really luxurious red-and-black dress—a sign of her decadent double life with James Mason—and it's all pretty uncomfortable because now Cary is dirty, a DIRTY MAN loose in civilization, too easily spotted... But the *suit* gets rescued here! Eva Marie tells Cary she'll have dinner with him if he'll let the valet clean it! Cary tells her that when he was a kid he wouldn't let his mother undress him. Eva Marie says, 'You're a big boy now'—Cary's growing up, from an impressive but essentially childish New York executive and, you suppose, a playboy, into a man taking charge of his life. He *grows into his suit* over the course of the adventure and finds a life (and wife) to suit him. In another sense, though, he maybe has a BONER—he's been sniffing round Eva Marie and suggesting a skirmish. This is all very good neurotic Fifties movie dialogue. I don't know who suffered more, who was the more repressed: the writer, the actors or the audience in those days.

So Cary takes off the suit, goes into the shower; she gives it to the valet and she splits! The suit is not there, so Cary is not there. We get to see that he wears *yellow boxers*, another sign that he's a daring guy in a 'creative' profession—whew!

Once Cary gets to the auction house the suit is *perfectly restored*. That valet is some little 'sponger and presser'. Eva Marie and the bad guys are bidding on a pre-Columbian figure. It's not very well dressed. It's only wearing shorts. Cary gets in a fist fight (no blood), is arrested, taken to the airport, put on a plane to Rapid City... The next day it's hot as blazes at Mount Rushmore, but the shirt is clean, the suit's fantastically smooth, a hot breeze rustles it a little. The monument itself is wearing a rock-like suit in solidarity with Cary. He's turning into a patriotic rock, too (ignore what I said up there).

Eva Marie arrives in mourning, essentially—black and dove grey; she's about to have to leave Cary and her entire life behind. James Mason is in a weird English fop get-up, to suggest, I guess, he's never been one of us, he's not long for these shores now. He's *frail*. Eva Marie 'shoots' Cary: no blood again, of course, as it's a charade, but wouldn't you think the CIA would have some *fake blood*? How else are they going to put this over on James Mason? He's not an idiot. But you can't do this to the suit.

4.

Now the suit is in the woods for the reconciliation scene with Eva Marie. This suit doesn't look too bad in the woods, and you reflect that Mount Rushmore seems a very *formal* national park, there were a lot of people dressed up in the cafeteria, paying their respects… Cary gets punched out for trying to interfere between the Professor and Eva Marie, AND WHEN HE WAKES UP THE SUIT HAS BEEN CONFISCATED! The Professor has locked him in a hospital room with only a TOWEL to wear! He's not going anywhere! (Although you feel a lot of relief that he's had his second shower of the picture.) But then comes the real act of betrayal: the Professor brings CARY GRANT a set of *hideous* clothes from some awful 'menswear shop' in Rapid City (you can just imagine the smell of it, Ban-Lon shirts and cheap belts). He gives him an *off-white* white shirt, a pair of black slacks, white socks and icky black *slip-on* shoes.

You get the creeps because this whole thing is about insecurity, exposure, *clothing anxiety*. When Cary escapes out to the window ledge he's inching his way along in a pair of brand-new slip-ons which may not fit! Your feet and hands start to sweat at this moment. But something major has occurred: *Cary is now in black and white*. Everything is CLEAR to him, and he can act decisively OUTSIDE the suit, in order to be able to win it back. It's all wonderfully Arthurian. Now he knows 'what to do'. And for us there's the thrill of a badly dressed Cary: the situation is now a real emergency.

Now Cary crawls off the hospital lintels and up the stone wall of James Mason's millionaire's-hideaway. It looks like the face of the office building in the beginning, the rectangles of a snazzy suit. And in this white shirt with no jacket, Cary is a sitting duck in the bright moonlight! *A New Yorker without a jacket on*. It is too frightening.

Delightful, though, to discover that in the end, when Cary and Eva Marie are on the train back to New York (she in virginal white nightie), he's got his suit back! He's not wearing the jacket (woo-hoo!) but those are definitely the suit's trousers and his original shoes and the gorgeous socks. The shirt has remained impeccable. Like Arthur, he needs a woman to be safe, to be alive and to be a king, even on Madison Avenue. Now he really knows how to wear that suit.

I managed to acquire a pair of trousers several years ago that were somewhat like Cary's. They weren't tailor-made, and weren't the same quality of material of course, but the colour was really close and the hang of them wasn't bad. And they turned out to be Lucky trousers, very Lucky. Until I burned a hole in them. The veneer of civilization is thin, fellas. Exceeding thin.   □

ISSUE **2**

FICTION
POETRY ARGUMENT
OPINION

A
PUBLIC
SPACE

APUBLICSPACE · ORG

GRANTA

ACROSS ELEVEN TIME ZONES
Simon Roberts

Russia cannot be understood with the mind,
Nor can she be measured with the ordinary yardstick.
There is in her a special stature:
You can only believe in Russia.
                              Fedor Tiutchev, 1886

Simon Roberts

In July 2004, I set out on a year's journey across Russia, the largest country in the world. I wanted to travel to some of its most isolated regions and to experience it during every season and in every kind of location. I travelled for over 75,000 kilometres, to the Far East—Sakhalin Island, Magadan and Chukotka—through the Siberian provinces, across to the country's westernmost point, Kaliningrad; then down to the Caucasus, along the Volga River and to the Altai Republic where Russia borders China, Mongolia and Kazakhstan.

The logistics alone guaranteed an unforgettable year. I crossed eleven times zones and travelled on fifty-five buses, thirty-six trains, twenty-two trams, sixteen aeroplanes, nine ferries, eight reindeer, seven trucks, six helicopters, six horses, three jeeps, three speed boats, two cargo planes, two cable cars, one cruise ship, one motorbike and sidecar and in one armed convoy. Along the way, I stayed in fifty-two hotels, twenty-one sleeper trains, ten campsites, nine homes, four B&Bs, two rented apartments, one ship container and one cruise ship cabin.

Being a photographer brought its own problems. Every security official in every obscure airport was at a loss when they saw my camera bag and hundreds of rolls of film. The cameras survived a five-day horse trek in Kamchatka—my companions Pavel and Sasha are pictured in bucolic surroundings (page 140). More miraculously, the same cameras worked in temperatures of minus fifty celsius in a remote village near Yakutsk, where Matryona and her family were my hosts (page 147).

Meeting people like these, and many others, led me to think about what it meant to be Russian. The idea of a Russian identity seemed to be so important to the people that I met. Most of them were patriotic, intensely proud of their homeland's beauty and its size. The concept of the motherland—*rodina* in Russian—wasn't just about the enormity of Russia's landmass or about its future potential. The concept of *rodina* insists that Russia is an exceptionally spiritual place: soulful, mysterious and holy.

The more I photographed, the more I came to believe in the aesthetic viability of Russia. I discovered scenes of unexpected beauty and humanity, often in the midst of great hardship. I wanted my photographs to explore Russia's many conflicts: economic, cultural and social, but continually to insist on its ability to be dignified and spiritual. □

The town of Binibino celebrates its 50th anniversary, Chukotka Autonomous District, September 2004

Kupol gold mine,
Chukotka,
September 2004

Magadan, Kolyma Region, September 2004

'Drivers! You are answerable for the lives of the inhabitants of Kolyma,' September 2004

Departure lounge,
Magadan airport,
September 2004

Grocery store overlooking the Nagaev Bay, September 2004

Display of Soviet military equipment, Magadan, September 2004

Tatiana Filatova selling pies at a roadside cafe, Kamchatka, October 2004

Drunk Evenki teenagers, Kamchatka, October 2004

Camping with Sasha and Pavel, Kamchatka, October 2004

Man fixing his car, Kamchatka, October 2004

Rusting trawlers
off the port of
Alexandrovsk,
Sakhalin Island,
October 2004

Kolendo, uninhabited since an earthquake on March 29, 1995, Sakhalin Island, October 2004

Soviet-era apartments, Okha, Sakhalin Island, October 2004

Yakutian village of Magarass, Yakutia Province, November 2004

Fedya Danilovs, his wife Matryona and son Valentin, Magarass, November 2004

Murmansk, January 2005

The US warship Daniel Morgan, torpedoed by the Germans in 1942, abandoned in the Barents Sea, Murmansk, January 2005

Alexei and his children at the Hotel Intourist, Pytiagorsk, Caucasus, March 2005

Slava, Yuri and President Putin, Pytiagorsk, Caucasus, March 2005

Temporary housing for Chechen refugees, Ingushetia, April 2005

Hadijhat, a Chechen refugee, with her children, outside their temporary housing built inside a derelict factory, Ingushetia, April 2005

Picnickers celebrate Victory Day, May 9, when Russia defeated Nazi Germany in the 'Great Patriotic War', 1945, Yekaterinburg, May 2005

Swimming in the River Volga, Volgograd, June 2005

On board a cruise ship travelling from Moscow to Astrakhan, June 2005

A new
development of
luxury apartments,
Moscow 2005

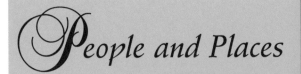

GRANTA

TRENITALIA
Tim Parks

Verona to Milan

Italians commute. Every September I receive a letter from the administration of the university where I teach, in Milan, reminding me that, since I am not resident in the city, I have to apply for a *nullaosta* for the forthcoming year. This piece of paper, signed by the rector himself, will say that *nulla ostacola*...nothing prevents me from working in Milan while living 150 kilometres away in Verona.

What on earth could prevent me? Only Trenitalia.

As so often in Italy, there is no official form to fill in; you have to make up the request yourself. This can cause anxiety when Italian is not your mother tongue and you are aware that there may be special formulas and terms of address. A university professor does not wish to seem inept.

'What if I just ignore it?' I asked a colleague, since it's only a formality. This was many years ago. I was innocent. It was explained to me that in Italy a formality is a sort of dormant volcano. It might seem harmless for years, then suddenly blow your life away. So, one day, if I misbehave in class, or support the wrong candidate in some hotly disputed faculty election, someone might decide that Trenitalia really isn't reliable enough for me to be resident in Verona and work in Milan. In the same way, in Italy, after years of neglect, certain laws on accounting or political-party fund-raising might quite suddenly be vigorously enforced for reasons that have little to do with someone's having broken the law.

Never say 'only a formality'.

Rather discouragingly, the colleague who told me about the dormant volcano later suggested that I might want to apply for an available professorship in Lecce. Disturbed, I pointed out that if Milan was 150 kilometres from Verona, Lecce was a thousand. At that point surely the *nullaosta* would not be a formality at all. 'There's an overnight train, Verona to Lecce,' I was told. 'No problem. You could go twice a week. Or stay there during the week and come home at weekends.'

It was a serious proposition. So many Italians do this. In Milan I have colleagues who are resident in Rome, in Palermo, in Florence. I have students who return to Naples or Udine every weekend. Thousands upon thousands of kilometres are travelled. Italians like to live where they live, where they were born, that is, with Mamma and Papà. Then they commute. Even when it offers no work, your home town is always the best town; a thick web of family ties and bureaucracy anchors you there. Trenitalia connects these city states. It makes the nation possible and allows it to remain fragmented, allows people to live double lives. Not for nothing is Trenitalia's holding company called *Le Ferrovie dello Stato*. State railways. *Nulla ostacola.*

To be present at a nine o'clock lesson or thesis commission in Milan, I have to get the 6.40 Interregionale from Verona Porta Nuova. It's the train of the living dead. But at least when I leave home at six many of the city's traffic lights are still only flashing yellow. You can move. You can even park.

Verona's main station was rebuilt, like the roads around it and the nearby stadium, for the 1990 World Cup. The tournament took place before the roads were finished, at which point urgency if not interest was lost. As I recall, Uruguay and Belgium played. I can't remember the names of the other teams. Did anybody go to watch? In all my years as a season-ticket holder at the stadium no one has mentioned these games. Yet the hastily conceived road system with its underpass on a tight bend will be with us for decades to come, as will the beautiful stone floor inside Verona Porta Nuova station.

Alas, even at 6.15 in the morning there's an impossibly long queue to buy tickets. The serious commuter has to have a season ticket. But what kind of ticket? In England now there are different tickets for different trains run by different companies. There is the confusion and clamour of free enterprise. And, in an attempt to balance supply and demand, there are differently priced tickets for peak and off-peak travel. This is annoying, but comprehensible and all very Anglo-Saxon. In Italy the complications are of a different nature. Truly to get a grip on them would be to understand Italian politics and social policy since the war.

First and foremost, train tickets must be cheap, or be seen to be so. People's desire to live in one city while working in another requires this. It is the structure of Italian nationhood. Which leaves little room for the market. A student has to be able to afford to travel home every weekend. The friends you make at primary school are your friends for life, you can't be without them. And who will do your laundry if not your dear mother? There are very few laundromats in Italy. So to travel from Verona to Milan—148 kilometres my ticket tells me—costs only 6.82 euros, peak or off-peak, weekend or weekday. About £4.50. It's a joke. And there are big reductions for students, for conscript soldiers, pensioners and a variety of other groups, needy and not. Priests and nuns travel free.

At the same time, the railways have traditionally been used as an organization to absorb excess labour and keep unemployment down. 'What a lot of officials!' wrote D. H. Lawrence on the station in Messina, Sicily, in 1920. 'You know them by their caps. Elegant tubby little officials in kid-and-patent boots and gold-laced caps, tall long-nosed ones in more gold-laced caps, like angels in and out of the gates of heaven they thread in and out of the various doors.'

Having shed 100,000 staff in the past twenty years, Trenitalia is no longer so dramatically overmanned, but still employs far more personnel per kilometre-travelled than France, Germany or Britain. Ten thousand of the 99,000 rail workers are considered unnecessary. And the officials still have pretty caps, and golden buttons on their green jackets.

It's clear that if ticket prices are to be low (less than half the prices on Deutsche Bahn) and manning high, that will make the train service expensive to run. How can a country with a national debt running at more than one hundred per cent of GNP deal with this? One answer is: *il supplemento*.

If to take an Interregionale to Milan costs 6.82 euros, to take the faster Intercity costs 11.05, or rather a supplement of 4.23 euros, and a Eurostar a further 58 cents. Once upon a time the supplement formed only a small percentage of the ticket, but since basic rail fares are taken into account to calculate national inflation rates while the more expensive rail fares are not, the supplement has tended to grow in relation to the basic ticket. A great deal of Italy's inflation is hidden with such ruses.

So on the first day of the new academic year I buy my annual season ticket to Milan. There is no special window. There is no special ticket. You queue up for ten or twenty minutes at the line of ticket windows. Four are manned, four are not. A couple of years ago they introduced a single queuing system at Verona Porta Nuova, a long winding snake between rope barriers, but then failed to block off entry to the windows to people who had not queued. A man leans against a pillar, chewing gum, watching, then, when a window is free, strides rapidly towards it and pushes in. The ticket seller knows what has happened but does not protest. The people in the queue grumble, but they don't protest either.

It's extraordinary how regularly Italy creates these areas of uncertainty: how is the law to be applied? Personalities form around these complications. The *furbo* is the one who will try to get round every rule; the *pignolo*, the one who will apply the rules most determinedly, even where they are most inappropriate. The *pignolo* always believes that everybody else is *furbo*, the *furbo* that everybody else is *pignolo*. The general resignation in the face of the *furbo* in Italy has always surprised me. It is always worth trying it on here. You can always protest that you didn't understand the rules.

A notice tells you that you're not supposed to ask for information at the ticket window, just buy your ticket and go, but people are asking for the most detailed information. 'How much would it cost to switch from second to first class on an overnight train to Palermo with four people taking into account reductions for the family and the granny over sixty?'

The ticket sellers are patient. They don't have a train to catch. Perhaps they like giving out information, they like demonstrating knowledge and expertise. At the place where the official queue emerges from its serpent of ropes, where you're first in line so to speak, it's impossible to see the ticket window furthest to the left, because it's hidden behind a pillar clad for the World Cup in a highly polished brown stone. If you don't know that the window behind the pillar is there, you don't go to it. And the ticket seller doesn't call to you. He has a newspaper, but no buzzers to push, no warning lights to attract his customers. Trenitalia does not want to spoil us.

At the window to my right, someone is asking for the timetable for a complicated series of connections to a town in Liguria. The queue frets. And if I take my bicycle? Another *furbo* manages to sneak in when the window near the exit is momentarily free. This time the ticket seller protests, but half-heartedly. 'I'll be quick,' the *furbo* says. 'Otherwise I'll miss my train.'

Nobody shouts. There is a slow, simmering resentment, as if the people who had behaved properly were grimly pleased to get confirmation that good citizenship is always futile, a kind of martyrdom. This is an important Italian emotion: I am behaving well and suffering for it...a feeling that will justify some bad behaviour at the appropriate time.

To cope with this stressful situation Trenitalia recently introduced the *Sportello Veloce* or FastTicket, as it's also called. This is a window that you're only supposed to use if your train departs within the next fifteen minutes. Sensibly, they placed the *Sportello Veloce* in the position where people usually sneak in to beat the single queue.

But what if my train leaves in half an hour? I wait for fifteen minutes in the main queue, I see things are getting tight. Do I switch to the fast queue, where there are already four people? What if one of them asks for information? What if everybody decides that they can now arrive only fifteen minutes before the train leaves and use the fast queue? This would be a problem, because whereas at least two of the main windows are always open, the FastTicket window is frequently closed.

Or what if I start queuing at the *Sportello Veloce* twenty-five minutes before my train leaves but get to the ticket seller eighteen minutes before it leaves? Will he serve me? Probably yes, but he would be within his rights not to. So do I have to go to the back of the queue? Can I keep him arguing for three minutes, at which point he would no longer be able to deny me a ticket? Or, since a standard rail ticket is valid for two months, what if I say I'm getting the Intercity to Bolzano leaving in five minutes' time, when in fact I'm planning to get it in two weeks' time? Is somebody going to check that I actually board today's train? These are unanswered questions. FastTicket has not made ticket buying easier. A child could see this. So why was it introduced?

Use of English is always a clue. Only the slow trains now have Italian names, the Interregionale and, slower still, crawling doggedly from one watering hole to the next, the Regionale. These are the trains which need not be presented to the outside world, to the foreign businessman and the credit card-holding tourist. The rolling stock is old and rattly. In summer you roast and in winter you freeze. The seats are narrow and hard, the cleaning...well, take a deep breath before passing the loo. But as soon as you start paying supplements you are in the territory of English, or at least international-speak. The proud old categories of Espresso, Rapido and Super-Rapido have largely disappeared. Now we have the Intercity, the Eurocity and the Eurostar. What we are dealing with here is an essential Italian dilemma. Are we 'part of Europe' or not? Are we part of the modern world? Are we progressive or backward? Above all, are we serious? There is a general perception that the Italian way of doing things, particularly in the public sector, is sloppy and slow, compromised by special interests and political considerations; hence an enormous effort must be made to work against the Latin grain and emulate a Teutonic punctuality, an Anglo-French high-tech.

This unease goes right back to the making of the Italian state. It is there in the patriot Massimo d'Azeglio's famous remark, 'We have made Italy, now we must make Italians.' It is there in Mussolini's obsession that 'our way of eating, dressing, working and sleeping, the whole complex of our daily habits, must be reformed'. To make the trains run on time would be proof that Fascism had achieved this, that a profound change had occurred in the national character. '*Abassa la vita commoda!*' proclaimed one Fascist slogan. Down with the easy life!

But at another level, and quite understandably, Italians have no desire at all to change. They like the easy life. They consider themselves superior to those crude and fretful nations who put punctuality before style and efficiency before digestion. A compromise is sought in image. Italy will be made to look fast and modern. There will be FastTicket windows even if they make the process of buying tickets more complex and anxiety-ridden than before.

Suddenly, I become aware that there is a man sitting at one of the four or five ticket windows that was previously closed. A man in uniform. I'm second in the queue now. The man sits there quietly, unobtrusively. He has just started his shift. He looks at the queue, where people are anxiously focused on the windows that are busy. He scratches an unshaven neck and turns the pink pages of his *Gazzetta dello Sport*.

I nudge the man in front: 'That window's free.' He looks at me suspiciously, as if I were trying to get him out of the way to grab the next free window. 'Are you open?' he calls. The man raises his eyes to gesture to the electronic display at the top of his window. 'It says open, doesn't it?' As a result, just a few minutes later, I find myself going to the window behind the pillar, where I discover that my one-time neighbour Ruggero is serving.

Fifteen years ago Ruggero gave up a promising and remunerative life as a freelance electrician to take up the dull job of serving at the ticket windows in Verona Porta Nuova. He had applied for the job when temporarily unemployed some years before, surviving a long admissions process and time on a waiting list. When the offer finally came, it was an opportunity his wife and parents wouldn't let him pass up: a meal ticket for life. This is how a railway job is seen. It is decently paid and as irreversible as a place in paradise. In the 1960s there was even the suggestion that railway jobs might be made hereditary.

Another friend, who once specialized in making handmade harpsichords, gave up his little workshop to become a railway carpenter, repairing vandalized carriage fittings. Peer pressure to take these sad decisions is considerable. Job security is placed beyond every other consideration. Ruggero, I know, finds his work at the ticket window desperately tedious but hangs on with bovine good humour. 'These are hard times,' he says, if you ask him about it. Though one of the hardest things these days, it seems to me, is to find an electrician in a hurry. Handmade harpsichords are not widely available either.

'An annual season ticket to Milan.'

'Interregionale, Intercity or Eurostar?' Ruggero asks.

I explain that I take the Interregionale going and the Intercity coming back.

My old neighbour shakes his head, rubs his chin in his hand. 'Complicated.'

Five or six years ago, as part of an effort to make *Le Ferrovie dello Stato* lean and mean, or at least not quite so bonnie and bountiful, the monolith was split up into various companies under an umbrella holding in which the state is by far the majority shareholder. Each company must try not to lose too much money. As a result, the Interregionali and the Intercities are now accounted for separately, and the Eurostars separately again. One can no longer buy a regular ticket plus a separate supplement and decide at the last moment which train to get. Now you have to tell the ticket seller what train you'll be travelling on (time and day) and he has to locate that train on the computer screen before printing the ticket so that the money you pay can go to one company rather than the other.

Strangely, though, the ticket you buy is valid for two months and hence it's perfectly legitimate not to get on the exact train you referred to when you bought the ticket.

However, Ruggero tells me, if I get an annual season ticket for the Interregionale, I will be allowed, as a special favour, to buy separate *supplementi* to travel on Intercities for individual trips, if, at the moment of purchase, I am able to show my season ticket and a valid ID. The ticket seller will then type into his computer (using two fingers) my name and the number of my season ticket so that the journey can be moved in accounting terms from one service to another, thus making the railways more efficient.

It's a drag, but I agree to this. I can buy half a dozen *supplementi* at a time, restricting my trips to the ticket window to a minimum. For 670 euros, then, Ruggero gives me a ticket that looks exactly like any other Trenitalia ticket and indeed any other supplement: a piece of soft cardboard about seven inches by two-and-a-half with a pink-and-blue-patterned background and faded computer print above. The only thing that distinguishes this ticket from the one that costs 6.82 euros is the word ANNUALE, which occupies approximately one hundredth of the ticket's surface area. It's clear I'll have to stick a piece of coloured tape on the thing to distinguish it from the *supplementi* I buy. I'll have to cover it in polythene to stop it disintegrating in my wallet.

Ruggero wanders off to take a photocopy of the ticket in case I lose it. In fact he takes two photocopies, one for me and one for the ticket office. That's generous. They keep a file. He opens an old metal cupboard. All this takes him five minutes and more. The photocopier has to warm up. Then he starts to ask after my family, and he's expecting, of course, that I'll ask after his. I do. I'm getting embarrassed because the queue behind me is long and there is a mill of worried people round the FastTicket window. The train of the living dead has been announced as *in partenza*. His son is doing very well at school, Ruggero is explaining. I fear that if I protest that we can't or shouldn't be exchanging pleasantries in these circumstances, he will imagine that I don't want to talk to him. His daughter less so, he says. She doesn't seem to take her teachers seriously. Ruggero would never really understand that I was worried about the others in the queue behind me. Why should I be? Personal relationships come before civic sense. *Salutami la Rita*, he calls. My wife.

One of the great advantages of the 6.40 is that it departs from Verona. You don't have to hang about on the platform or in the waiting room. Even if you're fifteen minutes early, you can go right ahead and sit on the train. I head for the last carriage. It has a very particular smell that always affects me deeply when, after the long summer holidays, I return to the trains and another year's teaching. It is a mix of urine and disinfectant and tired synthetic upholstery impregnated with the smoke of years ago. You can't smoke on the trains any more, but the smell lingers on. There are smudgy neon lights which offend the eyes without giving the impression that the space is properly lit. Here and there a seat is occupied: by a student returning to college with his laundry, a man in overalls constantly clearing his throat, a black girl, plump and clearly exhausted, a prostitute perhaps, on her way home after a long night.

It's an open-plan carriage, no compartments, and I choose a seat as far away from the others as possible. At 6.42 or 3 a faint tension is transmitted through the hard seat to the loins and the thighs. No train overcomes initial inertia as reluctantly as the 6.40 Interregionale to Genova Piazza Principe via Milano Centrale.

Then a late arrival bangs into the carriage and comes to sit down right next to me. Her Discman is tinkling, she wears a sickly perfume and a jewel in her navel, she carries a noisy paper bag with a sticky croissant. Why does this happen so often? There are people who want to be on their own, to mark out their own territory and be quiet there, and there are people who are eager to invade that territory, to sit close to someone else. There seem to be a disproportionate number of the latter in Italy. You sit in an empty compartment in a whole carriage of empty compartments, a whole train of them, and someone comes banging in and sits opposite you.

Once, during a strike, I found a completely empty Intercity at Milan station, a ghost train. Eventually, an announcement said that the train might leave in two hours' time and then again it might not. The voice apologized for any inconvenience this uncertainty might give rise to. Having no alternative, I decided to sit in the train and read. I chose a carriage halfway down the long platform. Since it was an Intercity, there were compartments. Suddenly, a man was tugging open the slide door to join me, a rather sad, lanky middle-aged man in a grey mac with a slack, worried mouth and thick spectacles. He had a huge suitcase, the sort of suitcase that has you wondering where on earth its owner can be going and for how long. Are these all his worldly possessions? Is he a refugee?

With some effort the man swung the suitcase up on to the luggage rack, sat down, brushed imaginary crumbs from his trousers, looked at me, smiled and began—I knew I couldn't stop him—to talk: about the strike, he shook his head sadly, about a difficult change of trains that awaited him in Venezia Mestre, it was going to be a close shave, about the impossibility of ever knowing what would happen in Italy when you began even the most banal of journeys. Wasn't that so? Italians like to refer to their country as if it were foreign to them, inhabited by people who are inexplicably unreliable. I barely nodded. 'Ecco il capotreno!' he suddenly shouted, the chief ticket inspector, and he jumped up and hurried out of the compartment and down the corridor to talk to a man in a smart green cap walking along the platform.

This was my chance. Furtively, I picked up my own small bag and headed the other way up the carriage. I must have walked through about four completely deserted carriages, going towards the locomotive. Since the electricity in the train hadn't been turned on, I was looking for a place where one of the big floodlights high up in the station outside would give enough illumination to read by, even through grimy windows. Here. Good. I sat down. For perhaps ten minutes I read. I was happy. The truth is, I really don't mind sitting on an empty train for a couple of hours and reading. If a book is good enough, it doesn't matter where you read it. There are times when I have even welcomed train delays.

All at once, breathless, anxious, the same man reappeared.

'There you are!' he cried. He sat down. He resumed his conversation. He began to tell me what the ticket inspector had said. The train would be leaving, but only when they found a co-driver. They were having trouble finding a co-driver. As for Mestre, heaven only knows. His last train, for some mountain destination, departed at 8.15. 'Who knows where I'll be sleeping tonight?' He seemed quite pleased with this melodramatic reflection. But anxious too. Then, glancing up at the luggage rack, he asked, 'Where's my suitcase?'

I shook my head. 'You left it in the other carriage.'

'What other carriage?'

The man hadn't realized that he was now four carriages nearer to the locomotive.

'Oh.' He squinted at me. 'I knew something was odd,' he said. 'But why on earth did you move?'

'I want to be alone,' I told him.

Alarmed, he jumped up and hurried back down the train to reclaim his suitcase. For a moment it crossed my mind he might be a ghost who haunted this train, and to avoid trouble I moved again, this time into first class. They can't fine you for being in first class until the train actually starts moving.

At 6.50 the landscape slips away outside smeared windows. To the left is the *pianura padana*: a ribbon of low factories beside the line and long stretches of vines, orchards and maize beyond. It's flat and dull, foggy in winter, steamy in summer. The replacement of the old wooden vine supports with a harsh geometry of identical grey cement posts is depressing, likewise the huge expanses of protective black netting now stretched over the cherry orchards. No more the white, spring blossoms. This countryside has a dogged, industrial, rectangular look, as if nature had been carefully parcelled out in discrete units to make it easier to count the cash. We're riding across one of the wealthiest areas in Western Europe.

But to the right of the line, the north, the land rises through the terraced hills of the Valpolicella to the mountains of Trentino. Here the vineyards have a more traditional aspect and on a clear day white peaks are visible along the whole alpine arc. You can even make out the wolfish pine woods, far away, the grey rock faces and dark resiny valleys. It's good to glance up from a book and see the mountains, to imagine you can smell them. They afford an illusion of drama and, for someone who grew up in London, the assurance that I now live far from home. Then, at Peschiera, the train begins to fill.

Peschiera and Desenzano, the first two stops, lie on the southern shore of Lake Garda. Peschiera is where you get off for Gardaland, the Italian version of Disneyland. The pretty provincial station, with its dark maroon stucco and unkempt flowerbeds, is marred by a series of colourful wooden facades mimicking a main street of the American Far West inhabited by cartoon characters. During the summer holidays, the train will be packed with adolescents come to spend their parents' money. This morning, incongruously, a police car has parked on the platform, as if Paperone and Topolino had really been shooting it out.

The train rattles along a low ridge and you can look down across old terracotta housetops and the concrete sprawl of hotels, pizzerias and gelaterias to the big lake, brightly grey in the morning light. A fishing boat trails a long wake but seems to be fixed there. The surface is very still and solid-looking. A couple of backpackers clamber into the carriage, arguing in German. The Interregionali have rather cunning swing doors between carriages: you can never quite figure whether you're supposed to push or pull. The backpackers have a tussle, then almost fall over each other into the carriage.

To the left of the train are the low hills of Custoza, rounded morainic mounds of silt and rubble brought down by the glaciers when the lake was formed. Here in 1866 Victor Emmanuel II led his Italian troops against the Austro-Hungarians, then masters of the Veneto. Austria had offered to hand over the territory in return for Italian neutrality in its war with Germany, but Victor Emmanuel felt that the honour of his ancient family and new nation demanded that he win the territory by force of arms. His army of 120,000 was defeated by 80,000 Austrians. Thousands of men died. Their skulls are on display in an *ossario*. You can see where the bullets passed.

A significant part of that victorious Austrian army of 1866 was made up of local Italians who were not greatly inspired by the idea of national unity and even today on walls between Peschiera and Desenzano you can read such graffiti as CALL ME A DOG BUT NOT AN ITALIAN. And: FREE US FROM SOUTHERN FILTH. Some tourists and ingenuous foreign journalists might imagine that these slogans indicate that there is a serious separatist movement here. But they are just a rhetorical flourish, not unlike 'FastTicket'. People like the idea that there is a separatist movement, they like hating Rome and the south, and then they travel Trenitalia to work in distant towns, or to their favourite holiday beach in Sicily, where quite probably they have friends and relatives. In much the same way people like the fact that a Pope is against contraception and abortion but then continue with their sensible, hyper-controlled sex lives. In every aspect of Italian life, one of the key characteristics to get to grips with is that this is a nation at ease with the distance between ideal and real. They are beyond what the British call hypocrisy; quite simply they do not register the contradiction between belief and behaviour. I have always envied this mindset.

At 7.40 the train stops in the town of Brescia. This is Lombardy now. Suddenly, a middle-aged man a few seats down from me comes to life. He jumps up, slams down the window and is leaning out, beckoning to friends on the crowded platform. '*Qua, qua. In fretta!*' He is saving seats for them, a coat on one, a bag on another, a newspaper on the next. In less than five minutes the train is crowded, it's packed. People are standing, pushing. No one can find space for their bags. Worse still, everybody is talking. Everybody seems to know each other.

This is something I have never observed in England. In England, on a commuter train, most of the passengers are shut away in themselves, in a newspaper, a book, or trying to prolong the dreams of an hour before. There's a pleasant melancholy to the journey. But not on the Interregionale to Milan. These dead are alive. Either the travellers are neighbours in Brescia or work colleagues in Milan. They form knots of animated discussion all down the carriage. Some knots know other knots and intertwine and snag. Students swap study notes. Football, politics and the proper way to prepare an asparagus risotto are urgently discussed. I insert a pair of yellow sponge earplugs.

But it isn't enough. Half a dozen men and women in their early thirties are crowded round me. There is usually one who does all the talking while the others offer occasional confirmation or objection. When the sexes are mixed, the one talking is invariably a man. 'Juve were let off an obvious penalty again. Did you see? *Una vergogna.*' It's a suit in his thirties with a nasal voice, a scrubbed, bank clerk's face, an earring, a sneer, a bright red tie. He laughs and jokes constantly. The women exchange indulgent smiles. Two of them are standing arm in arm, touching each other. There's a strange collective consciousness to these groups, something quite physical. They like their bodies and they like their accessories, their handbags and laptops and mobiles and tiny designer backpacks. 'Look at this I bought. Look at this.' They finger the new material and touch their friend's arm.

'Joke,' begins the red tie noisily. 'Listen up. So, Berlusconi's son asks his *papà* how he is to go about laying some girl he's hot for, right? And Berlusca tells him, "Stefano, first you buy her a diamond necklace, *va bene*? You take her to an expensive restaurant, book a room in a five-star hotel and make sure there's a chilled bottle of the finest champagne on the bedside table. And she's yours. Go for it." "But, *Papà!*" his son protests. "*Papà*, isn't love supposed to be free? I don't want to offend her by throwing money around. I don't want her to think I'm buying her." And what does Silvio reply?' The man smiles brightly before the punch line. 'What does *il buon Silvio* say? "Free love, son?" he says. "Romance? That was just a story the Commies invented so they could fuck for nothing! The cheapskates! So they could fuck for nothing!"'

The others titter and groan. Someone remembers something a talk-show host said the previous evening about the way referees were selected for Serie A games. I resign myself to an hour of forced listening, albeit with the pleasant muffling effect of the earplugs.

About a year ago, prompted by God knows which hypersensitive traveller, Trenitalia began to talk about the possibility of a 'quiet carriage' for those who didn't want to talk. But before going ahead with this revolutionary project they decided to carry out a survey of passengers' attitudes. The newspapers published some responses. Most fascinating were the people who simply didn't understand. 'If I don't want a guy to talk to me,' one woman said, 'I know how to tell him to leave me alone.' 'People can talk or not talk as they choose,' observed a student. They simply could not grasp the idea that some of us might want to be quiet to read and work in a carriage where nobody talks. 'What happens if I'm in the quiet carriage and my phone rings?' somebody objected. With this simple observation he was sure he had demonstrated the folly of the entire project. And perhaps he had. No more was heard of it.

The hills above Brescia are particularly gloomy. A nondescript grey-green vegetation scarcely covers looming mounds of chalky limestone, giving the landscape an odd, threadbare look. Here and there the slopes are broken by the white scar of a quarry, its vertical face scored with horizontal lines. Shapelessness alternates with grid-like geometry: shopping centres, walled cemeteries.

On the other side of the train, a fat man in a white vest cleans his teeth on a balcony. There are factories mixed up with modern apartment blocks: towering industrial silos, rusting cylinders and storage tanks, kitchen gardens with canes for runner beans, fig trees leaning on sagging fences. A tiny vineyard—just three rows of a dozen poles—is choked between two cathedral-size warehouses of prefabricated concrete panels. A tractor toils in the mud around what must be a pile of hay bales under a great white plastic sheet held down by used car tyres. Just here and here, like postcards stuck on a cluttered backdrop, fragments of the old picturesque Italy hang on: a baroque church façade up on the hillside; the ochre stucco of a villa glowing in the morning sunshine.

Comes a powerful whiff of burned brake fluid and the train screeches into Rovato. These are the satellite towns of Milan now. Chiari, Romano, Treviglio. More people push in. The phones begin to trill. The group beside me passes a mobile around, chattering and laughing. The caller is one of their company who is two carriages up the train but unable to push his way through the crowd to join them. 'Excuses!' a bright young woman protests. 'Who are you with?' She's boldly made up, dressed in pink with pink handbag, pink-and-white sweater, pink-and-white bracelets. The friend sends a photograph through the phone to show how blocked the corridor is. Even the ticket collector can't get through! Everybody is pleased to have found this use for the new technology.

Here and there someone manages to unfold a newspaper, the *Manifesto*, *Unità*, *Repubblica*. The left-wing papers are prevalent on the Interregionali. Somebody is reading out an article about the iniquities of the present government. There's a general strike next week; that's one day off work.

The train slows as it approaches Lambrate, the first station on Milan's underground network. The rails around us multiply and switch over each other as lines from all directions are gathered together for the final few kilometres to Milano Centrale. For perhaps five minutes the train plays at going as slowly as a train can go without actually stopping. All around us there are flyovers, gritty playgrounds, tenements. Many of the windows fly fading rainbow flags with the word *pace* written in white. Peace. Everybody loves to display their good sentiments and anti-Americanism. The graffiti are more interesting. EVVIVA LA FIGA! someone has written. 'Long live pussy.'

177

I put my book in my bag. There's an extraordinary tension for me in these last moments of the journey as the Interregionale grinds to a stop on another ordinary day of my life. The world appears to be suspended; for a few awful seconds you can't help but be aware of the horror of routine, the days and years bleeding into a past as cluttered and unstructured as this railway landscape. Nobody else seems concerned. Two girls are teasing a third over a new tattoo she has, a little rose just above her bare hip. They touch it with manicured fingertips. The flesh is firm and brown. 'Let me see,' one demands, but now the train jolts to a stop and everybody is piling off. Nothing could be slower than the Interregionale on those last two kilometres into Milano Centrale. Better take the metro at Lambrate.

Milan to Verona

If I climb on the dawn train half asleep, I return late in the evening wired up and exhausted. Italy being run at every level as a series of secret societies, networking is high priority, and since I'm in Milan only a couple of times a week I'm more or less obliged to spend the early evening conspiring with university colleagues or other contacts, usually over a *prosecco* at one of the city's endless 'appy ow-ers. When finally I dash for the metro and the train, I'm accused of being a snob, living so isolated away in the Veneto.

This time I head for Milano Centrale, surely the most monumental station in Western Europe and one that never fails to give a traveller the impression that he must be setting out on a very serious journey. I love the place. Contrary to popular belief, however, it was not dreamed up by the Fascists. The design dates back to 1912, ten years before the Great March on Rome. But the project was interrupted by the First World War and by the time the funds were there to resume the Fascists were in power and the look of the thing, if not the essential shape, was radically altered.

It's the combination of massive volumes and highly stylized ornamentation that does it. As you approach the main entrance, two solemn horses bow their necks down at you from forty feet above. Between them, over the central arch, huge letters read NELL'ANNO MCMXXXI DELL'ERA CRISTIANA. 1931 of the Christian era. The monumental inscription is full of tension and unresolved polemics, and tells us so much about Italy's relationship with Catholicism. To challenge the stranglehold that the Church had on people's minds, Mussolini had spoken of 1922 as the advent of a new era, the Fascist era. He referred to it as Year One. School children's copybooks had space for the Christian date on one side, the Fascist date on the other. 1931. Year IX of the Fascist era. Why not write NELL'ANNO IX DELL'ERA FASCISTA on the station, then? Fascism was at its zenith. The tenth anniversary celebrations were being prepared. Why accept the Christian date? Because try as Il Duce might to superimpose state on Church, it was a battle that couldn't be won. The Italians were and are Catholic, this quite aside from any question of religious belief. All Mussolini could do was to remind people of the challenge, remind them that the Church wasn't everything. The Roman numerals recalled an era before Christianity when Italy was great. The reference to the Christian era obliged people to reflect that officially this was now the Fascist era.

Beyond the arch there is the great *porticata* where the taxis wait, then the ticket hall. High, high above your head as you pass from one space to the next, dozens of statues and friezes of classical warriors alternate with bas-reliefs of trains and planes and motor coaches. It's Fascism's double gesture of looking back to the glory that was Rome and forward to some unimaginably efficient, technological Italy of the future. Aesthetically, at least in this space of greyish-white stone with coloured marble and granite inserts, it works wonderfully.

But you see all this beauty only if you lift your eye. And it's amazing how rarely the eye lifts when you are commuting. 'Each man fixed his eyes before his feet,' Eliot said of the crowd flowing over London Bridge. It's no different in Milano Centrale. It was years before I noticed the zodiac signs in small stone squares all up one wall of the ticket hall. To make it even less likely that you will really see the building, its grand spaces are being invaded and broken up by aggressive advertising campaigns involving huge poster panels suspended from the high ceiling to swing only a little way above eye level.

The archetypal images that were to establish a sense of Italian nationhood, of continuity between past, present and future, are thus eclipsed by fizzy drinks and fashion goods. A sticky film of post-modern parody wraps round everything that was supposed to be uplifting, majestic. Today Naomi Campbell is much in evidence. How short a skirt looks on those long legs. Mussolini was enthusiastic about this station and a sworn enemy of international capitalism; when the Americans occupied Rome, what distressed him most was the thought that black-skinned soldiers should have captured and, as he saw it, defiled the monuments of ancient empire.

So much of Italy's new immigrant life revolves around the railways. You see Indian families on the move with all their belongings, you see Slav and black prostitutes and their pimps with their colourful shirts, you see Arabs and Turks opening kebab places in station car parks...yet you never see an immigrant working for Trenitalia.

The truth is that a law passed by Mussolini still prevents foreigners from taking many public-sector jobs, notably in transportation, while another rule requires that for certain state jobs candidates be in possession of an end-of-school certificate. From an Italian school, of course. Whenever one admires the homogeneity and apparent dignity of a society like Italy's, a society that has retained a cohesion and identity largely lost in metropolitan England, one must always remember that it is constructed around such mechanisms of exclusion.

Those immigrants who have not studied in Italian schools will not be permitted to collect Italian garbage, or drive Italian buses, or sell tickets for the train of the living dead. The unions, so ready to strike and raise their voices about every move the government makes, do not seem to protest very loudly about this. It will be interesting to see what happens in the next few years as the first immigrants' children arrive on the job market with Italian nationality and Italian school certificates. It will be a great day when a black *capotreno* tries to fine me for not having stamped my *supplemento*.

Up on the platform, the trains have splendid names: Ludovico Sforza. Andrea Doria. Leonardo da Vinci. Tiepolo, Giorgione, Michelangelo. The station announcements are pre-recorded in segments and then tacked together, presumably by computer, as appropriate. As a result the words come in little mechanical rushes—*diprimaesecondaclasse*—pause—*conserviziodiristoranteeminibar*—pause—and then a dramatic flourish when one of the big train names is pronounced—MICHELANGELO!—VIVALDI!—since it was clearly impossible for whoever recorded the initial pool of information not to read out such glorious names without intense and understandable pride.

One has to listen to all kinds of information that is absolutely standard for all Intercity trains (first and second class, buffet, minibar, etc.) before they tell you where the thing is actually going. People stand on the platforms in rapt attention, listening to this fanfare of efficiency, waiting patiently for the only pieces of information that matter: the time, the destination, the platform. For who has any notion of the code numbers of the trains, or even their names? And since no one pays any attention to this information, but again no one complains about having to listen to it any number of times, you can only assume that these formulas have taken on a sort of liturgical function, not unlike the use of the names Hang Seng and Dow Jones in more or less every news bulletin, as if any of us cared what the Hang Seng had done today or might do tomorrow.

This constant, reliable, decorous repetition perhaps transmits to the harassed passenger the sensation that, rather than simply heading home a little the worse for wear and tear after another dull day at the workplace, he is in fact part of some grandiose, never-ending ceremony. This is not such a zany idea in the lofty temple that is Milano Centrale.

The 21.05, the last Intercity of the evening, is almost always fifteen, if not twenty minutes late. I've found an empty compartment, hung my coat on one of the hooks provided, taken a seat by the window facing the direction of the locomotive. Other people look into the compartment, weigh me up and move on; clearly I am sending out the right signals. I pull out a book, or students' work. There is a little Formica-topped table, or flap, that folds out of the wall under the window—I can put papers on that—then an old ashtray-cum-litter bin which has to be tugged open with great caution. Offering considerable initial resistance, it is capable of suddenly flying out and dumping damp tissues and banana skins on my trousers and shoes.

I check that I have my stamped *supplemento* at hand to show the inspector when he comes. I open my book. The lighting is decent and has three settings—off, medium and bright—which can be operated from a knob above the compartment door. This knob has a delightfully old-fashioned design of a light bulb beside it, with radiating lines to suggest the bulb is emitting light, though in fact the light source is neon.

There is also an individual lamp clamped to the lower of the two luggage racks above my head. It has a brass, trumpet-shaped shade that looks like it was designed in the Sixties. Sometimes there's a bulb inside. But however much I toggle the little stick switch below, it never works.

No, that's not true. Not quite never. These lamps have been out of action for decades, they are not maintained, yet once in a blue moon you do come across one that still responds to the click of its old metal switch. The light they cast, like that of the blue moon, is negligible; all the same, these rare occasions when you find something working that shouldn't be inspire a strange, wistful sort of tenderness. It's endearing that Trenitalia hasn't simply removed all the lamps to have the metal recycled. I like to think that someone somewhere has appreciated their ornamental value.

Another thing I like is the way the Trenitalia maintenance staff mend the vandalized armrests. Covered in imitation leather, these rests, which fold up for those who wish to lie across the seats or to lean heavily against each other with the curtains drawn, are frequently slashed, perhaps by football fans or passengers angry at yet another delay. Instead of replacing them, Trenitalia has a worker somewhere who sews up the tears using a thick orange-coloured tape which, applied in a crude cross-stitch, stands out against the dark polished brown of the fake leather and gives the impression that the repair is actually a fashion element. You have to admire this kind of solution.

At around 21.20, the train has begun to pull out of the station and I'm just settling down to read when an ear-splitting voice erupts from a loudspeaker in the panel over the door, the panel with the knob that adjusts the neon.

'*Benvenuti abbordo a treno seicentoventiquattro Michelangelo per Venezia Santa Lucia!*'

This is not the mechanical-speak of the station announcements, but the would-be friendly voice of the *capotreno* who has his hideaway in the last compartment of the front carriage, a sacred space where no passenger is allowed to sit, even if the train is bursting at the seams. He lists the stations we'll be stopping at. He informs us that there's a minibar. At a volume that has the compartment wall-panels trembling, he encourages us to turn down the volume on our mobile phone ring tone. 'Thank you for choosing Trenitalia,' he concludes, and *'buon viaggio!'* Who else could we have chosen? The voice is silent for a moment. Then he starts again in another language. 'Leddies and genlmen!' Next it will be *Mesdames et messieurs*, then *Meine Damen und Herren*.

I jump to my feet. Beside the knob that controls the lighting, there are two other knobs above the compartment door. They too are of quaintly old-fashioned design, black plastic hemispheres sprouting little pointy fingers. One controls heat and cold. Supposedly. I know that because there are two small thermometers, one each side of the knob, the one to the left coloured blue, the one to the right red, with, over the top, a widening curved line to suggest the gradual passage from blue to red, cold to heat, as the knob turns. It is pointless to fiddle with this knob since it just turns round and round and round and makes no difference at all to the temperature. This service, like the individual lamps, has long been discontinued, the temperature is centrally controlled, though the passenger isn't informed of this, just as he isn't informed that the image of a smoking cigarette on the glass door of the compartment no longer means that you can smoke in here. 'Ave a good journey!' The *capotreno* winds up his English performance. If I'm quick I can still escape his French.

The volume control can be recognized by the design of a little loudspeaker emitting radiating lines and tiny quavers and semi-quavers, though I can't recall music ever being played on the train. The knob has three clicks, supposedly loud, medium and off, though again, you will get little joy from moving it to these settings. Yet the volume control does work in its way: if you can get the knob to stick between any two clicks, the sound abruptly disappears. The thing has a propensity to slip, so this adjustment is a delicate operation. *'Mesdames et messieurs! Bien...'* Done it. The voice is only a rumour in the distance, a radio in someone else's apartment. Finally, I can read.

And I do, for perhaps five minutes, until, just as we ride past the crowded platforms of Lambrate, the door is hauled open and, with a great clattering and banging and a frightening fit of coughing, in comes a truly pantomime figure: a towering, bulky man with a massive head, no neck, a monumental paunch and an ankle in plaster up to his knee. He is walking with the help of a single aluminium crutch but despite this handicap carries a backpack and a very large, very old holdall. Panting hard, with the look of someone who has just escaped death by the skin of his teeth, he drops the bags on the floor and collapses with extravagant theatre on the seat by the door, his back to the direction of the train.

Without even looking at me, the new arrival starts to moan: '*Dio povero*, how they make you run!' He coughs and splutters. 'But how they make you run, *Dio santo, Dio povero, Dio santo!*' His accent is Veneto. He gasps, brings up some phlegm, swallows it and now pulls a clown's cloth handkerchief from the pocket of his voluminous trousers to wipe the sweat from his forehead. His face is red and steamy and very big. His eyes are glassy. His hair sprouts unkempt from a baseball cap, his whole body exudes discomfort and stickiness. '*Ma quanto ti fanno correre! Ma Dio santo.*' Then he stops, holds his breath, his eyes opening wider and wider until, without any attempt to cover mouth or nose, he produces a deafening squeeze, aaaah-choooo!

My fight with the PA system is now only a happy memory.

The sneeze is repeated. He sucks up hard through his nose, then begins his monologue again. '*Ma quanto ti fanno correre! Bastardi!* If only you knew! *Dio povero.* If you knew! How they make you run!'

I go back to my book. I can sense he is looking at me now, no doubt disappointed that I haven't responded. After what might be two minutes, despite all my instinctive resistance, I'm obliged to exchange glances. The width of the man's nose is disturbing. I raise my eyebrows in polite acknowledgement of his presence, but I absolutely refuse to say anything. I must not give him an excuse for carrying on. The expression in Italian is *dare corda*, to give someone string, meaning to offer them the conversational opportunity to talk to you. *Non mi dai corda*, you don't give me string, is one of the classic Italian complaints. The refusal to chatter is a breach of etiquette.

With or without my assistance the new arrival goes on talking. I knew he would. He has travelled, he says, *santo Dio*, from Genova. From Genova, *Dio santo*! The train was late, *Dio povero*. He had to make this connection with the train to Venezia. *Va bene*, so the Venezia train waited for the Genova train, as it should, no, *caspita*, as it must! But he had to get from platform 17 to platform 8 in just two minutes. '*Dio santo!* Two minutes! With my foot in this state,

Dio povero. There should be a law,' he says, '*santo Dio*. There should be damages.'

I'm thinking exactly the same thing. Again, he bursts into a fit of coughing. Again, there's something willed and theatrical about it: he's auditioning for a freak show. Then he bends down, unzips his holdall and pulls out a monstrous sandwich wrapped in the noisiest layers of paper ever manufactured. A smell of mortadella invades the compartment. It's uncanny how swiftly the air is saturated with spices and fats. Still spluttering, he opens a mouth from which various brown teeth are missing and takes a savage bite, contriving at the same moment to wipe his nose with one arm and fish about in his holdall with the other. For a can of beer.

He belches.

That does it. Ten years ago I would have sat and suffered, I would have listened to the story of how he had broken his ankle, of why he was travelling so far, to visit his mother or auntie, or for his niece's first communion; I might even have expressed sympathy. But times have changed. The repetition of similar experiences in a controlled environment like a railway compartment allows you to experiment with a variety of solutions and techniques. Very calmly, I close my book, I pack it away in my bag, I slip my pen in my pocket and get to my feet. For the first time, he looks at me with curiosity. He is puzzled. '*Ma quanto ti fanno correre, Dio povero*,' he mutters. There are shreds of mortadella between his lips.

'In the state you are in,' I tell him, '*Signore*, I fear you need a whole compartment to yourself.' I pull open the door and step into the corridor. As I do so, I can see him straining to watch me, extreme perplexity on his face.

Two compartments up, I find a pale young man, alone, sitting in the seat near the door, bent forward over a book. It is the perfect way to discourage a new arrival. This is my sort of companion. I open the door. He sits up. I read disappointment in his eyes. '*È libero?*' I ask. The enquiry, of course, is only a courtesy. He nods. He has a thin, studious face. In his hand he holds a fountain pen with which he has been writing notes on an exercise book held under the book he is reading, a rather old book by the looks. I sit down by the window. Despite the rush of the train I can still hear the coughing of that terrible man two compartments away. The earplugs should eliminate that.

We read. Sometimes I think I should have kept a list of all the books I have read on trains. Certainly most of the books that have been important to me would be there. Perhaps I just read better on rails. A book has a better chance of getting through to me, particularly when I'm in a compartment, and at night. This hiss of metal on metal, the very slight swaying of the carriage, the feeling of being securely enclosed in a comfortable, well-lighted space while the world is flung by in glossy darkness outside, all this puts me in a mood to read, as if the material world had been suspended and I were entirely in the realm of the mind.

Some forty minutes into the journey, having put the trauma of the fat man behind me, I look up and watch my new companion. A pleasant intimacy can settle over two people reading together on a train, even, or perhaps especially, if nothing is said. Finally the young man shifts the book in such a way that I can glimpse the title. *Le confessioni di Sant'Agostino*. He has round rimless glasses. His hair is that blond that is almost colourless, like greyish honey, slightly curly, cut tight to his head. He puckers brow and lips as he reads, he has thin lips, and makes sudden rapacious movements when he wants to jot down a note. Perhaps he's studying at a seminary.

I turn my head and through the big black pane of the window spy a small walled cemetery on a low hillside. It's uncanny: though I never think of it until I actually see it, I always seem to turn my head exactly as we pass this cemetery. It's on a low hill near Brescia. What is the mechanism that makes this happen? Do the dead call to us? There's the glow of our Intercity windows in the night, a dark field, then the old cemetery beside a newer section added on. In the new section, where the coffins are slotted into cement drawers in the high walls, you can see the flicker of the little red lights that keep the dead company, *lumini* they're called, as if the tenants of the place were all lying quietly there, reading together as they decay.

But at this point I must have fallen asleep. It's so often the way: the book, the cemetery, this quiet companion, the rhythm of the rails, the prosecco and snacks in Milan. On almost every homeward journey, I fall asleep at some point. Perhaps I shamed myself by snoring. In any event, I'm woken providentially by the sound of the PA system crackling into life. '*Avvertiamo i signori viaggiatori che tra pochi momenti arriviamo alla stazione di Verona Porta Nuova, Verona Porta Nuova!'*

Resurrected with a start, I gather my things. Already you can see the town's stadium, the suburban apartment blocks, the ugly round sanctuary of Our Lady of Lourdes floodlit on the hill above the river. I stuff my book in my bag and stand up.

When you get off a train in Italy it's a point of politeness to say *buon viaggio* to those around you who remain. I like this little ritual with its discreet invitation to recall the long journey we are all on, the daily meetings and partings in trains and bars and books. '*Buon viaggio,*' I tell the seminarist, sliding back the compartment door. The young man looks up from St Augustine. For a second his pale blue eyes hold mine. '*Buona sera,*' he gravely replies. □

GRANTA

LAVANDE

Ann Beattie

Some time ago, when my husband went to stay at the American Academy in Rome in order to do research, I accompanied him because I had never seen the Roman Forum. I had a book Harold had given me for my birthday that showed how the ruins looked in the present day, and each page also had its own transparent sheet with drawings that filled in what was missing, or completed the fragments that remained, so you could see what the scene had looked like in ancient times. It wasn't so much that I cared about the Forum; in retrospect, I wonder whether Rome itself hadn't seemed like a magical place where my eye could fill in layers of complexity—where I could walk the streets, daily performing my personal magic act.

At dinner, our first night there, we were introduced to other visitors, and here is where the story starts: they were the parents of a young man to whom our daughter, Angela, had briefly been engaged at the end of her senior year at Yale—so briefly that I had never met his parents, though Harold and Donald Stipley had a passing acquaintance. The engagement itself had not lasted the summer, and though Harold and I were never sure why they became engaged, let alone why they called it off, we remembered that period as the time when bright, energetic, pretty Angela began to sink into lethargy and pessimism, forgoing graduate study at UCLA and choosing, instead, to work at a salad shop on Madison Avenue. ('Salad shop' does not do it justice, but Harold always called it that, so that is the way I think of it.) This was in the mid-Eighties, when many people in New York City had money, and for a while the salad shop did very well. Things fell apart a year or so later when her partner, a man she had met at Yale, fell in love and relocated the business to Philadelphia. Angela would not consider moving. She lived in a second-floor walk-up in Chelsea and had a dog named Busy Man, who was in love with the dog next door, Benito (a female dog; I don't know the explanation of the name). When Harold suggested that Angela go along on the Philadelphia venture, she responded caustically, 'Should I also buy snow shoes and go to Alaska, if he moves there next?' She intended to find other employment, she told her father heatedly. But she did not—whether because she failed in her search, or because she never seriously set about the task, I don't know—and before the year was over, it became apparent to us that Angela had a problem with drugs and alcohol. At Thanksgiving, she left a rolled cigarette on the edge of the bathroom counter, and on Christmas Day she did not show up at all, arriving two days later with alcohol on her breath and a friend who stole Harold's Waterman pen, his sterling-silver business card case, and even a pair of Hermès suspenders.

If you are smiling, that is because we were the people to hate in the Eighties, Harold and I: stuffy people who never set foot in a disco, drank moderately and altered our alcohol preference with the season, and listened almost exclusively to classical music. Harold requested that the family doctor speak to Angela, but instead of keeping her appointment, she went to his office on Park Avenue and left a canister of tennis balls with the receptionist, along with a gift card that said 'Carry on'.

Then (details interchangeable with the problems of so many others who have been in our situation) began the late-night phone calls accusing us of things we never did, followed by requests for money. At first, it was paying her rent. Later—though it was for drugs, we knew—it was a 'downpayment on a car'. How was she going to garage a car in Manhattan? Well, maybe at night she could stick it up her father's ass, she suggested. We did not hear from her at all for six or seven months, then came home one day to find her sitting in the living room, reading a magazine. She was dressed nicely in a blue skirt and white blouse and blazer and said that she now worked as a secretary for a firm on Wall Street. She asked for a loan to pay the rent until she got her first pay cheque. Harold agreed to lend her the money if he could sleep on her fold-out couch. What he thought I was going to do while he was camped out, I don't know, but clearly he thought it would be a way of monitoring her. There was a long, loud argument— much of it ridiculous accusations by Angela—followed by (another opportunity for me to provoke a smile) her shutting herself in the bathroom and shoving Harold's silk bathrobe into the toilet. She also left her pumps behind, opening the door and running from the apartment in her stockings. It would be funny to anyone, if it was not their child. Some time during this period, she gave her dog away.

At any rate, there we were in Rome, years later, being served pasta—delicious hand-formed ravioli stuffed with unusual ingredients, served with a simple brown butter sauce—when Donald Stipley was joined at the table, a bit late, by his wife. She immediately exclaimed that we had a connection, though it seemed Donald had not realized his son had ever been engaged. He asked twice if his wife was sure it had been an engagement. She was adamant, and I backed her up, though she remembered the ring in far more detail than I did. Donald and Harold took to shrugging and laughing a bit nervously, suggesting that the whole matter was nothing they knew much about. In the back of my mind, and perhaps in the back of Harold's, was the question: had Angela been all right then or, even earlier than we knew, had something already been going dreadfully wrong? We discussed the qualities of Chuck Close's portrait of Alex Katz in the room outside the dining area. In winter, Donald Stipley's wife exclaimed, there was nowhere she would rather be than in front of the fireplace at the American Academy. Oh, perhaps Paris, she admitted, when her husband raised an eyebrow. They seemed to get along well, in that comfortable but vigilant way married people pay attention to each other after living together for years.

The next day, at the guard's gate in front of the lovely McKim, Mead and White main building, I ran into her again. The guard was calling a cab for her. Her name was Lavande. She had on a Chanel suit, black with white trim, and fashionable black boots with a higher heel than I'd been able to wear for years. Her pearl choker was certainly real, with pearls tinged ever so slightly pink to complement her complexion. The night before, when she'd discussed Angela's engagement ring, my eyes had fallen to her own hand: an emerald-cut diamond in a wide band, either white gold or platinum, with baguettes at either side. She was on her way to shop near the Spanish Steps. Wouldn't I like to come along? I was a bit tired from my trudge up the steep steps from Trastevere, but yes, I decided; yes, I would go along.

In the cab, we talked about Rome, and I mentioned the book that had made me so curious I'd come along. She said she had never seen such a book. We walked to the American Express office, where she paid a bill, then decided to have an espresso before shopping. 'To think we might have been related, all these years,' she said, 'and that we still might never have met, if not for a book you looked at.' I agreed that life was often a cat's cradle of attachments and missed connections. 'You don't often accompany your husband on trips?' she said. No, I told her: as an art historian, so much of his day was spent in research, and I hated just tagging along, biding time. She said— how, exactly, did she put it?—that she was always expected to accompany Donald. The trick was to pack light, she said, and to bring Woolite. This hardly explained the perfect condition of her suit, but seasoned travellers did have their short cuts and secrets, of course. Even her purchases were small and lightweight: a gorgeous camisole; a pink cashmere scarf. I asked if her son had married. I remember the moment I spoke, where we were walking, even that a little wind had blown up, so that I'd seen some grey in her almost-auburn hair. She stopped, seemed momentarily puzzled, then said, 'Oh, let's have our own connection, let's not have it depend on children.' Well, yes, I thought; why move inevitably towards a discussion of the pain Angela had caused her father and me? Lavande even spontaneously squeezed my hand, and I remember thinking how nice a gesture that was. How girlish it made me feel. At a newsstand, she bought the *International Herald Tribune* and I watched her out of the corner of my eye to see if she was surprised that I bought *Hello!* magazine. Instead, she squealed with delight, as if I'd done something slightly wicked. I felt young, would be the way I'd describe the afternoon later, to Harold. His response those times I said that was always the same: 'You're younger than me, so you mustn't complain.' Did he ask whether the subject of Angela and their son had come up again? I think I remember that he seemed a bit disappointed I'd gathered no more information about the past from Lavande.

They stayed a week, but because of Harold's schedule and my own ineptitude with the buses, we did not see them every day. The only other time I spent alone with Lavande was after she put a note under our door inviting me to a 'girls' afternoon' of herbal tea she'd brewed and a cucumber mask from a homeopathic pharmacy she'd discovered not far from the Academy. After they left, I went looking for the *farmacia* and wondered what other things she might have bought. I found some tiny scissors, almost as lovely as jewellery, and couldn't resist buying them. Back then, of course, you could still travel with such things on airplanes. I also bought rosewater, mixed with something unusual, such as lemon verbena: an after-shave spray, a beautiful little bottle closed with sealing wax and narrow silver cord that I gave to Harold, who would appreciate the packaging, if not the contents.

The evening before they departed I wrote my name on one of Harold's business cards, and she gave me—on a perforated page torn from a small notebook—her information, writing only her first name and a New York and Connecticut phone number. Both numbers turned out to belong to someone else, who had never heard of her. 'Westport', she had written with calligraphic swashes. Instead of writing Manhattan, she had written, 'Upper East Side'.

'It's one of the things I love about you,' Harold said. 'How could you be this astonished that someone you hardly knew gave you a made-up phone number? It's a well-known trick of dating, though I suppose it happens far more often to men.'

'But why would she do it?' I said. 'If it had been one phone number, I'd have thought she wrote a wrong numeral.'

'Good it was two, then! That way, you got the point.'

'Why would you want me to be disappointed?' I said.

'Well, truth be told, I thought there was something strange about her. Not the best person for a friendship, perhaps. I don't expect either of us thought they'd become close to us, did we?'

Sometimes I was not sure if Harold was obfuscating, or being entirely direct. In a way, I could understand Angela's frustration. Her father could be maddening when he was reading, as he so often was, and one didn't have his full attention. I was allowed to persist, even when he was busy; she had been trained not to.

'Harold, it's just very strange that someone who seemed friendly would provide false information.'

'Well, people are strange,' he said. 'Did you see how she ate the edges of the ravioli and left the good part? Picked at her entire dinner.'

'Oh?' I said.

He nodded. Still, I knew I did not have his full attention. Since it was the newspaper and not a book he was reading, I decided to ask one more question. 'Did he give you a business card?' I said.

'What's that? I don't remember.'

'Might you look in your wallet?'

He rolled his eyes, slid forward and extracted his wallet from his trouser pocket. He made quite a show of examining every piece of paper. Then, he found the business card and handed it to me, saying, 'You're acting like a teenager, refusing to take the hint.'

I could remember his frustration when Angela was a teenager and he'd tried to instruct her in nuance, subtleties, social subtexts. How quiet she'd been, before she began to argue.

'If she'd wanted you to call her, she would have provided the correct numbers,' Harold said. 'You will embarrass yourself less if you write, and accept silence for an answer.'

I wrote, and she was silent.

A year later, Angela became engaged to her psychiatrist. We hadn't known she had a psychiatrist, but then, we hadn't known for much too long about her earlier substance abuse problems. We were also confused—deliberately, by her, we thought—about where she lived. She had another dog, a little pug-looking thing, named Mr Jones. She and the psychiatrist, Dr Mark Clifford, paid us a visit to announce the happy news. They passed the little dog back and forth as if they were playing 'hot potato' in slow motion.

Angela came into the kitchen to help me make coffee. Usually she avoided being alone with me, as if I conspired to put her in chains, but I had liked Mark Clifford instantly, and I think her relief made her feel warmly towards me. The minute I spoke to her in the kitchen, though, I realized that I'd said the wrong thing and risked alienating her: 'When you were engaged before, Angela, was that a real engagement, or one of those sort of, you know, loose engagements that people had at the time?'

'Excuse me?' she said.

'I shouldn't bring it up, I quite like Mark Clifford, but I don't remember things as clearly as I once did, and I was just wondering...'

'Loose,' she said.

'Oh, really?' I said, surprised she'd answered at all.

She was a tall girl—almost as tall as her father. She had lovely eyes and brows, but she'd inherited my mouth, so that it seemed she regarded everything slightly grimly.

'You don't remember his name, do you? Your only daughter, her first great love, and you don't remember his first name.'

She'd provoked me enough that the name suddenly sprang into my mind: Steven. I stabbed with it, épée.

'Good for you,' she said. 'Yes, Steven. He was bi. I guess in the long run your conservative upbringing had an effect. You know what bi means, right?'

'Bisexual,' I said.

She nodded. 'And do you get the joke about what Mark and I named the dog?'

I thought about it and shook my head, no.

'It's a Dylan song. "Something is happening here, but you don't know what it is, do you, Mr Jones?"'

I smiled. 'I see,' I said. Recently, Harold and I had watched Martin Scorsese's documentary on Dylan—whose name I suppose I should have known had been selected, not given. I'd been surprised that Harold thought the documentary so fascinating. Though he said he found it informative about America's sub-culture at a particular time, I'd noticed his foot tapping to many songs. I, myself, had liked Joan Baez's perspective, and her sense of humour.

'That's great,' she said. 'You get that it's funny. I won't press my luck with your husband.'

'Oh, Angela, your father loves you,' I said. 'He's fifteen years older than I am, and from a very different background.'

'Yeah, repressed rich WASP snobs,' she said. 'His background is that you drop the maid off at the bus stop and think you're a hero for going out of your way. Do you know how to make coffee? Can I help?'

'Of course I do,' I said, flustered. 'Our Melita broke, and it's just taking me a moment to remember—'

She walked over to where I stood and opened the top flap. She filled an empty vase from the dish drainer with water and poured it in the back. That was Angela: always grabbing what was at hand, always improvising. Her father used to maintain that was part of the reason she got in so much trouble. I measured coffee into the filter and pushed the little drawer into place.

'What's your interest in ancient history?' she said.

'Ancient history?' I asked.

'My engagement to Steven. I wasn't suggesting you were an archaeologist.'

'Hardly that,' I said. 'A few trips to accompany your father on business, is about it.'

She was standing there with her arms folded across her chest, looking at me. She said, 'Steven Stipley. I wonder if he's sorted out his own sexuality. His mother used to dress him like a girl. He showed me a baby album filled with pictures of him with long hair, wearing dresses and Mary Janes. When his father left, she started calling Steven Sally.'

'Left them?' I said. 'But we met the Stipleys. They were together, at the American Academy. And I have to tell you, Angela, that she did not strike me as the sort of woman—'

'You look like a wet bird about to shake its feathers mightily,' she said. She had found the tin of cashews, opened it, and begun eating. She laughed, amused at her observation.

'What I mean,' I said, 'is that all reports are not to be believed, or at the very least, you might be overstating the case. I know many mothers find it difficult to send their sons for a first haircut.'

'Whew,' she said, pulling out a kitchen chair and sitting down. 'Didn't you hear me? Can I be any clearer? She dressed him as a girl, and when I met him, he couldn't have sex unless he had on women's jewellery, or women's underwear. What I'm saying is that—'

'I understand what you're saying, but I'm telling you that Dr Jekyll and Mr Hyde aside...'

'She rhymes! She laughs! She gets everything.'

'Whether you wish to cut me off or not, Angela, I'm telling you that I do not believe Lavande dressed her son as a girl.'

'Lavande! You met the mistress. You've outdone me and met the famous Lavande! Steven's mother died when he was thirteen. He prayed every night she'd die, and when he was thirteen, she did. Then his father sent him to boarding school. Groton. It was the one thing he could talk to Harold about. Don't you remember?'

'No,' I said miserably.

'You met Lavande,' Angela said, relinquishing her mocking for true fascination. 'She was a runway model in Paris. Steven had a picture of her from some fashion magazine. Gorgeous. Legs a mile high. So the great Donald Stipley—who wouldn't listen to what his son had to say any more than you would, by the way...he finally married her?'

Well, what did I know? She had on a diamond ring, but had Donald actually said that she was his wife when he'd introduced her? Whether he'd married her or not was a technicality; he was lucky to have her as a companion, because she'd been sophisticated and confiding and fun—we had had such fun looking in the shops near the Spanish Steps, we'd been like schoolgirls, free for the day. She had pointed out birds, and known their names in Italian. Returning to the Academy, we had seen what looked like a waterspout of black birds in the sky, taking every imaginable shape as they flew.

Angela was pouring the coffee into mugs. It seemed in all ways inferior to espresso—standing at the coffee shop with Lavande, who whispered that Italians thought Americans were too stupid to know that if they sat, instead of standing at the counter, the coffee would be twice the price. Since she took cabs and wore expensive clothes, I'd been surprised, at first, that she thought about what she spent, but I'd quickly understood: it was the principle, not the money.

I realized I'd had it in the back of my mind to go to the Forum with Lavande only when Harold said he had a free hour the next morning, so we should go together. Of course, there was no reason not to go with him: he knew that too much information bored me, but was usually clever enough to present a detail or anecdote that would lead me to ask questions. I knew some things from the guidebook I'd flipped through in the Academy living room, and of course I'd also been fascinated by my birthday book, with its transparent pages. Rome had ruled the civilized world for almost five hundred years, but then, when the empire fell, the Forum had been forgotten. It was buried in river mud and cows had grazed there in the Middle Ages.

I was surprised, though, that so very little remained. It was good I'd read something about it, because it seemed to me more like a deserted battlefield than a place that had once been the centre of the world. We stood by what Harold said was the Arch of Septimius Severus. Below, a tour guide led a group of Asians through the ruins. 'Well, they had a good run, I have to say. Five hundred years, give or take,' Harold said. 'Lucky it was buried, or there'd be less to see than is here. Horrible, the things carried out before there were any restrictions. Still, it's very moving, don't you think?' Since he had walked a bit ahead of me, he didn't really expect an answer. None of the Asians seemed to be couples; standing here and there, I could rarely match one with another with any certainty. I thought Asians were always taking pictures, but then the tour guide stopped speaking and many cameras were raised. A man in a camouflage hat sat at a French easel, painting something in the direction of—Harold said—the Arch of Titus. 'In that direction is the Temple of Vesta, and the house of the Vestal Virgins,' Harold said. 'Eternal flame isn't just an idea of our century, you know. The virgins were its keepers—over there, guarding the eternal flame.' The sun was weak in the sky, the area quite crowded. 'You need a permit to paint here. A *permesso,*' Harold said. 'Not that the need will arise for you or me.' He winked. I smiled. Harold was in his element when he was outdoors, in a historic place; he was being nice to refrain from giving me a history lesson.

Someone was handing Harold his camera, pantomiming in the universal language. He'd selected the right person: Harold was an accomplished photographer. He took a step back, made some adjustment to the camera, gave the universal nod for 'I'll take the picture now.' How sophisticated all this would have seemed to the Romans. A camera? Tourists? They were just Vestal Virgins, guarding the flame that would become extinguished.

I had no idea why the Spanish Steps, where Lavande and I had shopped, were called the Spanish Steps, but asking would reveal that my mind was not on what was being shown to me. Harold had returned the camera and was waiting for me with his arm slightly outstretched; he lightly guided me on with his hand cupped around my elbow.

For our anniversary, Harold booked tickets on a cruise ship. Early August found us in JFK, in the first-class lounge, spending an hour or so having coffee and reading the paper before boarding the plane for Miami. We now had a grandchild, Emily, whom we adored. Since retiring the previous year, Harold travelled infrequently. We had bought a house in Maine, two hours away from Angela and Mark— close enough, but still far enough away—and they had kindly moved into our house to tend the garden for the two weeks we'd be gone (though Harold maintained that Mr Jones would do more damage digging than our abandoning the plants and seedlings).

I was cradling a mug of coffee in both hands when I noticed someone wearing a pair of very fashionable high heels walk past, and looked up to see that it was Lavande. After my conversation in the kitchen the day Angela announced her engagement, I had more or less stopped thinking about Lavande, though the moment I saw her I realized that I had assumed, somehow, I would see her again. She was gone and could have stayed gone for ever: she had not seen us; Harold had not seen her; her husband was nowhere in sight. But yes, he was. At the opposite side of the lounge, a hand reached up from behind a tall chair back, and she handed him a cup of coffee. Donald Stipley. It popped back into my mind. Her name, I had most certainly not forgotten.

I might have expected to feel angry, but instead I felt almost preternaturally calm. Those times I had thought of her, I'd wondered—with no expectation of an answer—whether she might have found herself in a situation she knew little or nothing about to this day—Donald's first marriage, his crazy wife, the child—or whether they both knew everything, and had put it behind them.

I watched her sit down, seeing only her profile, and that indistinct without my distance glasses. It came to me, then, that she did not know—that her behaviour towards me had been only about being his mistress, so that she must have felt badly when his wife died prematurely, though she didn't know the extent of it—what other suffering had taken place. If I'd been Harold's second wife and he'd had a child, would I have wanted that child out of the picture, in boarding school? It was possible that I would have, though I thought that was based on the fact that I hadn't been very effective or able to communicate well as a parent. What would Harold have done if he'd discovered I was quite crazy, and that I had some perverse scenario in which I'd involved Angela? He would have every reason to hate me. It seemed impossible, but probably everyone marries thinking such a thing impossible. It was a shame, however well things had turned out, that as a child Angela had thought the slightest criticism was contempt towards her, and that she thought in stereotypes, so that her father and I could do nothing right, being of a particular time and class.

'Harold,' I said, 'Donald Stipley and Lavande are on the other side of the lounge. We must go say hello.'

Harold was immersed in the book he'd brought to read on the plane: *On Beauty and Being Just*. The small book almost disappeared in his big hands. 'Do what?' he said, looking up.

'Across the way,' I said. 'It's Donald Stipley and Lavande.'

He turned in their direction. 'Well, for heaven's sake. Not friends of mine, mere acquaintances,' he said.

I stood. 'Come with me,' I said. 'She acted like my friend in Rome and—'

'God! This again!' he said. 'Yes, I remember the situation.'

He tucked the cover flap in the book to mark his place, but did not stand, and two things quickly occurred to me: first, that his lower back had ached for days, and that he wanted to pretend that the two of them were of no consequence so he would not have to rise; next, that he really was a historian, and once he had decided how something was—in this case, not mysterious—he had satisfied his curiosity. I could arouse his interest, but I would never, ever be able to bring myself to tell him the tawdry things Angela had told me in the kitchen.

As I walked towards them, I sensed Harold behind me, the way you sometimes sense shadows you do not see. I felt that he had risen and was going to appear at my side, and I was right. He walked more quickly than I would have expected. He stood beside me as I said, 'Lavande.'

She looked up, half-glasses on the bridge of her nose, her hair falling in perfect waves to her shoulders. She smiled, momentarily confused. She put down her coffee and stood to take my hand. The ring had been joined by another couple of bands. Diamonds sparkled.

'Rome,' she said simply. I suppose she had forgotten my name. 'Darling,' she said to the man in the chair. 'You remember our friends from Rome.' Since Donald Stipley only frowned, she looked at Harold, with an expression that was pleading. What he had to understand, what we both had to acknowledge, was that Donald Stipley was old, frail, handicapped. She had said loudly into his hearing aid that we were their friends from Rome.

To my surprise, Donald Stipley erupted. 'Harold! Put 'er there,' he said. He raised his left arm slowly. Harold took his hand for a firm shake, then more or less guided the arm back to the chair rest. Donald's right arm remained across his chest, immobile.

I felt panicked, as if I didn't have much time. 'Why?' I said to her, just as suddenly as Donald had spoken.

'Why?' Harold echoed quickly, as if coming to my rescue. 'Well, Don, I don't know about you, but when you get to be our age, it's why not, isn't it?'

Donald Stipley nodded and laughed. A bit of drool rolled to his chin. Lavande leaned forward with a napkin. 'Excuse us,' she said quietly. Then she turned to me. 'Because, if you must know, I didn't think I'd have a life in which I could ever see you again. I'm not his wife, and on the Rome trip we'd decided to separate. On the flight back, he had a small stroke. Then two others.'

It was clear Donald had heard every word. He lowered the napkin to his lap. He said, 'I never told you you had to go.'

'All but,' she said.

'Let bygones be bygones,' Harold said. He took me by the elbow. 'Good flight,' he said. 'Lovely to see you again.'

'How can you, Harold?' I said, shaking off his hand, and in that second I knew exactly the frustration Angela had felt all her life, diminished by his exquisite manners, his implacable sense of timing, which meant whatever was necessary to maintain the status quo.

'Because we're all too old, and it's too late,' he said quietly. 'You got your answer.'

What went unsaid was that nothing could console me, I had needed a friend so very much.   □

GRANTA

WE HAVE
NO MINORITIES
George Bowater

In the old Armenian city of Kars

1.

It was spring and I was in a minibus leaving the town of Mush, in south-eastern Turkey. I was glad to be out of Mush, an ugly place, a place so poor that a turned-up collar is the only defence against the perpetual rain, a place so pious that there is nowhere to get a drink. In Mush, I had felt hemmed in—looking no further than the next puddle, the next grimy address to visit, seeking out the plain-clothes policeman I knew to be following me. Now, as the minibus bounded along, I stared at a stupendous landscape. South-eastern Turkey has the vastness of the Central Asian steppe but none of its tediousness. It is jagged like Colorado but doesn't parch the throat, far less the spirit. It has Somerset's lushness and twice the virility. Brooks meander glassily through spring grasses embroidered with flowers and rivers scoop nutrients from the soil. The sun strikes the turf-clad roofs of distant huts and steam rises into the sky.

This is a rebel landscape. The people know the redoubts, a shelter from unexpected snowfalls, the almost inaccessible summer pastures. The government officials do not. The state can burn houses but it can't stop the rain, can't round up all the sheep. It isn't an easy place to control.

After about an hour and a half, we rounded a bend and I saw my destination: an inviting little town with two well-stocked markets at different points along the main street and minarets rising before a green backdrop of gently sloping hills. There was no sign of the five- and six-storey apartment blocks that distinguish rich Turkish towns from their poor equivalents. The houses were simple, with slanting roofs, respectful of the grandeur all around. And there were beer signs, a bar or two, some women strolling bareheaded.

A man was waiting to meet me. He was burly and he wore a leather jacket of superior cut. 'Welcome!' he said with a smile. Another man, balder and taller but similarly attired, stood behind him. The tall one put my bag in the back of a dirty white Fiat. I sat in the front passenger seat, next to the burly one. 'Celal the accountant?' he asked, gunning the engine.

The white Fiat; the jacket; the paunch accumulated over fifteen years of sitting behind a desk, behind the wheel of a white Fiat, of eating greasy *börek* on the go; the narrow, placid gaze of someone who knows how to damage a man without leaving traces for the human rights lawyers—such are the markings of the Turkish intelligence agent. You may not spot him in his home town on the prosperous Aegean coast, but here, in the mountains of eastern Anatolia, he is a conspicuously superior specimen, better paid and better padded than the stringy malcontents he has to deal with. For all that, you will occasionally notice a flicker of doubt cross his features; although he represents the mighty Turkish state, he himself is weak. He has been sent to the Kurdish south-east against his will, in the face of his wife's objections. It's a bum posting, this unknown town in the middle of nowhere. And while he tells himself that this is his country and that he should feel at home here, he does not. At the local school, his daughter's excellent grades stand out like her dazzling smile beside the neglected brown teeth of her classmates. But she derives no satisfaction from these and other distinctions. At the school gates on their way home, the other children stop speaking Turkish and revert to their own languages, and she wonders if they are talking about her.

The burly one was called Sedat, and there was no need for the Fiat because Celal the accountant's office was barely a hundred yards from the patch of open ground that served as the bus terminal. Celal, Sedat told me in the car, used to be in business with his cousin, also called Celal, but they had fallen out and the first Celal was no longer working as an accountant. He was busy with the affairs of the Pir Sultan Abdal Cultural Association, of which he had recently become the local representative. It was in this connection, Sedat ventured to guess, that I had come to see Celal.

Pir Sultan Abdal was a sixteenth-century poet and mystic who was executed by the Ottoman authorities for inciting rebellion. Even today, his followers, the Alevis, remain distrusted for rejecting orthodox Sunnism, for their traditions of profane music and poetry and for their periodic rebellions against central authority. There are about twelve million Alevis in Turkey, and the Turkish Republic, which Kemal Atatürk founded in 1923 from the ruins of the Ottoman Empire, does not quite know how to deal with them. The Alevis tend to be secular in outlook, which makes them useful allies in the state's campaign against militant Islam. But lots of Alevis claim Kurdish ancestry, and many are socialists. This is awkward, for the state is sensitive about people who trumpet their Kurdish identity, and it doesn't care for socialism at all. In the 1980s and 1990s, thousands of Kurdish Alevis joined a separatist rebellion by the Kurdish Workers' Party (PKK), a rebellion that seemed to have been defeated in 1999 with the capture of the PKK leader, Abdullah Ocalan, but is now showing signs of coming to life again. Some Alevis have links with illegal left-wing organizations that launch bomb attacks on civilians.

Celal wasn't at the association. Sedat said we would wait. We sat down and made conversation with the three or four other people in the room. They didn't seem surprised that Sedat had paid them a visit, or that he had brought a foreigner with him, and they contributed to the bonhomie that Sedat deemed appropriate to the occasion. There was a pleasant rattling conversation in which the state's representative and a group of suspect citizens expressed their mutual affection and regard, and vowed to put previous misunderstandings behind them. Was this for my benefit? I think not, or not entirely. I have met plenty of Turks like Sedat, people who harbour cynicism and idealism without distinguishing between the two. Sedat had a fantasy that the joshing could be for real, that all obstacles could be removed and the Alevis would realize how lucky they were to be Turkish citizens. If only!

My attention was caught by a slight, balding man in early middle age, as grey as cigarette ash. He wore a badge with an Atatürk profile and his eyes glittered with a pained, ironic intensity. Sedat followed my gaze and said by way of introduction, 'Mr Ombudsman! How are you?'

Without waiting for an answer, Sedat explained to me, 'Mr Bulent here is our ombudsman, and he's also the head of the local branch of the Communist Party. Now, you may have heard from certain foreigners who understand Turkey only very superficially about our Kurdish brothers and our Alevi brothers, but what the foreigners neglect to mention is that the majority of our brothers are not unhappy, that they don't regard themselves as minorities, that they have no truck with the terrorists and state-splitters. Take Bulent here. He's a Kurd, but that doesn't stop him being a Turkish patriot and a secularist, does it, Bulent?'

'And an anti-imperialist,' Bulent said, looking at me, and everyone laughed. 'The gentleman is from...?'

'Our foreign guest is a writer from Britain,' Sedat said, 'but tell him your views on the PKK, Bulent. I know he'd be interested.'

Bulent shrugged. He didn't like being paraded by Sedat. 'Mr Sedat, everyone here knows my views on the PKK, although many others do not agree. They're a creation of the Americans and other imperial powers and their aim is to divide the Turks and the Kurds so they can't form a united front against Western capitalism.'

Sedat and his colleague smiled indulgently, which irritated Bulent. He started speaking faster and he jabbed his finger as he spoke, poking an imaginary Sedat in the chest. 'This is why I wear Atatürk on my lapel, and why I'm a member of the Association of Atatürkian Thought. This is why I stand foursquare with the police when they prevent reactionary young women from entering the universities wearing the headscarf and propagating their reactionary Islamist ideology. This, Mr Sedat, is why I am for the reform of the state, so that it stops suppressing the legitimate democratic and socialist aspirations of the people.'

As the conversation petered out, I found myself recalling previous trips that I had made to the south-east, in the 1990s, as a reporter living in Turkey. For journalists and diplomats, 'the south-east' was code for the rebellion that the PKK had been waging since 1984, and for an older struggle over Middle Eastern land that started decades before Israelis and Palestinians went at each other's throats. And it was code for a largely ignored third party, the Armenians. The Ottoman Turks had solved the Armenian 'problem' during the deportations and massacres of 1915, in which at least one million Armenians—most of them living in the Turkish south-east—are thought to have lost their lives. Now, there were no Armenians; their skeletons lay below the surface.

My friends in Istanbul and Ankara had viewed my south-eastern trips with slightly bemused indulgence. They, westernized Turks living comfortable European lives, had no reason to visit this benighted region. They spent their holidays on Turkey's western coasts, drank their wine in sight of a Greek island. If they went further afield, they headed west, to Paris or New York. They had been taught to think of the south-east as a part of Turkey—it was the reason why so many conscripts were dying there—but they spoke of it as if it was a different country.

My view of Turkey was heavily influenced by these friends. I liked the idea of a secular Muslim country that was animated by the same ideals as Western, democratic nations. (It was the best riposte to those who argued that Islam and the West would always be in conflict.) Certainly, the country had problems, of which Kurdish nationalism and Islamic militancy were the most serious, but they would be solved, I believed, and Turkey would take its rightful place among the happy, powerful nations of the world.

The solution, of course, was for Turkey to join the European Union. There was a debate, inside and outside Turkey, over whether or not the country could be considered properly 'European'. Then, in the late 1990s, a Turkish prime minister called Mesut Yilmaz observed that Turkey's path to Brussels ran through the south-east. Yilmaz was widely pilloried and the reason, I think, is that he did not couch an awkward subject in the usual abstract terms. He was talking bluntly, about land and power, and saying that conflicts between the two must be resolved before a country can be at peace.

2.

The door of the Pir Sultan Abdal Cultural Association opened and Sedat exclaimed, 'Here he is! Celal!' Celal was a slim man with wary eyes and a left-winger's moustaches. (They droop morosely, unlike an Islamist's, which are prim and sandpapery, or a Turkish nationalist's, which follow the arabesque of the mouth.) Sedat gestured in my direction. 'We've brought your British friend. He is here to study the question of minorities. He has heard that we have Kurds and Alevis in our little town, and he has heard that we used to have Armenians, and he thinks that this is very interesting.'

It is interesting; this is one of the most disputed regions in the world. To the Turks, this is Turkey; to the Kurds, Kurdistan; to the Armenians, Armenia. The land is old and thick, but the people move fast when occasion demands. You will be hard pushed to find a village whose inhabitants have been in the same place for more than two generations, where there haven't been looting and burning, forced marches, expulsions and counter-expulsions. In times of trouble, the men head for the hills with the family Kalashnikov, and vow to take back what is theirs.

You can't rationalize an attachment to land. You can study its effects on people, see it in their histories and self-image, in their memories—ingenious vacancies when you ask them about their own atrocities, encyclopaedic when discussing the cruelty of others. In this corner of the south-east, you will find Alevi villages and Kurdish Sunni villages. You will find two separate Kurdish languages and, in the towns, Turkish as well. You will come across Cyrillic carving on stones that lie embedded in the wall of a hut and you will know that this village, or part of this village, once belonged to Armenians, and that the village had a church. The world knows that the Armenians were deported by the Istanbul government and massacred, by Kurdish tribesman and government forces, as the Ottoman Empire collapsed during the First World War, in what many historians regard as a genocidal foretaste of the Holocaust. But you should pause before remarking on these stones to your hosts; they may think you are accusing their grandparents of stealing the homes of others, of putting women and children to the sword for a swathe of nice pasture. They will tell you of an infamous incident in local history, when the Armenians herded several dozen Alevi women and children into a barn and set the place on fire, and you will take the hint and shut up.

This corner is full of battlefields. To the west there is Tunceli, where a Kurdish rising in the 1930s was brutally put down, and where Marxists competed with the PKK to torment the state in the 1990s. Close by lies the ancient Armenian monastery of Surp Karapet, which was much admired by European travellers such as Jean-Baptiste Tavernier and H. F. B. Lynch in the eighteenth and nineteenth centuries and now consists of a single wrecked apse that the Kurdish villagers, refugees from the PKK rebellion, use as a woodpile. To the east there is the great Lake Van, scene of some of the worst atrocities against the Armenians, and, to the north, Erzurum, where Turkish nationalism begins and hundreds of local lads fell fighting the PKK. At Erzurum's Atatürk University, under a Turkish flag the size of a block of flats, professors are hard at work to prove that it was the Armenians, collaborators in the Russian invasion that took place in the First World War, who perpetrated the worst massacres—against Turks and Kurds. They dispatch intrepid parties to discover mass graves and then pronounce, using their knowledge of skull types, that these are Turkish bones. No one listens—the number of parliaments across the world that have recognized the events of 1915 as genocide is well into double figures—but the patriotic work must go on.

Sedat was a true patriot. He followed Celal and myself when we drove out of town to visit the tomb of an Alevi saint, or to a Sunni hamlet that once belonged to the Armenians. He joined us when we followed the river into the dense forest to eat trout and drink raki at a restaurant that belonged to a friend of Celal. Glancing in his rear-view mirror, Celal would curse Sedat, but I could not wholeheartedly dislike him. Behind the slow smile, you sensed someone who had been tainted by dark memories and decisions. One day, I vowed, I would sit with Sedat and he would tell me of his colleagues who had been killed by the PKK and the Marxists, and of their wives who had been widowed. And then I would feel sympathy for him, and perhaps look at Celal—generous, humorous, pitiable Celal—in a harsher light.

Between them, there was a fine balance of power: over me, over their little town, over the whole of south-eastern Turkey. Upsetting the balance, bringing unpleasant things into the open—everyone knew the cost of that. You did that only if you were prepared for the consequences.

Sedat stayed at the door when Celal and I entered the office of the district administrator, or *kaymakam*. Lynch visited this man's predecessor in the last years of the nineteenth century, but I don't suppose the present *kaymakam* has read Lynch, or even heard of him. There was a tart philistinism to him, not because he hadn't a sense of culture—he had, as I would discover later—but because he had decided not to dignify *this* culture, the murky whatever that lay around him, with his critical attention. The *kaymakam* was in his late twenties but he looked nineteen. He wore a dark blue suit and a white shirt and a blue tie with a big knot. His father was a businessman on the Black Sea coast. The *kaymakam* was nervously superior, a Sedat without balls.

Celal had accompanied me so he could invite the *kaymakam* to an evening of Alevi music. Celal had recently been released from jail, where he had spent two years on suspicion of being a PKK member. I'm not sure if the *kaymakam* knew this, but his distant manner suggested that he regarded Celal as an unfortunate choice of host. As we talked awkwardly of this and that, the *kaymakam*'s phone rang. He spoke at length about which of his colleagues had been appointed to which provinces. 'Yes, I heard he got Isparta... Yes, it's hard, difficult... We'll see what happens when the next transfers come around.'

The *kaymakam* told me about the state's efforts to improve the local economy. He had personally distributed twenty-five rams to different villages; it was a way of replenishing stock that had been depleted during the conflict with the PKK. Private-sector incentives were in place. But the *kaymakam* did not seem hopeful. The tribal system, he rued, is very strong in Kurdish society. 'All the same,' he went on, 'they expect the state to do everything for them.' He smiled one of his unpredictable smiles, a smile that said: you see what we have to put up with here?

'And what is being done to satisfy the demands of minorities, for example...?'

The *kaymakam* cut in quickly: 'We have no minorities in Turkey. A lot of people talk about minorities but we don't have them. It's out of the question to have minorities. There is no discrimination in Turkey.'

We sat dully. Celal had crossed his arms and was looking intently at the floor.

I asked what proportion of the local population had moved abroad. The *kaymakam* said, 'I'm not sure we have those figures to hand, but I'll get them for you. It will be something for our statistics department to work on.' (Again, that unpredictable smile.) The *kaymakam* pressed a buzzer.

A man came in and the *kaymakam* asked for the population statistics. 'I want ages and place of residence.' The man looked puzzled. The *kaymakam* repeated what he had said and the man left the room. The *kaymakam* turned back to us and picked up the thread of his thoughts. 'As I was saying, we have no minorities.' He looked at Celal. 'Isn't that the case, my friend?'

Celal nodded sagely. 'Of course, Mr Kaymakam.'

A different man came into the room holding a piece of paper, but it contained the wrong information. Eventually, after more buzzing and toing and froing, the first man came back with the statistics that the *kaymakam* wanted. According to these figures, the district had several people in their mid-140s. The *kaymakam* saw nothing funny in this. 'Some people must have died without informing us.'

That evening, the *kaymakam* invited me to his house so that he could practise his English. He would utter the first two or three words of the sentence in English, finish it in Turkish and get me to translate what he had said. Then he would repeat my translation.

I remarked on the music stand next to his sofa. The *kaymakam* removed a violin from its case.

'I shall play,' he said, 'if you...' He said the rest in Turkish.

'...don't mind.'

'...don't mind?'

'...don't mind!'

He smiled. 'I shall play if you don't mind.'

The *kaymakam* played a piece by Zeki Muren, a composer who used to appear in drag on state TV every New Year. When he had finished, he lamented that, what with his duties, he rarely found time to practise. His teacher would be cross.

He laid down his bow and began to tell me about himself. I learned that every civil servant must spend at least five years in the south-east.

'How long have you been in the south-east?'

'Three years. I do not know how much...' He ended the sentence in Turkish.

'How much longer I can take it.'

'Yes! Take it for two years more.'

The *kaymakam* wanted to invite girls home, for tea and Zeki Muren. He wanted to stroll down clean streets, watch a film, eat lamb kebab without a bodyguard. He wanted to be liked, respected. He resented those of his colleagues who, by dint of their superior connections, had found a way around the five-year rule. I wondered whether it had ever crossed the mind of anyone in his position, anyone at all, to learn Kurdish—rather than English or another European language. It would facilitate communication, after all. It would show a bit of goodwill. But the *kaymakam* wasn't interested in that. He was interested in getting out.

I left his house at ten and found Celal and Bulent and some others sitting on stools in a small shop that sold alcohol. There was no need to put the beer in the fridge—even in May, the cans were cold when you took them off the shelf. Celal introduced me to a dapper man in a suit: Abdullah, the town jailer.

Abdullah gestured towards Celal. 'I locked him up. I've locked up most of my friends at one time or another, and my brother-in-law. You get used to it. Of course, you'd like to hand over the key and say, "Get out," but the authorities aren't going to like that. Celal knows the score.' He raised the can to his lips.

3.

When I lived in Istanbul, it was taken for granted that Atatürk would have approved of Turkey's campaign to become a member of the EU. It would be the natural culmination of the astounding project of social engineering that he had started. Within a few years of founding the Turkish Republic, he had set an Eastern autarchy on an enlightened Western course.

My Turkish friends loved Atatürk for emancipating women and for smashing the power of the Muslim *ulema*. They loved him for waltzing and seducing while he built Turkey anew; they forgave his vicious temper. During Atatürk's time, it became illegal to talk about the Kurds. He made it compulsory for men to wear Western-style hats. It was not good form to refer to the events of 1915. School textbooks taught that the Armenians had betrayed the Ottoman Empire; they deserved everything they got.

But when the EU and its member states came to review Turkey's membership application, they declared many of the dogmas to be at variance with the very European ideals—tolerance and respect for freedom of expression—that Turkey claimed to share. If the Turks wanted to the join the EU, the Europeans said, they would have to ditch the old positions, discuss the taboos, make peace with history.

Around the time that I left Turkey, at the end of the 1990s, the Turkish state started to do this. The Kurds were grudgingly recognized. The insurgency stopped for a time; thousands of guerrillas came down from the hills. The torture of dissidents started to happen less frequently. Some Turkish academics suggested that the Armenian massacres constituted genocide and were not arrested. Some Alevis started demanding special recognition. There was a clamour of voices claiming rights. 'Everyone,' an exasperated Turkish official told me, 'thinks they're a minority now.'

For the Kemalists, these new experiences were painful and disconcerting. Turkey had embraced the EU in the name of Atatürk and now the EU was insisting that they abandon him. The EU process meant acknowledging the untruth, or the incompleteness, of the history that was being taught at school. Moreover, there was no guarantee that, even if it took these steps, Turkey would be let in. Reflecting their electorates, some European leaders started speaking out against Turkish membership. When, in October 2005, the EU finally opened accession negotiations with Turkey, it did so with such an ill grace that many Turks felt confirmed in their conviction that the Europeans intended to string Turkey along, but never to admit it.

On that day in October, I happened to be in Yerevan, the capital of Armenia. Armenia is a small, poor and ruggedly beautiful country, the eastern limb of what many Armenians wistfully refer to as 'Greater Armenia'—a much bigger ancestral homeland that takes up a lot of eastern Turkey. From Yerevan's Genocide Memorial, overlooking the city, you get a superb view of Mount Ararat, which has an important place in Armenia's literature and mythology, but which lies across the Turkish border. In 1993, the Turks closed the border in protest at Armenia's annexation of an Armenian-majority part of Azerbaijan, which borders eastern Armenia, during a war that was marked by ethnic cleansing on both sides. Few of the non-official Armenians I met seemed inclined to distinguish between the inhabitants of Turkey and Azerbaijan. In their eyes, all are ethnic Turks who can be expected to manifest generic traits of treachery, fanaticism and cruelty. 'You have read *Karamazov*?' I was asked on more than one occasion. 'Dostoevsky understood the Turk.'

In the Armenian foreign ministry building, officials told me that they welcomed the start of Turkey's EU accession talks. Armenia's diplomats and politicians believe, probably with good reason, that the EU will not admit Turkey unless it apologizes for the atrocities of 1915 and accepts that a genocide took place. They also believe that pressure from the EU will force Turkey to end its trade embargo against Armenia. Turkey's EU process, they told me, can only be good for Armenia. Outside the government buildings, however, I found that feelings were more complicated.

One afternoon, I was invited for tea by a philologist and his family. The philologist's wife had baked a delicious apricot cake, of which I had several slices. While I ate, he told me that, for much of the Soviet era, the massacres of 1915 had been a taboo subject. The Communists had been wary of anything that might fuel ethnic nationalism. He also spoke of a 'national shame'—a traumatized reticence of the kind that one might associate with a victim of rape. There had been poets, he went on, who touched on the national tragedy, but a more general expression of interest came only in the 1960s. Young Armenians started pressing their grandparents, survivors of the deportations, to relate their experiences. The Communists allowed the Genocide Memorial to be built. In the 1970s and 1980s (though my host did not mention this) illegal Armenian groups in various countries honoured the dead by assassinating dozens of Turkish diplomats and members of their families.

Just as our tea seemed to be getting quite relaxed, I let on that I had spent five years in Turkey and that I had good friends who were Turks. This news nonplussed my hosts. It contradicted all that they knew about the Turks. They listened politely as I spoke of Orhan Pamuk's boldness in speaking publicly of the massacres, and of the readiness shown by many less-celebrated Turks to shoulder the burdens of the past. Then another guest, a middle-aged woman, held up her arms, squeezed her bare forearm rhetorically and exclaimed, 'No! The Turks do not bleed the same blood as us.'

During the week I spent in Yerevan, I got to know a courteous architect called Armen. During the 1970s and 1980s, when he was a young man, Armen spent many months travelling surreptitiously around eastern Turkey, taking photographs and recording physical evidence of the former Armenian presence—mostly churches, graveyards and ornate carved stones called *khachkars*. Armen and his companion, a Turkish-speaking European, were arrested several times; among the Kurds, they often met with hostility. Occasionally, they came across Armenians, or the children of Armenians, who had converted to Islam in order to save their own lives. The children of these people tended to marry each other; the Kurds, Armen was told, refused to marry converts.

It is several years since Armen was last in Turkey; younger men have taken over the detective work. Their findings have been gathered in a multimedia archive in Yerevan. From this, it is clear that, slowly but surely, all evidence for the Armenians' settlement of eastern Anatolia is disappearing. Here, the stone wall of a church is incorporated into a new house; there, a graveyard is ripped up and ploughed over. Armen told me of an eleventh-century Armenian church that he had seen before and after it was used for target practice by Turkish gunners.

Armen was such an engaging companion that it was unsettling to be reminded, as I occasionally was, that he was driven by a resilient hatred. One late afternoon, sitting in a room at the archive, I remarked that some Armenians I had met in Yerevan believed that relations between Armenia and Turkey should be allowed to normalize, provided the Turks apologized for the events of 1915. Armen's face darkened. 'They are fools,' he said. 'Do you think we will exchange one and a half million murdered ancestors for an apology? That's our land the Turks are sitting on.'

We sat in silence. Outside, in Marshal Baghramian Avenue, municipal buses were driving people home. Armen brought in coffee. As we drank, I mentioned some villages around Mush that I had visited with Celal. Armen nodded; he had visited the same villages. As a matter of fact, he went on, he remembered an interesting incident that had happened in one of them.

'It must be over twenty years ago. My friend and I were driving through, and we stopped for a glass of tea in a teahouse.'

'As soon as we entered the teahouse, the chatter died and everyone looked at us. We must have been the only non-Kurds. You know—those faces, those moustaches. We sat down on stools and ordered tea. We drank quickly because the atmosphere was hardly congenial, but as soon as we had finished that first glass, they brought another.

'I had been looking furtively around, and my attention had been drawn to something. There was a big Kurdish fellow sitting there; he was wearing a belt, and it glinted like silver. When they brought us our second tea, the serving boy pointed at the man and said that he'd sent it over to us. Then, before we knew it, the man had brought up his stool and was sitting next to us.'

Armen paused. The office was dark and silent; everyone had gone home. He finished his coffee and went on.

'This fellow had seen me looking at him but he thought I was interested in the revolver he was carrying. He whacked it down on the table so I could have a look. I spoke to him about the calibre and where it was made and so forth, and my stock rose because I know a bit about firearms. Everyone in the teahouse had gathered round to hear what we were saying. The place was an enormous cloud of cigarette smoke. But I was only interested in his silver belt.

There was more tea and more cigarettes and my friend kept looking at his watch and saying to me, "We should get going. We don't want to be on the road after dark." I kept having to shush him and say, "No! There's something I have to do here."

'Eventually, I summoned up the courage to ask to see the man's belt. He took it off and handed it over. It was composed of embossed detachable sections and had leather on the back. It was inscribed in Armenian and there was a date, 1902. I was sweating and trembling, but, in the end, I managed to buy the belt from that Kurd.'

Armen fell silent. He had become a silhouette in front of the window. After a few moments, I said, 'Presumably only rich men could have afforded a silver belt.'

He became animated. 'Not men! Men didn't wear such belts! These belts were given to Armenian girls when they got married. They were meant to last their whole married life; that's why they were made up of removable sections. During pregnancy, they added sections. After giving birth, when they were getting slim again, they took the sections away.' □

GRANTA

THE END OF TRAVEL
James Hamilton-Paterson

Ibegin writing this in an Austrian inn while a blizzard swirls noiselessly outside. It is nearly mid-March, and like the Austrians themselves I have been taken completely by surprise by the weather. The locals claim that by rights spring should be in the air, yet most nights the temperature sinks to minus nine celsius and it snows much of the time. Everyone is phlegmatic, but I am also stuck. Because I drove up from Italy on summer tyres my car, a white lump hunkered outside, has become a death trap. Tomorrow, inconveniently, the inn is closing until Easter and in one way or another I shall have to leave. My host blows apologetically through his moustache and plies me commiseratingly with *Obstler*, his home-made fruit schnapps. But go I must.

Mine is an old-style traveller's dilemma. This is not modern tourism, when stranded punters angrily besiege harassed guides and demand they lay on buses, Hummers, helicopters, *anything* to get them out and back on schedule. The essence of travel is that timetables do not matter. One does well to arrive where one hoped to go and even better to return. It is fatal to chafe when things go wrong, as I did for the very last time twenty-five years ago when I was at the end of a long sojourn on a small Philippine island. I had one of those bucket-shop air tickets that afforded no leeway or redress. Miss the flight and you lost the ticket. The evening before I was due to hitch a lift to the mainland in a fisherman's outrigger boat and begin the long, uncomfortable haul to Manila, the wind got up. All night long gusts banged my hut and now and then whole panels of palm thatch lifted vertically like air brakes to reveal rectangles of hurtling black sky. I lay unsleeping and through the bamboo floor felt the waves shake the shore. First light found me with my bags packed, watching hopelessly as the great rollers crashed and their spume plastered the clothes to my body. It was three days before my friend could take me off, by which time I was not a little hungry, had missed my flight and had had patience thrust upon me. In those parts survival itself goes from day to day and is something to be cheerful about. It is an unflustered habit of mind we are swiftly losing.

So I am not downcast by the minor inconvenience of being driven forth into the snow. Rather, it reminds me agreeably of the unexpected that always was a hallmark of my travels. In this snug wood room with its peasant-style wardrobe painted with naive sprays of flowers, I am suddenly overtaken with nostalgia for a lifetime of

223

uncomfortable journeys. This is partly made up of the conviction that they would no longer be possible today. Or even desirable, so much has the world changed. And lurking there somewhere is a vainglorious pleasure in having been a traveller rather than a tourist, whatever that could mean. The ancient Greeks used to go on sightseeing tours of Egypt, and in Europe tourism had noble origins when, between the seventeenth and early nineteenth centuries, the great British land-owning families would round off their sons' education by sending them with a tutor for a couple of years to France, Switzerland, Italy and back through Germany. Thomas Cook's commercial paraphrase of this Grand Tour took off in 1856, when he first led a party to Europe. Even then, the motives were educational and it would have been thought incomprehensibly frivolous to have admitted that one was travelling purely for 'fun' rather than self-betterment.

I was travelling for neither forty years ago. A recent house move has brought to light some reminders of my first journey to Brazil in 1968. As diary entries and letters reveal, I asked myself that hackneyed question 'What on *earth* am I doing here?' both frequently and plaintively, something I had never done a couple of years earlier while teaching in Tripoli. If one is drawing a salary from the Libyan government, however irregularly, the question of what one is doing doesn't seriously arise. But what I had repressed about my first Brazil trip was that I had gone with the intention of *emigrating*. An old passport reveals that I had an immigrant's visa and as far as I can remember I fully intended to become a Brazilian citizen. Why? No special reason, apparently, so it must have been a gesture of wanting to disappear—not the first in my life but by far the most dramatic to date. Why Brazil, particularly? I forget that, too; but I expect it was something I had read, such as Peter Fleming's *Brazilian Adventure*, that suggested a country ample enough to become lost in.

That was it, then: no job to go to and only the bare minimum of money to take with me to satisfy the Brazilians that I wouldn't become indigent within weeks. What would I be doing there? Just *being*, really: in its way the essence of one kind of travel. No zoo quest to find new animal or plant species; no anthropological fieldwork to do in a backwater of those *tristes tropiques*; no wretched tribe to evangelize; no gap year to dutifully fill; not even a notion of self-discovery, that bathetic trip to nowhere of interest. Simply an overwhelming urge to

"TOP-NOTCH JOURNALISM, MEMOIR, FICTION, ESSAY, AND PHOTOGRAPHY."

CHICAGO TRIBUNE, 2005

You get a good deal when you subscribe to GRANTA. One year (four issues) is just $39.95 (33% off the bookshop price). An additional gift subscription is only $31.25 (47% off). So if you subscribe to the view that good writing matters—that it can make a difference—subscribe! Or give Granta to a friend who shares your love of reading. Or, at these low prices, do both!

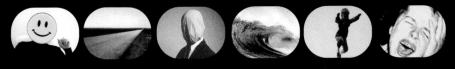

YES. I would like to order:

○ A one-year subscription for $39.95. This is: ○ A new subscription for myself ○ My renewal ○ A gift.
○ An additional one-year gift subscription(s) for $31.25 for the person/people listed below.

PAYMENT: ○ Check (US$ drawn on a US bank) ○ MasterCard ○ Visa ○ AmEx ○ Bill me (US only)

_____
Credit Card Number

_____
Expiration Date/Signature

$_____ total for _____ subscriptions/gifts (please add foreign postage if necessary*).

* Additional postage outside the US: Canada (includes GST): $12 surface, $20.50 airmail; South America and Mexico: $8.75 surface, $20.50 airmail; Rest of World: $20.50 airspeeded.

MY NAME & ADDRESS: _____

_____

City/State/Zip _____

GIFT RECIPIENT(S) NAME & ADDRESS (if ordering gifts):

GIFT 1: _____

City/State/Zip _____

GIFT 2: _____

City/State/Zip _____

➧ **FOR FASTEST SERVICE, FAX CREDIT CARD ORDERS TO (601) 353-0176.**

SUBSCRIBERS GET MORE.
FOR LESS!

GRANTA SUBSCRIBERS GET OUTSTANDING NEW FICTION, REPORTAGE, MEMOIR,
AND PHOTOGRAPHY FOUR TIMES A YEAR, AT AN OUTSTANDING DISCOUNT.
SEE OVERLEAF FOR PRICES, AND AN ORDER FORM.

be out of my own culture, beyond the reach of home, decisively elsewhere. The sparse letters I recently found reveal nothing of what drove me from England's shores, only the selfish zeal with which I went, not leaving poste-restante addresses, heedless of the worries I knew would (and did) plague my recently widowed mother. And for all the discomfort and ennui I must have loved it. Although I never became a Brazilian, I was to go back on two further occasions.

That first time I wound up in Manaos. In those days the nearest stretch of the fledgling Pan-American Highway was still hundreds of miles away and this provincial capital was only reachable by air or river. To travel in the Brazilian hinterland one could sometimes hitch a lift on a Brazilian Air Force flight if the plane had space to spare—and this during the charmless rule of the Colonels. Later, I availed myself several times of Força Aérea Brasiliera's public-spirited if unreliable service. But on that first occasion I hitched a lift on a boat simply by going aboard the Hamburg-registered cargo vessel *Hilde Mittmann* as she lay in Belém port and asking her master if I could work my passage to Manaos. I could and did, learning a good deal about the difficulties of navigating a river whose sandbanks were always shifting and necessitating stops to take on a series of local pilots. In between I scrubbed down the engine room bulkheads: a noisy and stupefyingly hot task in the tropics. That first visit to Manaos provided the backdrop for my novel *Gerontius* twenty years later, which described a trip Sir Edward Elgar had made from Liverpool to Manaos and back in 1923, because the town I found had changed so little since his visit. One could still walk from the centre for twenty minutes in almost any direction and be either on a river bank or in primeval rainforest. But already there were ominous signs of change to come. The place had just been designated a Free Trade Zone. On the outskirts of town bulldozers were beginning to mass restlessly like runners before the London marathon and an American missionary family with whom I lunched in their jungle home had been given a warning to quit.

Today Manaos is an industrial city with skyscrapers, firmly on Brazil's road and air networks, and I'm told the nearest virgin forest is now hours away. Quite as bad is that thanks to 'security issues' one can no longer hitch lifts on tramp steamers. Seamen's unions, insurance companies and containerization with smaller crews gradually made it harder; officialdom finally made it impossible. Yet those casual modes of travel were essential to most of my forty years' wanderings. They facilitated an urge to vanish which had made itself known early and insistently enough to shape my life. When I was an undergraduate, bored and disaffected, I sent away for information about joining the merchant navy and decided to run away to sea. My tutor was sensible. He told me to go right ahead, provided I had already lined up a job at sea more useful than that of getting an Oxford degree. He also gave me a copy of *Dauber*, a long and scarifying poem based on John Masefield's own victimization aboard a sailing ship in his youth. Feebly I stayed on and got a degree and a poetry prize, both of which, for all the good they have done me, I would willingly have swapped for an extra year of being alive. A lifetime's drift then set in. Drift, in the sense that regardless of what I would end up doing, I first needed to rinse England off me in tropic seas and the jetstream of long flights. It didn't much matter where.

For a while I kept returning to the UK, where I wrote documentaries for ATV, journalism for the *New Statesman* and scripts for commercial videos. Just temping, and I knew it. In the Seventies I even bought a house near Oxford. But I was coming and going the whole time: in Indochina and South America; later in Egypt for a year, ostensibly doing an Arabic course at the American University in Cairo but in fact goofing off in a country I became immensely fond of. In 1979 I sold my house and went to the Philippines, having been told by a US Medevac helicopter pilot years earlier that it was a strange and wacky place. It was there that I at last found islands and villages remote enough to satisfy my compulsion to become lost, a monkish tendency devoid of the slightest religious motivation. A couple of years later I bought a house for almost nothing on a mountainside in Italy. It was two miles from the nearest neighbour and had no electricity, no phone and no running water until I boxed a spring in the forest a quarter of a mile away and laid a hose from it. It was the happiest house I've ever lived in. A few years ago I sold it at 1,600 per cent profit because an American writer had proclaimed that its formerly unfashionable *commune* lay under a Tuscan sun and the area had become modish and grotesque. It was time to get out.

But for over twenty years until then I had one foot in the Far East and one in Europe. In a way both have become 'home' in the sense that I am enough at home almost anywhere except my native land.

And now, once more feeling the need for a change of culture, I am contemplating a move to Austria. 'You'll like the geology,' Wystan Auden assured me as he was nearing the end at Christ Church, Oxford. Maybe. I have liked the geology of half a hundred places. When I sift them in my mind's eye I wonder how much they have changed since I last saw them. So many will have become developed, touristed, too accessible. Even the way one travels to a place, the very mode of transport, affects it indelibly. The town one reaches by river steamer is a wholly different place from the one reached by a Ryanair flight.

Forty years ago the world was altogether less organized; and although politics made large stretches of it (the USSR, China) virtually out of bounds, much of the rest was protected by being off the beaten track. We forget that even in the 1960s air travel still felt like something of an adventure. Flights were fewer, destinations limited and fares proportionately higher. The flying public was infinitely smaller, with the result that even the humblest economy passenger was treated with the remnants of a pre-war courtesy. There was a good deal less hanging around, too. My handbook to London Airport, which internal evidence dates to 1956–7, casually remarks that a passenger arriving for check-in could expect to be sitting in the aircraft on the 'apron' outside, ready for immediate take-off, in twenty minutes. This booklet, with its heartrendingly optimistic Fifties' typography, reveals the ghost of the wartime RAF transport station at Hounslow Heath still lurking beneath the grand, Frederick Gibberd-designed main concourse of what was yet to be called Heathrow, and the place was clearly run with military as much as civilian efficiency. The Sixties, with its bigger aircraft like the Boeing 707, might have stretched that twenty minutes' wait to an hour, but no more. Nowadays we are resigned to almost any flight effectively occupying the best part of a day.

What I miss is the informality with which one could still flit about the globe in those blessed days just before mass air travel began, with its attendant controls, security checks, delays, bullyings, herdings and anxiety, all in the name of our 'safety and convenience'—that doxology of a secular age that brooks no argument. Bernard Levin, the often pompous and splenetic *Times* columnist, once put his finger on exactly what is so loathsome about modern flying. In one of his pieces he described the horrors of a perfectly ordinary flight he had just made, correctly identifying how the whole process was calculated to *infantilize* the passengers. He noted the constant bing-bong of nannyish announcements and instructions, the general chivvying and thinly disguised scolding that lie just beneath the airline personnel's rote gentilities. Most of the travelling public have colluded in the steady reduction of their status to that of mere bums-on-seats who are handed trays of dreadful fodder and effectively told to keep quiet and strapped in, like recalcitrant infants in high chairs. By sheer chance I recently flew first class to the Far East (for the first and doubtless the last time in my life) and can testify that the difference is quite remarkable. What really distinguishes first- and business-class passengers from the nursery herd only a curtain's thickness away is not the food and drink, which are neither here nor there; nor even the leg-room, vital though that is. It is the refreshing experience of being treated like an ordinary adult, as though having money automatically made one more grown-up (a fallacy if ever there was one). Not for first-class people the frequent hectorings by loudspeaker, the remorseless houndings out of lavatories.

One plausible distinction between travel and tourism is that the traveller makes his or her own way, whereas tourists' paths have been beaten into submission long before they go, whether singly or as a group. The elision between the two types has often been a consequence of pocket guides. In the nineteenth century the Thorough Guides and Baedeker's made it easy for the less intrepid to plan in advance, to know where they might stay, what to see, what to expect. The information acted as insulation against the threat of too much raw reality. In our day the Lonely Planet and Rough Guides have simply done for the demotic mass what the earlier guides did for the middle classes, now greatly aided by the huge expansion of cheap air travel in the last twenty-five years. The whole experience of dashing about the planet has become commonplace and increasingly standardized.

This fact barely conceals the uncomfortable point that one good reason for nostalgia about my early travels is not just that I was young (and the peculiar excitement of being young in a foreign land can never be repeated), but that I enjoyed a faint but unmistakable exclusivity. Comparatively speaking, there were many fewer of us doing it. One's costly flight was full of business people and returning citizens, but less frequently holidaymakers. The arriving aircraft's doors would crack open in the middle of the night somewhere hot, letting in that pulse-quickening smell of tropical rot like decaying sponge bags, and one would totter down the steps towards a small terminal building amid neon lights on concrete standards haloed by swirling insects and prodigious bats. Once past the dilatory passport and customs officials with moustaches and pistols, one's fellow passengers seemed just to melt away into the night. There was seldom a nexus of tired Brits complaining that the hotel hadn't sent a bus as promised. One was tinglingly on one's own.

Tourism changes all that by dint of sheer throughput. Officials may now barely glance at the passports or luggage of the incoming hordes. Weary men with belligerent anti-perspirants hold aloft rallying notices for the tour groups. The hotels' minivans and touts are lined up outside. There is nothing exclusive about tourism. Quite the contrary: it is primarily *in*clusive. It is an industry determined to embrace you. It wants you to check in to the right hotels; it wants you to spend as much as you can on fatuous souvenirs; it wants you to do Machu Picchu or the Taj Mahal; it wants you to have the Rainforest experience or the Mysterious East experience or the Rose Red City Half as Old as Time experience and it doesn't terribly mind if you also have the fleeced-by-muggers-on-Copacabana-Beach experience. And when your fifteen days are up it wants you to bugger off, taking with you no local currency and maybe the odd disgusting parasite or two.

It is extraordinary—and, to lovers of difference, extraordinarily depressing—the swiftness with which mass travel is ironing out variety the world over. (Just try buying a souvenir somewhere exotic that you can't find in a high street back home.) True, savvy travellers know it is still quite easy to avoid the backpacking and tourist hordes by buying a guide and noting where not to go. But there is an ironic sense that as travel expands, horizons are closing off. Our natural habitat, those beloved spaces in which we could once simply *be*, anonymous and observant, is everywhere shrinking. I no longer wonder why people have this restless urge to whiz about the world to places that are rapidly becoming harder to differentiate, to stay in the identical sorts of horrible hotel you can see advertised on CNN, to do and buy the same things they do and buy at home. This lemming-like urge to be constantly on the move to nowhere truly different congeals into its own way of life. Sun, sea and snow have each become a commodity. This turns travellers by default into mere consumers of climates and landscapes where they can disport themselves on tame terrain, chattering the while with their mates back home on mobile phones. Horace famously put his finger on the hidden dynamic here: *Coelum non animum mutant qui trans mare currunt.* Different landscape but the same dreary habits of thought.

Thus fashion shapes how we go and what we do. These days probably few oddballs go and live unobtrusively in the wilds of Kazakhstan and on their return have nothing much to say about challenges. Tourism apart, we note how much modern travel writing and media interest now concerns journeys apparently influenced more by the *Guinness Book of Records* than by a desire to travel per se. People aspire to be the first to swim the entire length of the Mekong backstroke or become the only dude ever to go snowboarding in Antarctica. Take a camera crew along to capture your waggish ego! See how extreme ironing smooths out the planet's landscapes! And why not hurry while stocks last and be the last person ever to ski on Kilimanjaro? For thanks to global warming the old world is fast fading away, its accelerating demise helped along by the mounting effluent of our journeys.

It is now clear that our collective desire to race ever faster and in greater numbers from place to place, whether by road, rail, air or sea, will lead to the end of this planet as a gracious and agreeable habitat for its dominant species. Everybody knows this but nothing will be done in time. Evolution has hard-wired us to worry about the morrow, or even the coming winter, but not about thirty or fifty years hence. Virtually all the UK's airports have expansion plans in the pipeline, the objections from those living nearby overruled. Just as it is now hard in much of Britain to find a place where one can't hear the constant rushing of a motorway or main road, it will soon be equally hard to find somewhere without an airline route slicing across its patch of sky. The environmental damage projected even by the UK's own Department for Transport is alarming enough, but it can't take into account as-yet-undiscovered consequences of high-speed, high-altitude flight. Jet airliners have an exaggerated impact because they spew their pollution into the delicate region between the upper troposphere and the lower stratosphere, between five and seven miles up.

Aircraft exhaust gases injected at high temperature into those icy regions produce their own clouds in the form of condensation, or contrails. Following the attacks of September 11, when all commercial airliners in the US were grounded, American skies were free of contrails and in only three days scientists noted a change in the mean temperature. The implication is that the cirrus clouds and upper-atmosphere haze caused by aviation trap outgoing radiation and block incoming sunshine, making the planet cloudier and warmer. It is now belatedly recognized that commercial aircraft are a major source of pollution (military aviation—itself a massive source—is never factored into this equation and remains unaccountable). Yet the volume of air traffic is projected to multiply by up to eight times in the next forty years, while aircraft fuel is zero-rated for taxation the world over on the unilateral insistence of the United States. Judging from their ads, BP now wants us to be conscious of our 'carbon footprint' on the ground, but it is notably reticent about our carbon trail in the air. And following the recent test of a scramjet (faster still, higher yet!), futurists are envisioning flying from London to Sydney in two hours. Evidently they live in an environment-free Neverland of their own.

The more we flock to view the disappearing glaciers, the faster they will vanish. So what should we do? In an article in the *Guardian* George Monbiot observed:

If we want to stop the planet from cooking, we will simply have to stop travelling at the kind of speeds that planes permit. This is now broadly understood by almost everyone I meet. But it has had no impact whatever on their behaviour. When I challenge my friends about their planned weekend in Rome or their holiday in Florida, they respond with a strange, distant smile and avert their eyes. They just want to enjoy themselves. Who am I to spoil their fun? The moral dissonance is deafening.

There is pathos in witnessing the genetic inability of a species to curtail its own self-destructive behaviour. The pathos naturally includes the rueful awareness that one is oneself a part of it, doomed to the impropriety of watching the steady eradication of so many species except the one that most deserves extinction. *That* multiplies horribly. Sometimes I have thought that a return to sea travel might be a way to recapture a calmer, more reflective mode of voyaging, but most people haven't the time and are too easily bored. The new breed of cruise liners offers a travesty of the voyage. Not only are the days of the great passenger lines as dead as those of stagecoach travel (as the final swallowing-up of the husk of P&O recently showed); the cruise ships coming down today's slipways were never designed to transport people eager to get from A to B. Rather, they function as idealized versions of everyday urban living with the added novelty of being at sea.

Their ugly, un-nautical design betrays this. One need only look through a book of photographs of the great Clydebank ships to appreciate the imposing elegance of vessels such as *Aquitania* (1913) and *Queen Mary* (1936), built for speed with their well-raked masts and funnels (not to mention the delicacy of *Aquitania*'s counter-stern). Even *QE2* (1969) has a beautiful bow and graceful upperworks despite a rather inelegant funnel. Compared with purposeful-looking liners like these, most modern cruise ships look exactly like what they are: hotels that happen to float. Their blocky, stack-of-apartments design makes them top heavy, thick and bulbous in the wrong places, like gigantic training shoes. Actually, of course, their design is as purposeful as the older ships'; it is just that the purpose has changed. With their non-stop restaurants, banks, shopping malls, games arcades, cinemas, gyms, saunas, swimming baths and all the rest, it must sometimes be hard for the tourists to live their lives at all differently from usual. The classic liners also offered such things, depending on whether your class of ticket gave you access to them; but they were temporary diversions to ease the tedium of the necessary days at sea. Cruise tourism's facilities are more an end in themselves, a way of seamlessly continuing the consumerist style of dry-land living.

These ships leave their own carbon wake, their massive engines and generators consuming tons of heavy fuel. Around ports where the vessels lay over, local residents have protested against the stench and soot from their auxiliary engines. Their main engines are vastly more polluting. Current vessels hold up to 5,000 tourists, but bigger ones are being built. At present an estimated seven million tons of rubbish are dumped at sea annually, of which seventy-seven per cent comes from cruise ships. The impact of these enormous ships is already taking its toll on delicate environments the world over, as is that of 5,000 people suddenly decanted into a small but picturesque place. Last year I was in Tallinn when a cruise ship put in as part of its 'Baltic experience'. The medieval centre's cobbled streets became suddenly jammed with people who descended like jackdaws on the shops and restaurants. At three o'clock an imperious hooting came from the harbour and the crowds hastily evaporated. Within minutes the old town was deserted and an uncanny silence fell as, down below, a white cliff of apartments made its way back out to sea. If it's Thursday, this must be Tallinn. Apparently this form of tourism, like that of the airlines, is going to expand enormously. It is not clear what purpose it serves beyond that of killing time, which doesn't seem a good enough excuse for killing the planet.

If old-style travel is dead, it is not just due to newer technology and more people with more time and income to dispose of. September 11, 2001 not only killed nearly 3,000 people; it effectively killed off any hope of old-style travel for nostalgics and the perverse. A stranger in a strange land is now a security threat and anathema to the new authorities. For the first time in human history no one is allowed to roam the earth in blessed anonymity. Even the Wandering Jew is at last confined to barracks unless he has computerized ID, the right visas and a good excuse. It is not that pre-war travellers like Robert Byron (*The Road to Oxiana*) never had problems with officialdom—they did, as I also did. But such difficulties could so often be sorted out by personal negotiation, which might involve money or a brief spell in jail or interminable cups of sweet tea. Now passports are no longer documents but are becoming mere vehicles for bar codes, chips-and-PIN and retinal scans. For our safety and convenience the new panicky and draconian security measures will never be repealed because the emergency will never be deemed to be over. The political and cultural alienation that engendered it now hobbles our travels as Communism once did.

Whether or not I find a suitable piece of geology to live next to in Austria, I shall henceforth travel less, though not from weariness and only partly from melancholy and distaste. A drawback to getting older is that we find ourselves compulsively skipping to the end of things and experiences out of sheer familiarity. We know in advance how most conversations, people, jokes and regimes will turn out. And even when they're a little different from expectation that, too, will fall within our bounds of recognized variables. Given the repetitiousness of public things, a place might qualify as my home if I can sit there in seclusion and enjoy being startled afresh by the music, books and piano that, after a lifetime's vagrancy, alone merit housing to the end. I shall keep an eye cocked to the seasons' changing outside with an affection for natural processes and a gleeful interest in whatever doom impends for all of us. □

GRANTA

MATRILINEAL
Tessa Hadley

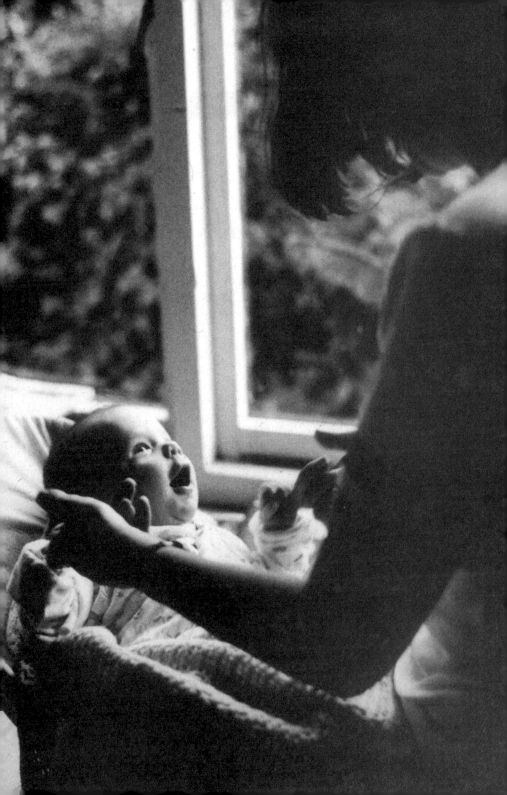

One night forty years ago Helen Cerruti left her husband. They were living together at the time with their two little girls on the top floor of a big Edwardian house, in a respectable street where the houses sat back behind well-tended gardens and knobbled lime trees with blotchy bark surged up like life forces out of the civilized pavement. The Cerruti girls taking in the terrain at pushchair level saw how dogs left their small calcinous offerings among the tree roots (the dogs in those days were only fed on bones and scraps). This was just at the end of the time when women walked and pushed pushchairs in those streets in gloves, with matching handbags and shoes, suffused in that vanished elegance at once studied and nonchalant.

Helen and Phil Cerruti didn't have much money—Phil was a jazz musician, who also gave lessons at the teacher-training college—but Helen had a gift for making herself elegant. She passed all her wisdom on to her girls, who later, in a different world, weren't really ever able to make much use of it: that it was better to have two or three good things in your wardrobe than to have it stuffed full with inferior items; that cut and line were important above all; that instead of washing your clothes to rags you should valet them carefully, taking out stains with patent cleaner from a bottle, repairing with a needle and thread, pressing everything through a wet cloth before you wore it. They had an intimation—seeing their mother in her petticoat pressing and steaming, pinning up and letting down and taking in, grimacing at her make-up in the mirror, practising postures—of the hidden heavy labour that underlay the nonchalant surface. Helen was a dancer; that is, she had been a dancer before she had her children. She still had a dancer's figure, driftwood washed to leanness. In 1965 she was wearing shirt-dresses and pale pink lipstick; her dark hair was cut short, backcombed up behind a broad hairband.

The access to their top-floor flat was up a metal staircase added on to the side of the house, which gave out a booming noise however quietly you tried to step. If the Cerrutis had too many visitors, or Phil ran back two at a time because he'd forgotten something, or Nia, rapt in one of her daydreams, came stomping up, a heavy stolid little thing, after playing out in the garden, then the retired Reverend Underwood, who lived with his wife on the floor below, would pull back the net curtains and rap on the windows at them. Helen made Phil climb up in his socks when he came in after playing late at night, with his shoes in his hand, unless it was raining. She also feared that if he'd been drinking he'd slip on those damn stairs and break his neck. And the stairs meant she had to keep Sophie's pushchair down in the garage, where Phil kept the car. Every expedition, even round the corner to the grocer's or to the clinic for Sophie's orange juice, was a performance; when they got home she had to climb the stairs with Sophie struggling in her arms, laden with her shopping bags, clinging on to the metal handrail, desperate not to look down. Nia would go first and be entrusted with the keys. Straining on her stout legs, she could just reach the keyhole. Solemn with her own importance, each time not quite believing that the trick would work, she would stagger forwards, hanging on to the keys, as the door swung in upon the familiar safe scene, extraordinarily unchanged since the moment they'd gone out, which would by now seem to Nia like hours and long ages ago.

Helen left Phil on an April evening, at about half past six. They had parted at breakfast on perfectly friendly terms; then one of Phil's lessons had been cancelled in the afternoon, which meant less money, and she had heard him bounding up the stairs, pleased of course at the release, a couple of hours before she expected him. She wasn't ready for him; she'd taken advantage of Sophie's afternoon nap to wash the linoleum in the kitchen, and was on her hands and knees in her oldest slacks, with her hair tied up in a scarf. Nia was leading one of her dolls on an adventure round the lounge, instructing it confidingly: along the bookcases made of planks and bricks, behind the jazz records, among the hilly cushions on the low couch covered in olive green, through the forest of the goatskin rug whose skin peeled in scraps that looked like tissue paper. The weather was grey, the clouds had been suffused all day with a bright light that never quite broke through them. Helen had all the windows open up here in the flat, she hated stuffiness; they were so high at the top of the house that they looked out into the hearts of the garden trees almost as if they were birds nesting. It was that suspenseful moment in spring when the cold has loosened its grip, the tender leaves are bursting out everywhere, the bitter smell of the privet flowers tugs at the senses. The adults are all poised for something momentous to happen to fill out the meaning of this transformation, anxious already in case another year is slipping past without certainty, without anything becoming clear.

—That's a very, very attractive proposition, said Phil when he came in and saw her scrubbing the floor intently with her back to him, her bottom stuck up in the air. He ran his hand suggestively around the curve of it under the tight cloth.

She looked over her shoulder at him, resting her weight on one arm, wiping her sweaty face on her shirtsleeve. —You're early.

—Cancellation, he said jubilantly. —Freedom! I've come home to practise.

Usually, when she was ready for him, Helen made an effort to be welcoming when Phil came home: to have a meal ready, to freshen her make-up and perfume, to take an interest in whatever he'd been doing. She had herself had a perfectly nice day. She had taken the girls to the park on the way back from the shops this morning; this evening, when Phil went to play, she was going to cut out the new chunky white cotton drill she had bought to make a suit to wear to his sister's wedding. She didn't even mind washing the floor. She was sorry for Phil, having to go out and teach when he hated it.

—But you can't practise here, she said.

This was their oldest quarrel, ever since they'd moved from their first flat to this one, after Nia was born.

—They won't be in, he said easily, as if they hadn't been over all this so many times before. —They won't mind.

—Why didn't you stay and practise at the college?

—Because I hate the college. Because I can't wait to shake the stinking dust of the college off my shoes.

—But at college they have soundproof rooms.

He stood quietly then for a few moments without moving; Helen pretended not to notice his portentousness, swirling the scrubbing brush in her bucket of water.

—Do you really hate my music so much, Phil said: not as a question but in a sort of wondering cold calm.

Phil Cerruti was a very good alto player, something in the style of Art Pepper but of course not that good. Art Pepper was his hero; he played his records over and over, he learned his solos off by heart. He got a lot of work, in the city in the west of England where they lived and the area round about, but not enough work yet to give up teaching. Helen loved him to play. She had fallen in love with him watching him on stage: his small loose-jointed body, its movements delicate and finished as a cat's, twitching to the off-beat. Moods passed visibly, like weather, over the transparent white skin of his face, blue under his eyes when he was tired. Men were drawn to Phil as well as women; his energy was a steady heat, a promise. He walked out of the kitchen without another word and went into the lounge. Helen went on scrubbing the floor for a while and then she got to her feet, with her scrubbing brush still in her hand, and followed after him as if she had something more to say. Phil was sitting on the couch beside the open alto case, wetting the reed in his mouthpiece. He had let his thick black hair grow recently almost down to his shoulders (the teacher training college had complained). Nia and her doll were paused en route around the room, looking at him; Helen knew she was surprised that her daddy hadn't greeted her with his usual exuberance.

—All day, Helen said, —I have to stop the children running round, in case the Underwoods start banging on the ceiling.

—Let them bang. We pay our rent, we have a perfect right for our children to run round, for me to practise my music if I want to.

—Don't raise your voice, she said. —They'll hear you.

—What the hell do I care if they hear me?

—I have to live here with them, all day every day.

—Then let's move. This is insane. I need to play. We need to feel free in our own home.

—We'll never find a flat as nice as this, in such a nice area, for this rent.

—What do I care about nice?

—I care.

—I can't live like this, Phil shouted. —You're killing me.

He dropped the alto on the couch and rolled on to the floor, shouting at whoever might be listening in the flat below as loud as he could, with his face down against the carpet. —You're bloody killing me! For Christ's sake!

Helen threw the scrubbing brush hard at him. Dirty water sprayed around; the brush bounced against his temple, wooden side down, and he yelped in real pain and surprise. —Jesus Christ! Nia looked astonished and embarrassed. Helen went into the bedroom and closed the door behind her and lay down on the bed. Sophie was still asleep in her cot in the corner, her breathing weightless and tiny as a feather on the air. The rank smell of Phil's hair on the pillow filled Helen's nose and senses; her heart seemed to be leaping to escape out of her breast. They quite often quarrelled; what she said to herself usually was that Phil was like a child, emotional and volatile. But today she believed it when he said she was killing him. She had been washing the floor so contentedly, and then in the space of a few minutes her body had been seized and occupied by this violent tempest; she saw starkly that their two lives now were set against one another, that he was desperate for freedom and art and that she needed to stop him having them. She had heard the scrubbing brush crack against his skull; she couldn't pretend that it wasn't true, that she didn't want to destroy him. It was horrible, that they were yoked together in this marriage. She thought that if they went on like this she might one day soon tear his saxophone out of his mouth and stamp on it and break its keys.

When Phil went out to play that evening Helen packed a suitcase and a bag and caught a bus with the children to go to where her mother lived, about three miles away across the city. She could only carry enough for one night; she even left behind the pushchair, which was too heavy and too difficult to fold down. She didn't mean, though, ever to go back to Phil. She had no idea of what lay ahead in the future, although she did think that if only she could get back her old job at the dance school, then perhaps her mother would look after the children while she worked. This wasn't likely, however, as the management at the dance school had changed and she didn't know the new people. She and Phil had eaten the tea she had cooked in silence; they hadn't said goodbye when he went out. Helen had thought, as she always thought when he left to play, that he might be killed that night and she might never see him again: he would be driving home when he was tired and had been drinking, on unknown roads in the dark. She always pictured these roads as twisting through forest or bleak moorland, shining and treacherous with wet. But even then she didn't run after him. The clamour of his footsteps on the staircase died away. She heard him open the garage door and drive out the car, then stop and get out and close the garage door behind him. Then he drove off.

The clouds that had muffled the day like a fleece broke up in the evening and floated as pink wisps in a high sunny sky; a thrush was joyous in the garden as they left. Helen had Sophie on her leading rein and could just manage the suitcase as long as she would walk. She didn't care if the Underwoods saw her go. The little girls loved catching buses. They had to get one down to the Centre and then change; Helen was only afraid that as it got past Sophie's bedtime she would grumble and rub her eyes and want to be picked up. But the girls seemed to understand that this evening didn't exist inside the envelope of ordinary time; they cast quick, buoyant, wary looks at their mother, as if they mustn't make too much of anything. Nia, who had seen Helen throw the brush, practised an air of easy adaptation. Sophie held on to the chrome rail of the seat in front and bounced. When Helen clenched her fist on the rail, so that if the bus stopped suddenly and Sophie flew forwards she wouldn't hit her face, she was surprised to see she was still wearing her engagement and wedding rings, distorting lumps under her glove. All that seemed left already far behind.

Helen's father had died three years before; her mother had sold the big house where she had lived for thirty-five years and gone to live above a hairdresser's. Socially, she had come down in the world. Her husband had been retail manager for one of the big department stores; she had used to come to this hairdresser's as a customer, to have her hair washed and set, preserving a proper dignified distance from the staff. Now she even worked as a receptionist for them several afternoons a week, drawn deeply and happily into the world of their gossip and concerns. The only entrance to her flat was through the hairdresser's; Helen had to ring the doorbell, then her mother peered down from between her sitting-room curtains to see whoever was calling at this time. She didn't have a telephone, so Helen hadn't been able to warn her. A few minutes later they could see her feeling her way along the row of dryers in the dim light from the stairs behind; she didn't like to use the salon lights because they weren't on her bill. No one knew that Nia's dreams were visited by dryer-monsters with blank skin faces and huge bald, egg-shaped skulls in powder blue. The glass door to the salon, hung inside with a rattling pink venetian blind, had 'Jennifer's' stencilled across it in flowing cursive script, and underneath that a pink silhouette bust of a lady in an eighteenth-century wig.

Helen and her mother weren't very alike. Everything about Helen had always been poised and quiveringly defiant; her mother seemed in contrast compliant and yielding. They didn't look alike: Helen had her father's stark cheekbones and strong colouring, her mother had been pinkly pretty and had faded and grown plump. But Helen was aware of a stubbornness deep down in her mother's softness; when you pushed, she didn't give way. When Helen was a teenager she and her mother had fought over every single thing—over dancing, over make-up, over Phil—as if one of them must destroy the other before it could end; Helen's father, who had always appeared to be the stern parent, could only look on in perplexity. It was through the birth of the babies that they had been reconciled; as if that blood sacrifice had satisfied both their honours. Now, as soon as she had undone the bolts and opened the salon door, Nana Allen seemed to know intuitively what had happened.

—You've left him, she said. —He didn't hit you, did he? Has he been drinking?

Helen gave a little bleat of laughter and pressed the back of her wrist against her mouth. —I hit him. I threw something at him and hit him on the side of the head.

—A scrubbing brush, explained Nia solemnly.

Nana Allen laughed then too.

—Oh, God, these children saw it, Helen said; and then for the first time tears spilled out from her eyes and ran down her cheeks.

—Sophie didn't see it, Nia corrected.

—Get them inside, her nana said. —Come on in, my little lambs. Come and get warm in Nana's flat. Have you eaten anything? I've got some casserole.

Nia got past the egghead dryers by clinging on to her Nana's skirt and burying her eyes in the familiar comfortable-smelling cloth. Helen couldn't believe these tears, now that they came; they hadn't been part of how she had imagined her exit, or her austere altered life. She hadn't even known she had inside her whatever deep reservoir of sorrow the tears poured from, flooding out of her, wave after wave, so that she was sodden, sobbing, helpless to speak. Her mother made her sit down in the corner of the sofa, wrapping her up in the old wartime quilt from home that she put over her knees in the evenings against the draughts (before Helen came she had been sitting reading her library book). She made cups of milky sweet tea for the children, made Nia a pickled onion sandwich, gave them the biscuit barrel full of lemon creams; she had a special pronged fork for the pickled onions, with a pusher on a spring to press them off on to your plate. Helen eventually was able to drink a cup of tea too. The women together put the children to bed: Sophie in Nana's bed because it was wider and she was less likely to fall out of it, Nia in the bed in the spare room, which they had to make up first. They left the doors just open, in case the children called out. Then they sat and talked together for hours. Helen's mother held her hand while they talked, and stroked her hair, and brought a cool flannel for her to wipe her face. Nia could just hear their voices, although she couldn't hear the words. She fell asleep and the voices became a loose safety net into which she fell, drooping and stretching under her, bearing her up, letting her go.

—I hate him, Helen said adamantly at some point that evening. —He hates me. We're killing each other. It's horrible. But I've seen through the whole thing now. I couldn't ever put myself back inside it.

She was pacing about the room then with her old, important restlessness, which still irritated her mother sometimes. She stopped to light another cigarette; the ashtray was already full, they were both smoking. Helen sucked on the cigarettes as if she was drinking the smoke down thirstily.

—Love is such a lie, she said. —In marriage, it's a lie. You kiss each other goodbye in the morning but actually inside you're both burning up with anger at things the other one's done or not done, and relief at getting rid of them for a few hours. I don't love him any more. I see right through him. All he cares about is his music, and actually I agree with him: why shouldn't he?

—You gave up your dancing.

Helen looked at her in surprise. —I wasn't very good. Not good enough. I wouldn't want Phil to give up his music. That's not the point.

—I thought you were very good.

(In fact she had exerted her utmost powers to dissuade Helen from a career in dance.)

—All those jazz standards about love and women, Helen went on, indifferent for the moment to the long-ago story of her dancing. —But actually they're only interested in each other, they're not genuinely interested in women at all. I mean, not once they've got what

they want. All they're thinking about when they play all those songs about the women they can't bear to live without, the beautiful women they've lost, is actually what other men think. Am I playing it as well as him? What does he think of the way I did that solo? Is he impressed?
—He does care about you.
—No, he doesn't. He thinks I'm his enemy. He wants to be free.
—It will seem different tomorrow morning.
—It won't. Or if it does, then it won't be the truth.

Nia woke up very early. She knew at once where she was, from the way a vague light was swelling behind her nana's lilac-coloured silky curtains. Even though Nia didn't go to school yet—she only went three afternoons a week to a little nursery where in fine weather they lay on mats in the playground to nap—that lilac-toned light already meant to her a precious freedom from routine. Usually the accompaniment to the lilac light at Nana's was the sound of car engines starting up in the street outside and then droning deliciously away into the distance; but it was too early even for that to have begun.

Helen was in the bed with her. She had forgotten to wonder where her mother would sleep. Once or twice at home Nia had been put into bed with her when she was ill; but it was a rare, strange treat. Helen had her back turned and her head buried down in the pillows. She was wearing her blue seersucker pyjamas, and snoring slightly; she smelled of cigarettes. Her hair still had some of its backcombed stiffness from the day, only matted and flattened; Nia reached out her fingers and felt it sticky with hairspray. She lifted herself carefully on one elbow, to survey her mother from this unaccustomed advantage of consciousness; everyone was asleep in the flat apart from her. Helen hadn't taken her make-up off before she came to bed: some of it was smeared on Nana's pillowcase. She radiated heat, and gave off her usual beloved complicated smell, like face powder and fruitcake. Shut up and inactive behind her closed eyes, frowning in her sleep, she seemed more and not less mysterious. Nia settled down again, pressing up cautiously behind her mother so as not to wake her. Through the puckery material of the pyjamas she could feel against her face the skin of her mother's warm back; she breathed in and out with her mouth open, tasting her. She wondered if their lives had changed, and if she would be able to sleep with her mother every night from now on. Anything seemed possible.

Some time later she was wakened again by a sound of knocking, then of Jennifer (who wasn't really Jennifer but Patsy) opening the salon door and speaking crossly to someone with a man's voice: her daddy. Then the doorbell rang up in the flat. Helen sat bolt upright in bed, as though she came from sleep to full consciousness in one movement; she slithered her legs over the side of the bed and dashed into the sitting room, where she collided with Phil, who had just dashed upstairs. She gave out a little moan: of subsidence, remorse, relief. Nia snuggled into the warm space her mother had left behind. She could hear Jennifer moving about downstairs, tidying up and running water. She knew that soon the bell on the salon door would begin to tinkle as the staff arrived, and then the customers. If she was lucky she would be allowed down later. The hairdryers were only harmless and comical during the day; she would sit out of the way and play with the perm papers.

Forty years later, only Nia can remember any of this. Sophie was too young to remember. Nana Allen is long dead; and Nia's father is dead too, in his fifties, of a heart attack. When Nia tells the story to her mother, Helen simply flatly denies it; and Nia is sure she isn't pretending, that she's genuinely forgotten. In her seventies, Helen is still elegant and striking-looking, with suffering deep-set eyes and beautiful skin ('Never use soap on your face, Nia'). She complains about her hairdresser, but he's good: she has her hair dyed a dark honey colour with silver streaks, cut to fall loose and straight in a boyish look she calls 'gamine'. People who meet Helen think she must have been something important, a broadcaster or a designer, although actually what she has mostly done in her life is that old-fashioned thing: being an attractive and interesting woman. She has had two significant relationships with men since Phil died, but she wouldn't marry either of them, although (she says, and Nia believes) they begged her. One of these men died too, and the other went back to his wife. The way she tells it now, the relationship with Phil Cerruti was the true love of her life, because Phil was a true artist. Nia isn't meaning to challenge this, either, when she brings up the subject of the time they ran away to Nana Allen's.

—I won't deny we did fight, Helen says. —We were both pretty passionate people. But no, I would remember it if I'd ever actually left him. I don't think the possibility would have crossed my mind. By the standards of today, of course I should have left. Everything in our family life had to be fitted around his music; you can't domesticate a real musician. But I was happy. The women of your generation wouldn't stand for it, darling, I know. But we'd been brought up to believe you stuck by your husband and that was it. You took the rough with the smooth.

On the other hand, Helen does now sometimes talk about her dancing. It has become part of her story, that she could have had a career as a dancer and she gave it up because that's how it was in then, if you married and had children; the way she tells it, you can't tell whether she thinks the sacrifice was a shame or a splendid thing. Helen and Nia get on reasonably well most of the time these days. When Nia was in her twenties she went through (as she sees it now) a drearily dogmatic feminist phase. She lived for a while as a lesbian and camped at Greenham Common. She gave herself a new name because she didn't want to use her father's, and then when Phil died (suddenly, so that she never said goodbye to him) she went into a depression for two years, and only came out of it with the help of therapy. Now she works as a therapist herself, and has a steady relationship with a man, Paul, although they don't live together and don't have any children. (Sophie has two boys and a girl, so Helen isn't cheated of grandchildren.)

Nia suggested to her mother last Christmas that in the spring the two of them should fly together to New York, to see the exhibition of Rubens drawings at the Met. The teacher at Helen's art classes had said how wonderful they were; and Helen had never been to America. It should have been one of those brilliant late-night inspirations that crumble to nothing in the light of practicalities, but somehow they really went ahead with this and booked their flights and their hotel. Then it was too late to change their minds, although in the week before they left Nia was consumed with doubt and dismay, imagining every kind of disaster. Her mother, who suffered from angina, wouldn't be able to walk anywhere; she would be taken ill, and Nia would have to deal with the American medical system. Or they would quarrel over something and not be able to escape from one another. On the flight over, Nia sat in the window seat and looked down at the unpopulated earth below, wherever it was, Greenland or Canada: for hundreds of miles, nothing but the black whorls and coils of rock, snow and winding rivers and frozen lakes. There was no cloud layer; there must be unbroken cold sunshine down there. She calmed herself by imagining she was translated down into that landscape; though not of course in her hopeless human body, which would only know how to stumble around in it and die.

They arrived in New York in torrential rain. The hotel in Greenwich Village, where Nia had stayed once before with Paul, looked rougher than she remembered. It was the kind of place she and Paul enjoyed, full of atmosphere and the traces of an older New York which they knew from films, with a marble-faced dado and huge gilt mirrors in the hallway, little metal mailboxes for the permanent residents, a lift painted around the inside with acanthus blooms, oddly assorted books on the shelves in every room. Now she could only see it through her mother's eyes. The furniture was cheap, made from split cane. They had to use a bathroom out on the corridor, and the first time Nia went in there she found a dirty sticking plaster on the floor. The breakfasts were awful, in a basement where a fierce Hispanic woman presided over thermoses full of coffee and hot water. Mother and daughter were both shy, transplanted out of the worlds they knew. Nia was often anxious, worrying about how to get from place to place, and where to eat, and whether Helen was tired; probably Helen was worrying too.

They were also always aware, however, that they would think about the things they were doing as wonders afterwards, when they got home. Their shared bedroom had a view on to the street of elegant and wealthy brownstones, where the trees were just coming into leaf. While Helen did her face and hair at the dressing table in the mornings, Nia (who only showered and towelled her short hair dry) watched out of the window, exclaiming at the New York dogs: extravagantly big or small or pampered, sometimes being exercised in gangs of five or six by bored professional walkers. They gave up the hotel basement and found a place round the corner which did breakfasts of rough peasant bread and seed bread with real fruit jam and café au lait in bowls; they made friends with the waiter. And on their second day the sun came out and was even hot; they took a boat trip to the Statue of Liberty and the Immigration Museum on Ellis Island; they marvelled at the Manhattan skyline. Helen persuaded Nia to let her pay for some oatmeal cotton trousers and a long moss-green cardigan; Nia in the expensive Fifth Avenue shops felt cornered and oversized and fraudulent. She longed for the new clothes to transform her, to prove that her mother's old instincts hadn't lapsed or fallen out of date.

After they had seen the Rubens drawings they had tea in the American Wing cafe in the Met, and watched through the glass wall a gang of workers in Central Park pulling the ivy off the bare winter trees. They tied ropes around it and heaved together until the ivy came away in heavy masses, which the men then fed on a conveyor belt into a shredder. Helen that day was wearing a grey suit and a silk scarf decorated with blue and yellow birds; the scarf had got somehow skewed sideways so that it stuck up rakishly behind one ear and made her look as if she was drunk or slightly dotty. Nia could see, too, where her lipstick was bleeding into the fine wrinkles at the edges of her lips. She talked about the mistakes Sophie was making with her children, in a tone of tactful light regret which Nia knew Sophie found particularly maddening. After tea, when Helen came out from the Ladies, where she would have checked herself in the mirror, the scarf was tidied into its usual casual elegance. She looked tired, though, and had to use her angina spray when they were walking from the museum to find a taxi.

—Don't those drawings simply make everything worthwhile? she said when they were back in their hotel room, groaning and easing her feet out of her shoes.

—Are you all right? Nia stood over her, frowning and surly because she was worried.

—Don't fuss, said Helen. —I'm an old woman.

She undressed down to her petticoat, so as not to rumple her suit, and lay on her back on her twin bed, her head propped on the pillows in the careful way Nia recognized as protecting her hairdo. The room was bright with evening sunshine. They had made its seediness homely with their clothes hung about, their scarves and beads and books mingled together, their flannels and bottles and sponge bags on the sink.

—Where would you like to go to eat tonight?

Helen sighed. —I'm so comfortable here.

—We don't have to go out, said Nia, full of doubt. —But won't you get hungry?

—I'm not worried about me. But what about you, darling? You'll need something.

Nia went to find the delicatessen they had noticed a few blocks away, to buy food they could eat in their room. It was the first time she had been out alone, and it was a relief to be able to use her long stride instead of continually adjusting her pace to her mother's. She felt as if she was really part of New York at last, choosing cold meat and bread and olives and fruit juice. She bought yoghurts, too, forgetting that they didn't have spoons; it was Helen who suggested that they could scoop these up with the wrong ends of their toothbrushes. While they ate their picnic they became deeply involved in a real-life courtroom drama on the television, debating it passionately. When that was finished they undressed and climbed under the bedcovers and fell asleep, even though it was very early.

Some time in the night Nia half woke and was confused, not knowing where she was. Outside on the street a car started up, and then the drone of its engine faded into the distance. She lifted her head off her pillow in the incomplete dark, and knew from the smell of face powder and cake and the light snoring that her mother was somewhere close by. She seemed to feel the radiation of her heat; and she remembered the seersucker pyjamas, dotted with little rosebuds.

—I'm still here, Nia thought, reassured and happy, falling back easily into her sleep. —She's still here.   □

GRANTA

HOMAGE TO MOUNT DESERT ISLAND

Selections from the Bar Harbor Times compiled by

Mark Haworth-Booth

BENT WIRE RD

Mount Desert Island, Maine

Homage to Mount Desert Island

They have reproached me for reading the police reports of Rome,
but I learn from them, all the time, matters for amazement.

Memoirs of Hadrian by Marguerite Yourcenar

Police investigated several reports of shots fired near Seal Harbor on February 6. Rangers were also notified because of the proximity to Acadia National Park. An investigation revealed that a local resident was shooting off a small novelty cannon every time the New England Patriots scored in the Super Bowl. No charges were filed.

Police checked on a teenage girl who was walking on Ripples Road barefoot, wearing only jeans and a T-shirt, on March 9. The girl was visiting a friend and was just fine.

There were several complaints this week about barking dogs, missing dogs and dogs running at large, and one complaint of a man barking like a dog.

A woman reported finding a suspicious-looking jug on the side of the Old Bar Harbor Road on April 2.

A bright light was reported in the sky over Somes Sound on April 11. A second caller in Blue Hill reported around the same time that a meteor-like object was falling over MDI.

There was a report of 'a kid on a skateboard drinking a Coors beer' on Main Street on April 14.

Pedestrians reportedly were playing in a flooded section of Eagle Lake Road on May 26.

A cow was on the wrong side of the fence on Crooked Road on May 26.

Squirrels running amok inside his home gave an Otter Creek resident fits this week. Police were called, and they saw an adult female squirrel running around the house; after a bit of looking, they found two baby squirrels nestled in back of the home's refrigerator. The officers took the babies outside, and the mother squirrel followed them, finally giving the homeowner some peace.

There was a puppy wandering loose on Park Street on May 27.

A driver stole a new road cone, replacing it with an old one, on June 1 on Crooked Road.

A report of suspicious goings-on turned out to be unfounded when the officer responding discovered a family roasting marshmallows in a controlled fire pit.

A worker at Big Apple said someone started drinking a beer in the store, then left in a taxi on June 4.

An intoxicated woman was reportedly harassing customers at Get Clocked on Main Street on June 8.

An unwanted raccoon was reported on the porch of a Ledgewood Road home on June 10, refusing to leave.

Gasoline was reported running down Rodick Street on June 15.

A fox attacked a cat on the porch of a Northeast Harbor business on June 16.

A person pounding on a back door on Ledgelawn Avenue was told not to return on June 16.

A man was standing near the public showers in Otter Creek on July 12, making visitors uneasy because he was uncommunicative.

A noise complaint was made about McKay's Restaurant on July 12. Someone was washing the exterior of the building, apparently in a manner that was considered too loud.

A Seal Harbor resident arrived home to find two men standing on her porch on July 16. She believed they were Jehovah's Witnesses.

Kids playing outside late in the evening on a trampoline were asked to move indoors on July 17.

A woman reported hearing a strange noise on School Street on July 17. She thought it might have been an alarm clock going off.

A can of Pringles chips was swiped at the Irving Mainway on July 20.

After someone called to complain, two men were told to stop bouncing a ball off a wall on Sea Street on July 24. The men said they often bounced the ball to unwind.

Somebody left a cardboard box with a flag in it at the Alternative Market on July 29.

A man who was walking around town pointing at people and talking to himself was told to knock it off on July 30.

A woman shoplifted a pink-and-blue bikini top at Village Emporium on July 30.

People who were not guests sneaked into a hot tub at the Regency on July 30.

Seagulls had been foraging in the trash at the transfer station on July 31.

The driver of a convertible that was idling loudly on Mount Desert Street on July 31 was told to move along.

Someone tried to steal some salt-and-pepper shakers on Main Street on August 1.

A strange letter was received by a Mount Desert Street resident on August 3.

Mark Haworth-Booth

A Forest Avenue resident told police her neighbour's dog was 'using her yard as a bathroom' on August 3.

Someone was sleeping in a restroom at the Bar Harbor Inn on August 5.

A caller complained about a megaphone being used at a party at Maine Sea Coast Mission on August 6.

People were talking too loudly on Myrtle Avenue on August 6.

What appeared to be molasses was found on Route 102 on August 11.

There was a seagull with a broken wing on the Shore Path on August 13.

Two dogs were chasing deer on Kitteredge Brook Road, one with porcupine quills in its muzzle, on August 14.

Police helped a family locate its eight-year-old son who had wandered away from them on Main Street on August 14. The child was found safe about a block away. □

All selections © The Bar Harbor Times, 2005